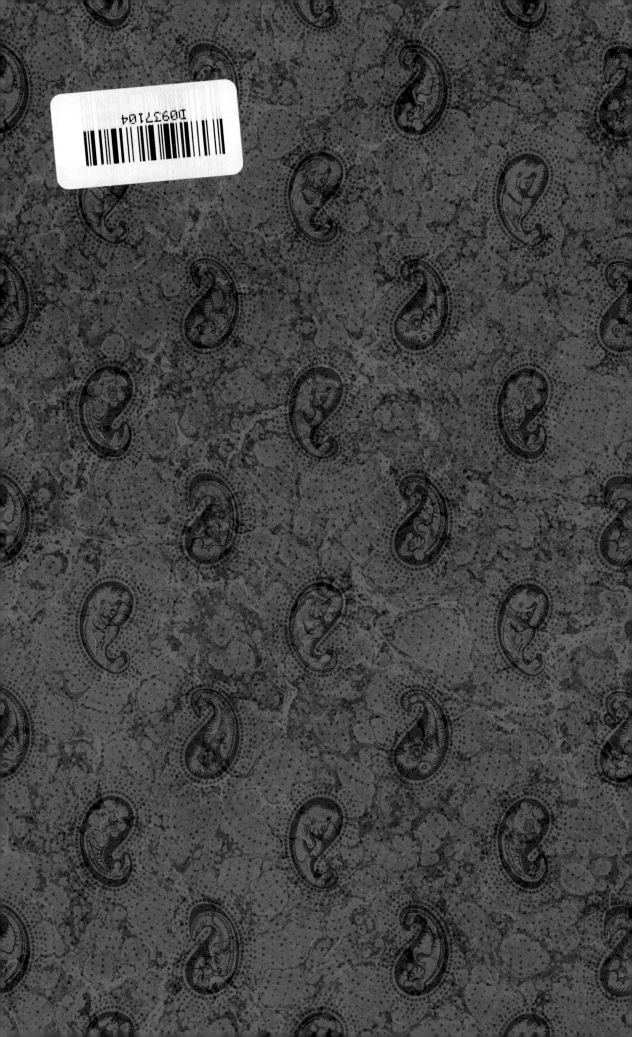

THE ILLUMINATI BALL

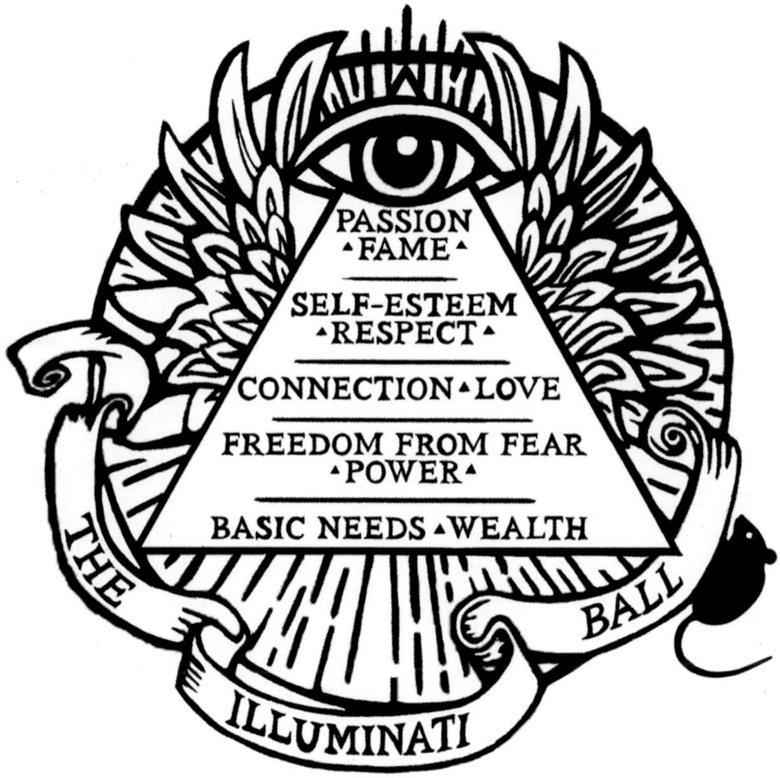
PASSION
FAME
SELF-ESTEEM
RESPECT
CONNECTION LOVE
FREEDOM FROM FEAR
POWER
BASIC NEEDS WEALTH
THE ILLUMINATI BALL

For Adonis and Persephone.

TITAN COMICS

THE
ILLUMINATI
BALL

TITAN COMICS

EDITOR
TOLLY MAGGS

MANAGING EDITOR
MARTIN EDEN

SENIOR CREATIVE EDITOR
DAVID LEACH

SENIOR PRODUCTION
CONTROLLER
JACKIE FLOOK

PRODUCTION CONTROLLER
PETER JAMES

ART DIRECTOR
OZ BROWNE

SALES & CIRCULATION
MANAGER
STEVE TOTHILL

PUBLICIST
IMOGEN HARRIS

DIRECT MARKETING OFFICER
CHARLIE RASPIN

ADVERTISING MANAGER
MICHELLE FAIRLAMB

HEAD OF RIGHTS
JENNY BOYCE

PUBLISHING DIRECTOR
DARRYL TOTHILL

OPERATIONS
DIRECTOR
LEIGH BAULCH

EXECUTIVE DIRECTOR
VIVIAN CHEUNG

PUBLISHER
NICK LANDAU

Thank you:

Editorial assistance: Adam Buhler, Charles Ardai

Actors/Models: Vincent Cinque (Pig King), Travis Moore (Chumanzee), Luka Fric (Vacanti), Kate Lori (Parthenope), Justin Moore (Bruno), Rachel Boyadjis (Aerialist), Erin Orr (Chef) and Persephone Pig (Herself).

Additional models: PJ Mead (Kamadhenu), Audrey Love (Demeter), Sxip Shirey (Jacob), Coco Karol (Mrs. Rubenstein), Chris Green (Dr. Rubenstein), Jesse Long (Alex), Andrea Danese (James), Charley Layton (Uncle Dougie), Jenne Hayden (Bruno's girlfriend)

Masks: Kat Mon Dieu, Kate Lori; Music: Prodigy of Mobb Deep; Poem: Paul Dunbar

THE ILLUMINATI BALL

9781787732216

Titan Comics is a registered trademark of Titan Publishing Group Ltd. 144 Southwark Street, London, SE1 0UP

The Illuminati Ball © Cynthia von Buhler, 2019

A CIP catalogue record for this title is available from the British Library

10 9 8 7 6 5 4 3 2 1
First Published October 2019
Printed in China

WWW.TITAN-COMICS.COM

 BECOME A FAN ON FACEBOOK.COM/COMICSTITAN **FOLLOW US ON TWITTER @COMICSTITAN**

For rights information contact jenny.boyce@titanemail.com

THE ILLUMINATI BALL

WRITTEN & ILLUSTRATED BY:

CYNTHIA VON BUHLER

LETTERING BY:

ADITYA BIDIKAR

CONSULTING EDITOR:

CHARLES ARDAI

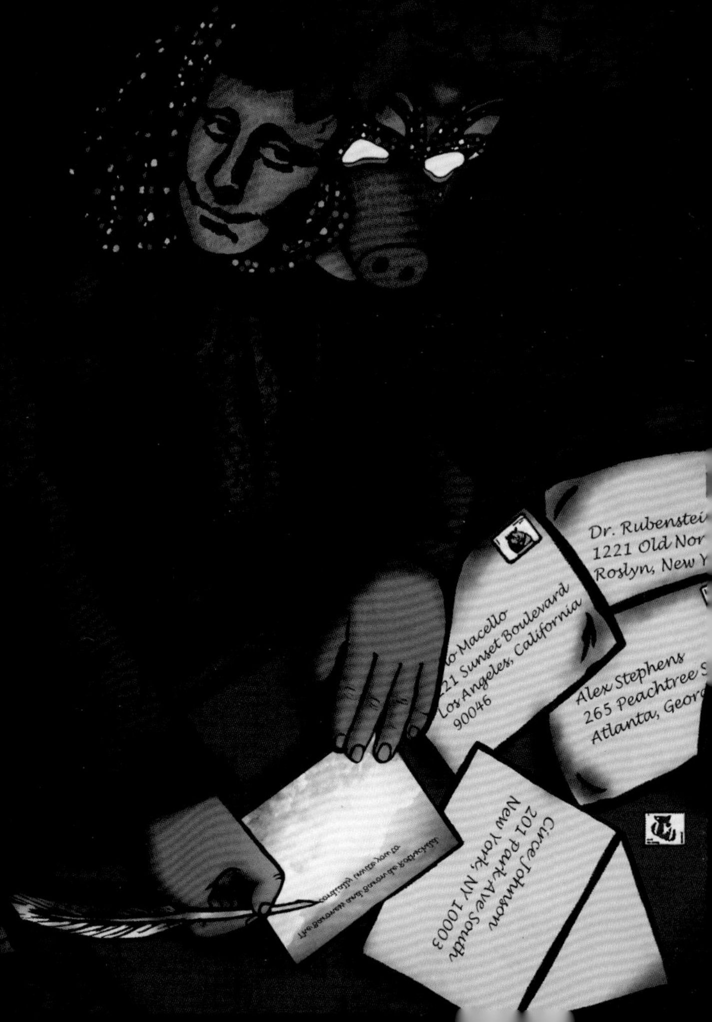
Dr. Rubenstei
1221 Old Nor
Roslyn, New Y
o Macello
21 Sunset Boulevard
Los Angeles, California
90046
Alex Stephens
265 Peachtree S
Atlanta, Geor
Circe Johnson
201 Park Ave South
New York, NY 10003

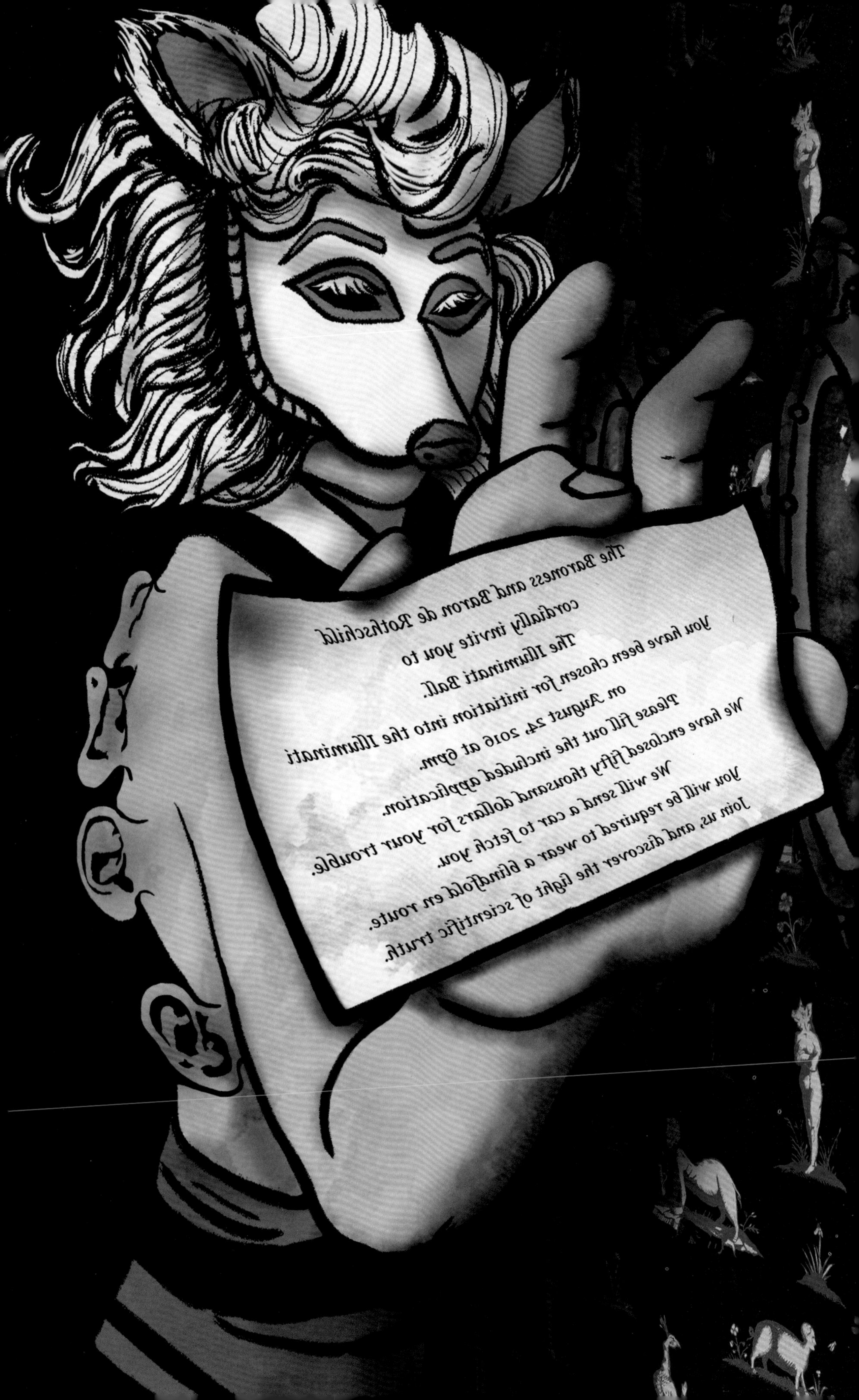
The Baroness and Baron de Rothschild
cordially invite you to
The Illuminati Ball.
You have been chosen for initiation into the Illuminati
on August 24, 2016 at 6pm.
Please fill out the included application.
We have enclosed fifty thousand dollars for your trouble.
We will send a car to fetch you.
You will be required to wear a blindfold en route.
Join us, and discover the light of scientific truth.

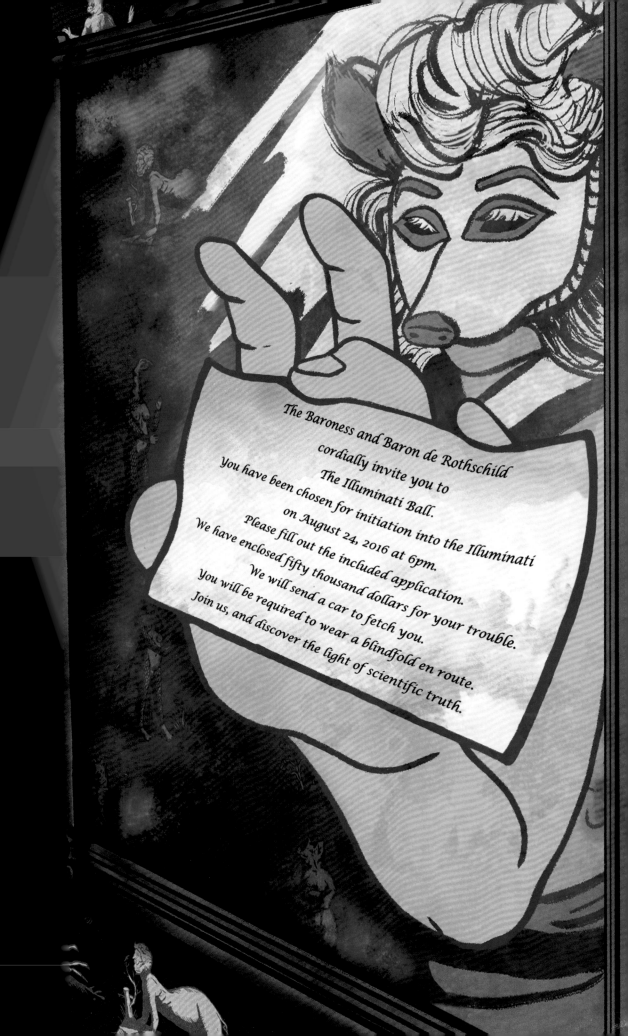

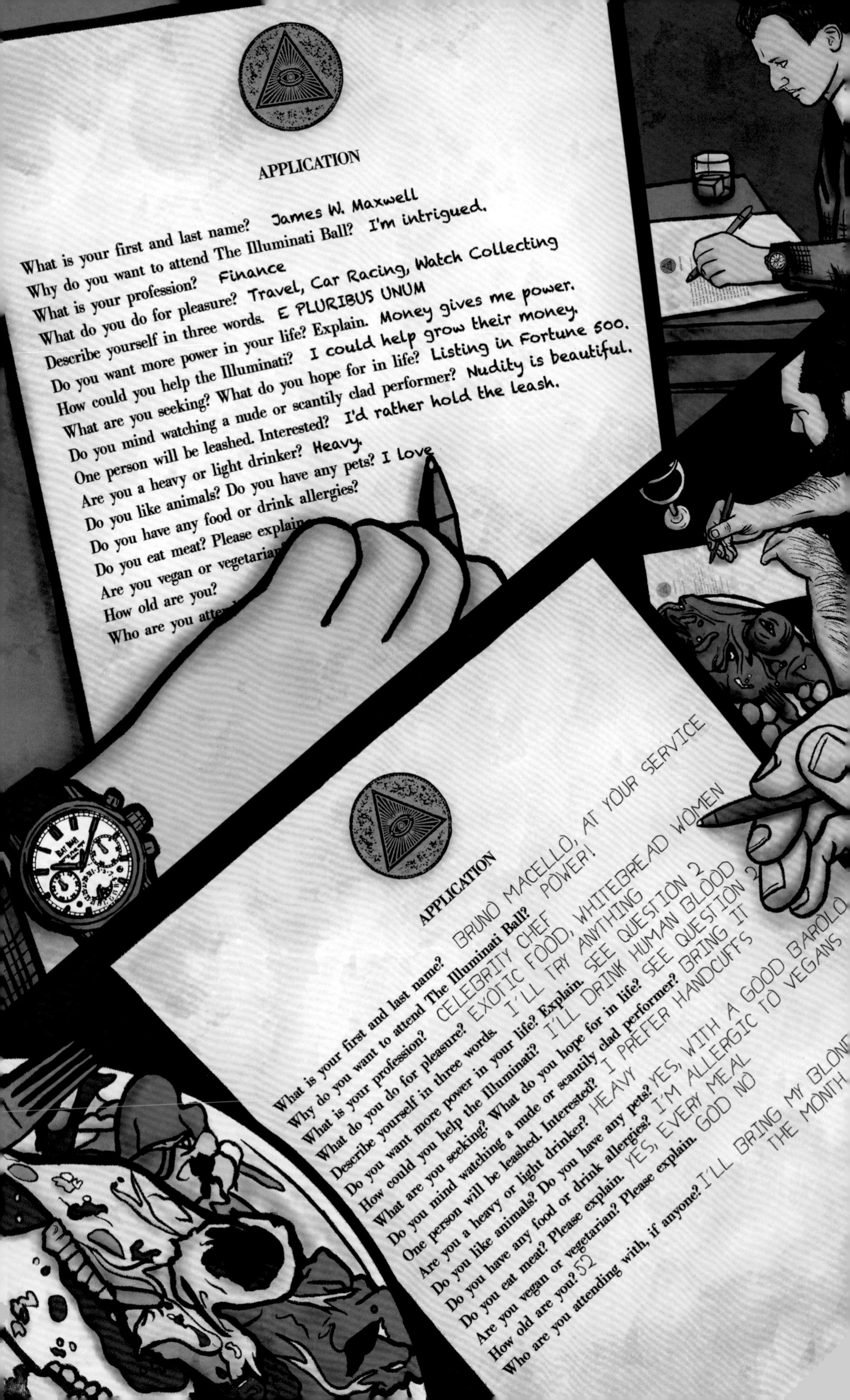
APPLICATION
What is your first and last name? James W. Maxwell
Why do you want to attend The Illuminati Ball? I'm intrigued.
What is your profession? Finance
What do you do for pleasure? Travel, Car Racing, Watch Collecting
Describe yourself in three words. E PLURIBUS UNUM
Do you want more power in your life? Explain. Money gives me power.
How could you help the Illuminati? I could help grow their money.
What are you seeking? What do you hope for in life? Listing in Fortune 500.
Do you mind watching a nude or scantily clad performer? Nudity is beautiful.
One person will be leashed. Interested? I'd rather hold the leash.
Are you a heavy or light drinker? Heavy.
Do you like animals? Do you have any pets? I love
Do you have any food or drink allergies?
Do you eat meat? Please explai
Are you vegan or vegetarian
How old are you?
Who are you atte
APPLICATION
What is your first and last name? BRUNO MACELLO, AT YOUR SERVICE
Why do you want to attend The Illuminati Ball? POWER!
What is your profession? CELEBRITY CHEF
What do you do for pleasure? EXOTIC FOOD, WHITEBREAD WOMEN
Describe yourself in three words. I'LL TRY ANYTHING
Do you want more power in your life? Explain. SEE QUESTION 2
How could you help the Illuminati? I'LL DRINK HUMAN BLOOD
What are you seeking? What do you hope for in life? SEE QUESTION 2
Do you mind watching a nude or scantily clad performer? BRING IT
One person will be leashed. Interested? I PREFER HANDCUFFS
Are you a heavy or light drinker? HEAVY
Do you like animals? Do you have any pets? YES, WITH A GOOD BAROLO
Do you have any food or drink allergies? I'M ALLERGIC TO VEGANS
Do you eat meat? Please explain. YES, EVERY MEAL
Are you vegan or vegetarian? Please explain. GOD NO
How old are you? 52
Who are you attending with, if anyone? I'LL BRING MY BLOND
THE MONTH

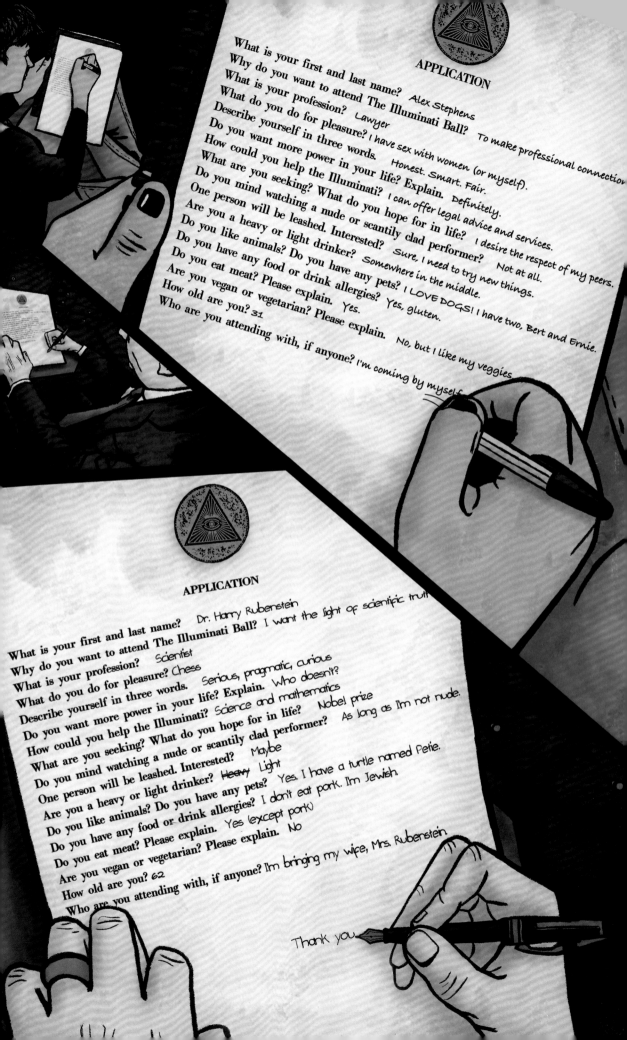

APPLICATION

What is your first and last name? Alex Stephens

Why do you want to attend The Illuminati Ball? To make professional connection

What is your profession? Lawyer

What do you do for pleasure? I have sex with women (or myself).

Describe yourself in three words. Honest. Smart. Fair.

Do you want more power in your life? Explain. Definitely.

How could you help the Illuminati? I can offer legal advice and services.

What are you seeking? What do you hope for in life? I desire the respect of my peers.

Do you mind watching a nude or scantily clad performer? Not at all.

One person will be leashed. Interested? Sure, I need to try new things.

Are you a heavy or light drinker? Somewhere in the middle.

Do you like animals? Do you have any pets? I LOVE DOGS! I have two, Bert and Ernie.

Do you have any food or drink allergies? Yes, gluten.

Do you eat meat? Please explain. Yes.

Are you vegan or vegetarian? Please explain. No, but I like my veggies

How old are you? 31

Who are you attending with, if anyone? I'm coming by myself

APPLICATION

What is your first and last name? Dr. Harry Rubenstein

Why do you want to attend The Illuminati Ball? I want the light of scientific truth

What is your profession? Scientist

What do you do for pleasure? Chess

Describe yourself in three words. Serious, pragmatic, curious

Do you want more power in your life? Explain. Who doesn't?

How could you help the Illuminati? Science and mathematics

What are you seeking? What do you hope for in life? Nobel prize

Do you mind watching a nude or scantily clad performer? As long as I'm not nude.

One person will be leashed. Interested? Maybe

Are you a heavy or light drinker? Heavy Light

Do you like animals? Do you have any pets? Yes. I have a turtle named Petie.

Do you have any food or drink allergies? I don't eat pork. I'm Jewish

Do you eat meat? Please explain. Yes (except pork)

Are you vegan or vegetarian? Please explain. No

How old are you? 62

Who are you attending with, if anyone? I'm bringing my wife, Mrs. Rubenstein

Thank you

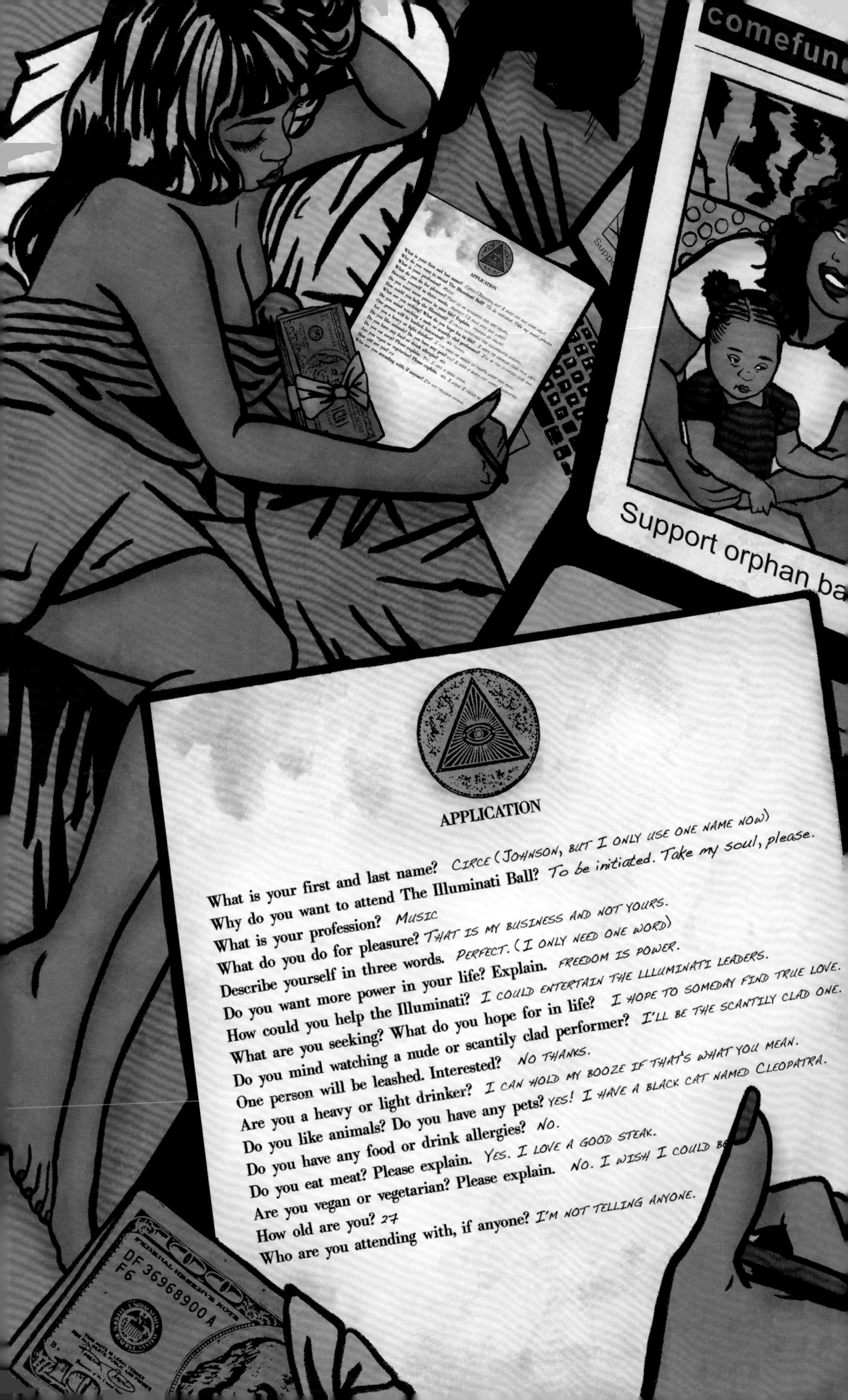
comefun
Support orphan ba
APPLICATION
What is your first and last name? CIRCE (JOHNSON, BUT I ONLY USE ONE NAME NOW)
Why do you want to attend The Illuminati Ball? To be initiated. Take my soul, please.
What is your profession? MUSIC
What do you do for pleasure? THAT IS MY BUSINESS AND NOT YOURS.
Describe yourself in three words. PERFECT. (I ONLY NEED ONE WORD)
Do you want more power in your life? Explain. FREEDOM IS POWER.
How could you help the Illuminati? I COULD ENTERTAIN THE ILLUMINATI LEADERS.
What are you seeking? What do you hope for in life? I HOPE TO SOMEDAY FIND TRUE LOVE.
Do you mind watching a nude or scantily clad performer? I'LL BE THE SCANTILY CLAD ONE.
One person will be leashed. Interested? NO THANKS.
Are you a heavy or light drinker? I CAN HOLD MY BOOZE IF THAT'S WHAT YOU MEAN.
Do you like animals? Do you have any pets? YES! I HAVE A BLACK CAT NAMED CLEOPATRA.
Do you have any food or drink allergies? NO.
Do you eat meat? Please explain. YES. I LOVE A GOOD STEAK.
Are you vegan or vegetarian? Please explain. NO. I WISH I COULD
How old are you? 27
Who are you attending with, if anyone? I'M NOT TELLING ANYONE.
DF 36968900 A
F6

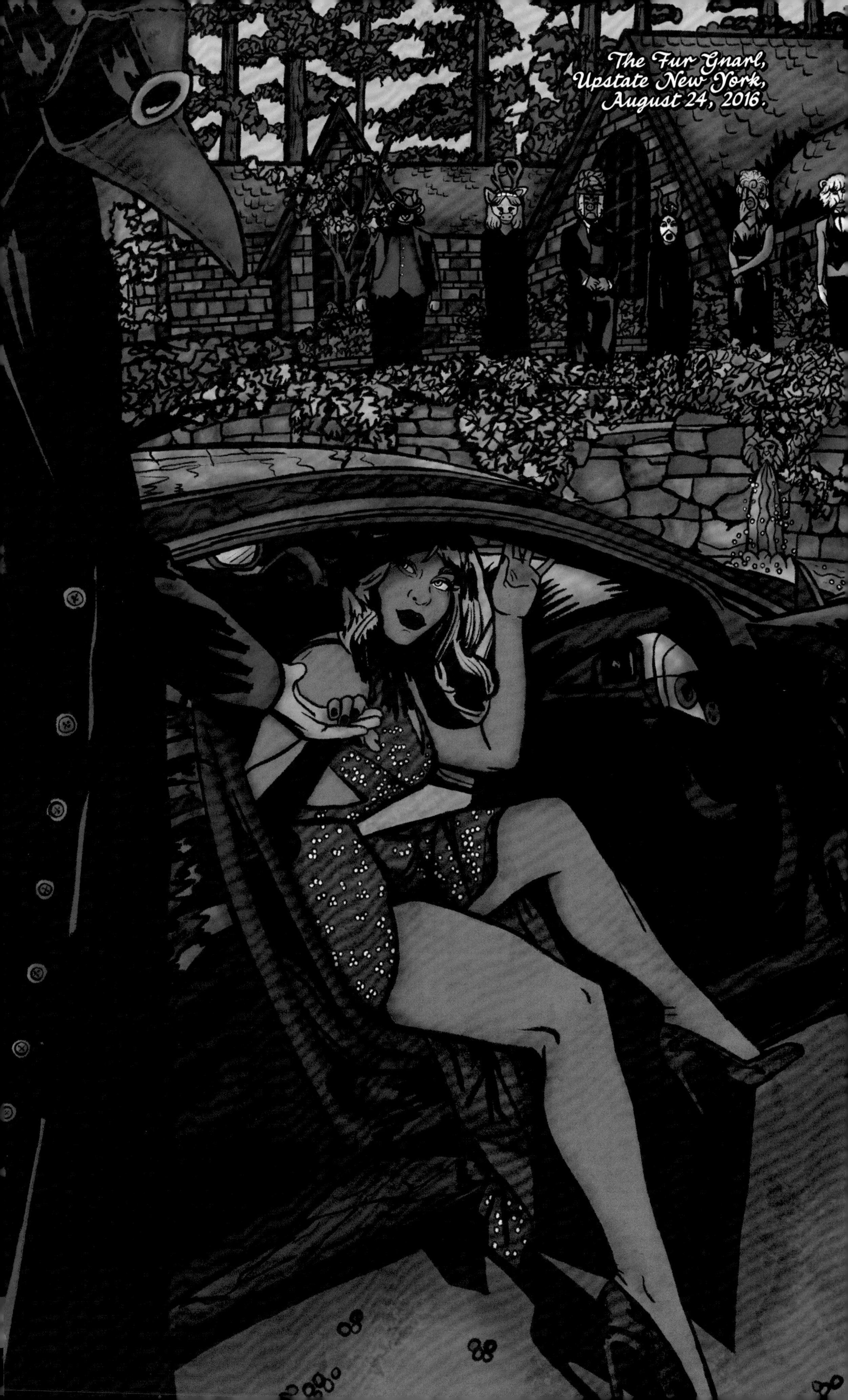
The Fur Gnarl,
Upstate New York,
August 24, 2016.

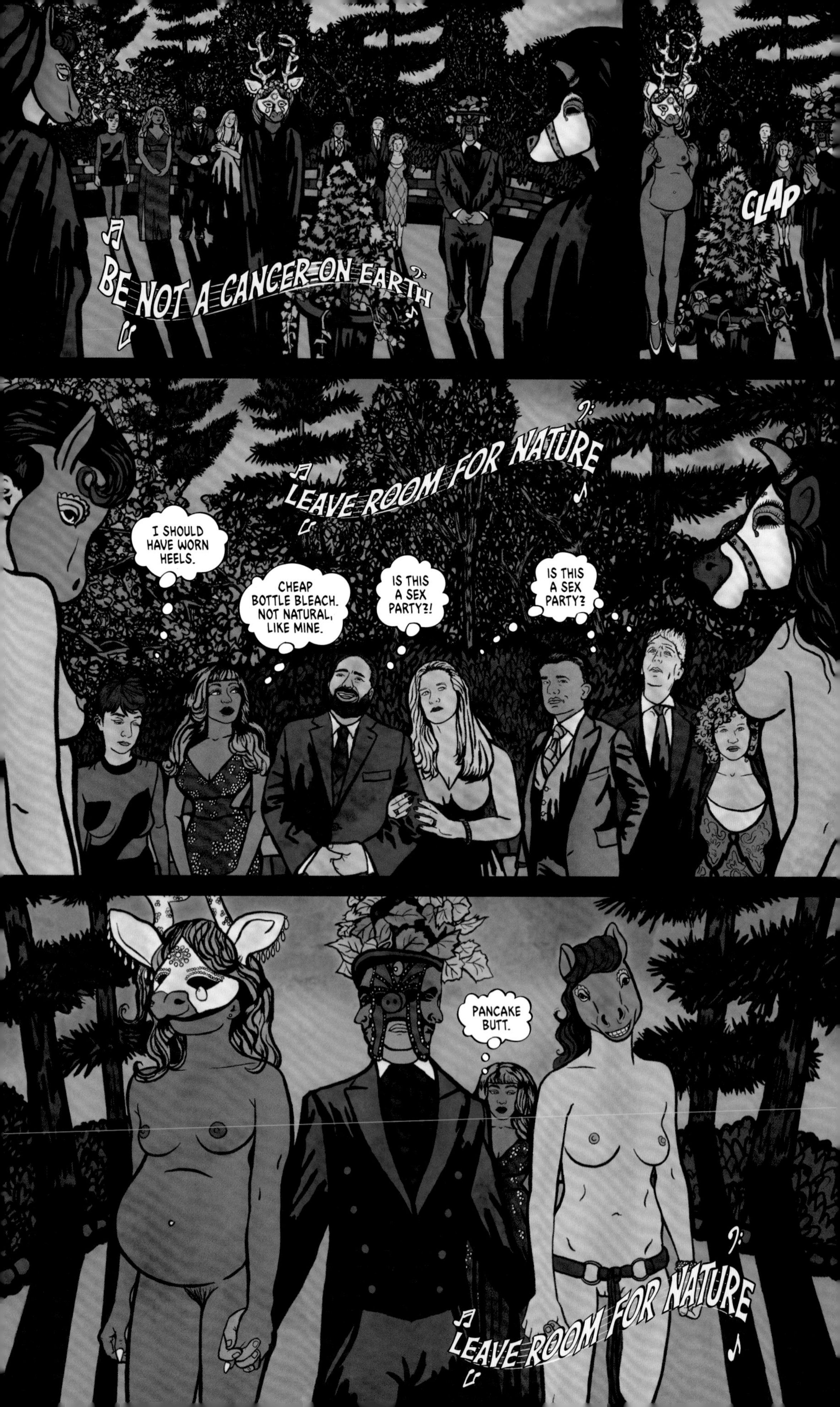
BE NOT A CANCER ON EARTH
CLAP
LEAVE ROOM FOR NATURE
I SHOULD HAVE WORN HEELS.
CHEAP BOTTLE BLEACH. NOT NATURAL, LIKE MINE.
IS THIS A SEX PARTY?!
IS THIS A SEX PARTY?
PANCAKE BUTT.
LEAVE ROOM FOR NATURE

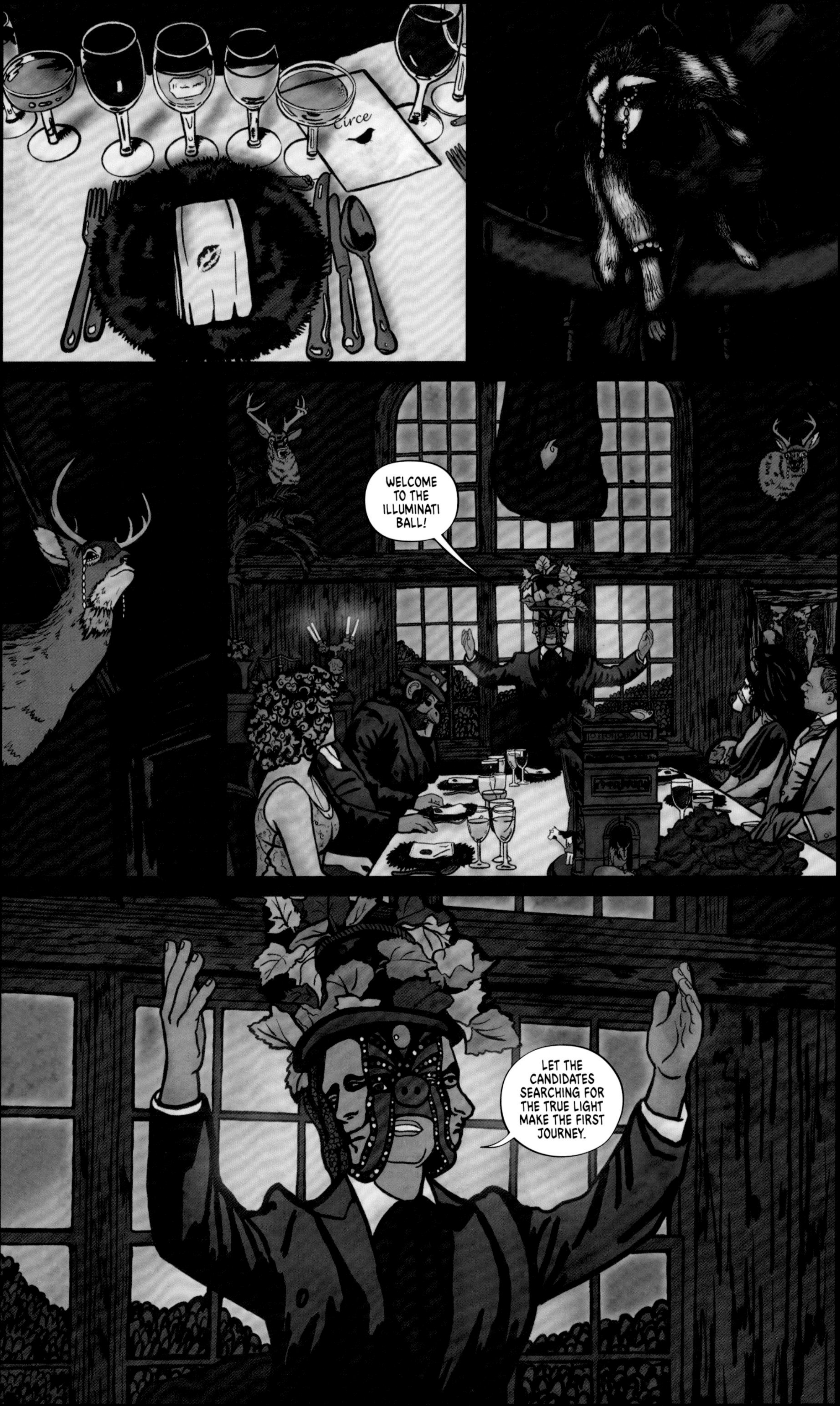
Circe
WELCOME TO THE ILLUMINATI BALL!
LET THE CANDIDATES SEARCHING FOR THE TRUE LIGHT MAKE THE FIRST JOURNEY.

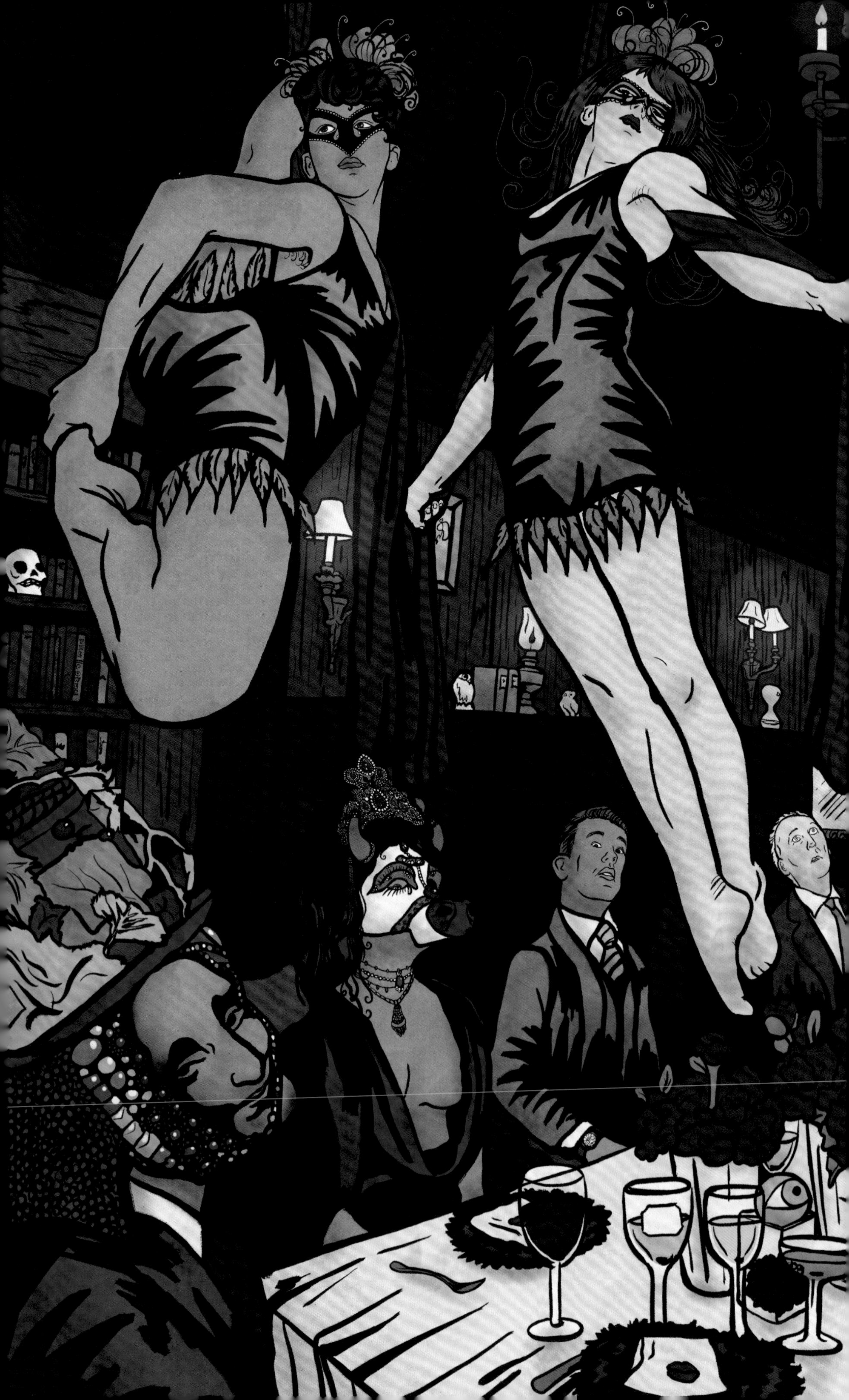

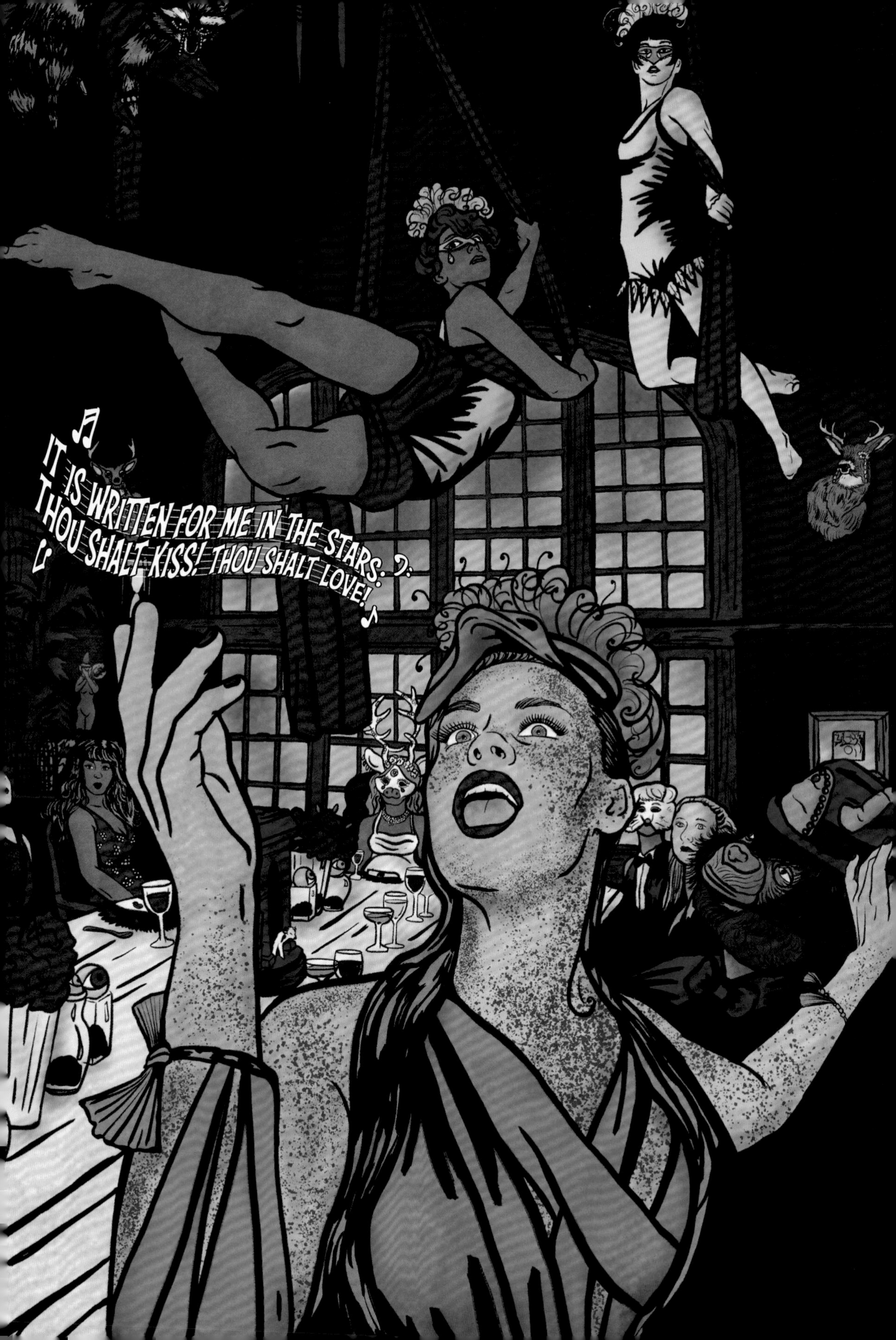
IT IS WRITTEN FOR ME IN THE STARS.
THOU SHALT KISS! THOU SHALT LOVE!

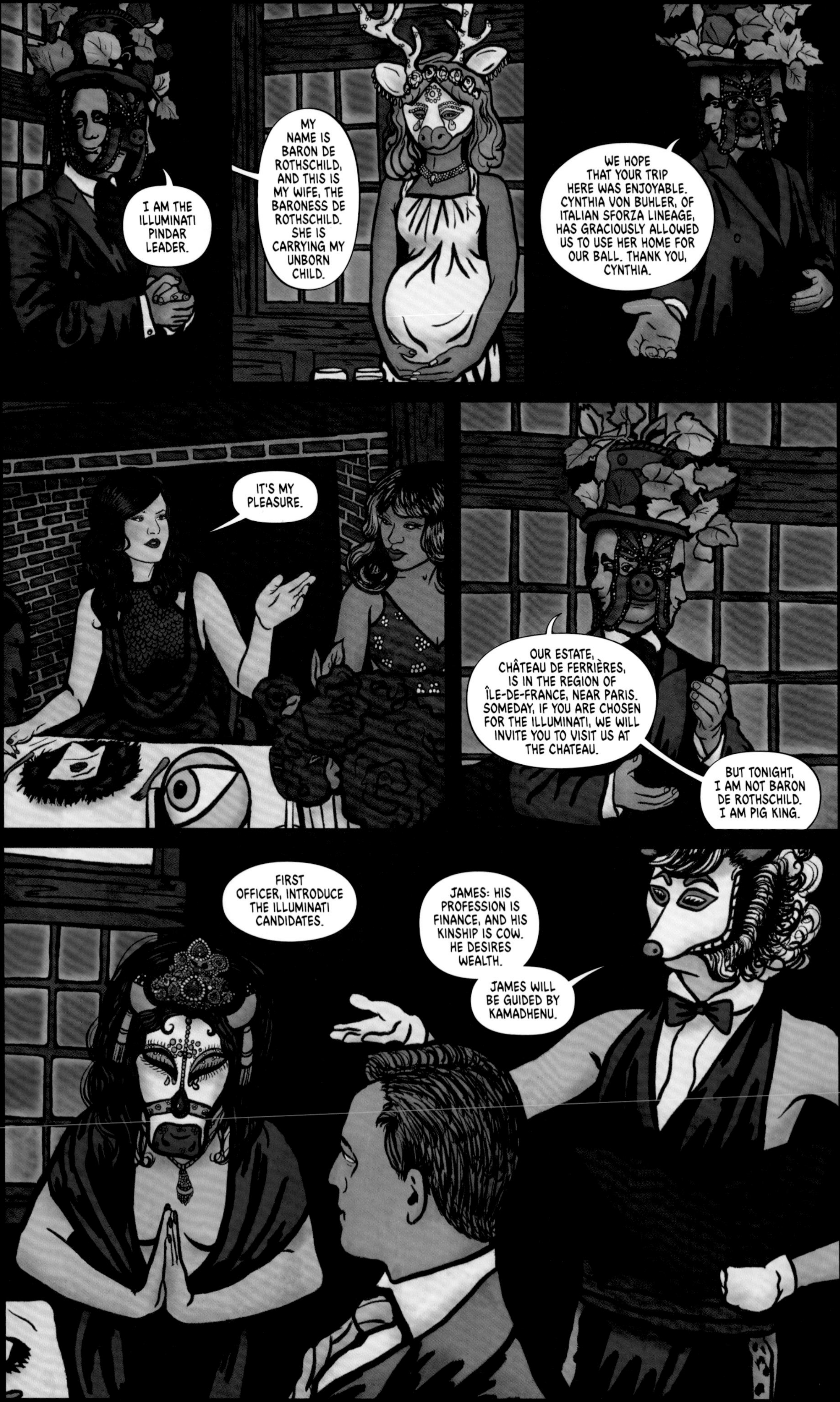

I AM THE ILLUMINATI PINDAR LEADER.
MY NAME IS BARON DE ROTHSCHILD, AND THIS IS MY WIFE, THE BARONESS DE ROTHSCHILD. SHE IS CARRYING MY UNBORN CHILD.
WE HOPE THAT YOUR TRIP HERE WAS ENJOYABLE. CYNTHIA VON BUHLER, OF ITALIAN SFORZA LINEAGE, HAS GRACIOUSLY ALLOWED US TO USE HER HOME FOR OUR BALL. THANK YOU, CYNTHIA.
IT'S MY PLEASURE.
OUR ESTATE, CHÂTEAU DE FERRIÈRES, IS IN THE REGION OF ÎLE-DE-FRANCE, NEAR PARIS. SOMEDAY, IF YOU ARE CHOSEN FOR THE ILLUMINATI, WE WILL INVITE YOU TO VISIT US AT THE CHATEAU.
BUT TONIGHT, I AM NOT BARON DE ROTHSCHILD. I AM PIG KING.
FIRST OFFICER, INTRODUCE THE ILLUMINATI CANDIDATES.
JAMES: HIS PROFESSION IS FINANCE, AND HIS KINSHIP IS COW. HE DESIRES WEALTH.
JAMES WILL BE GUIDED BY KAMADHENU.

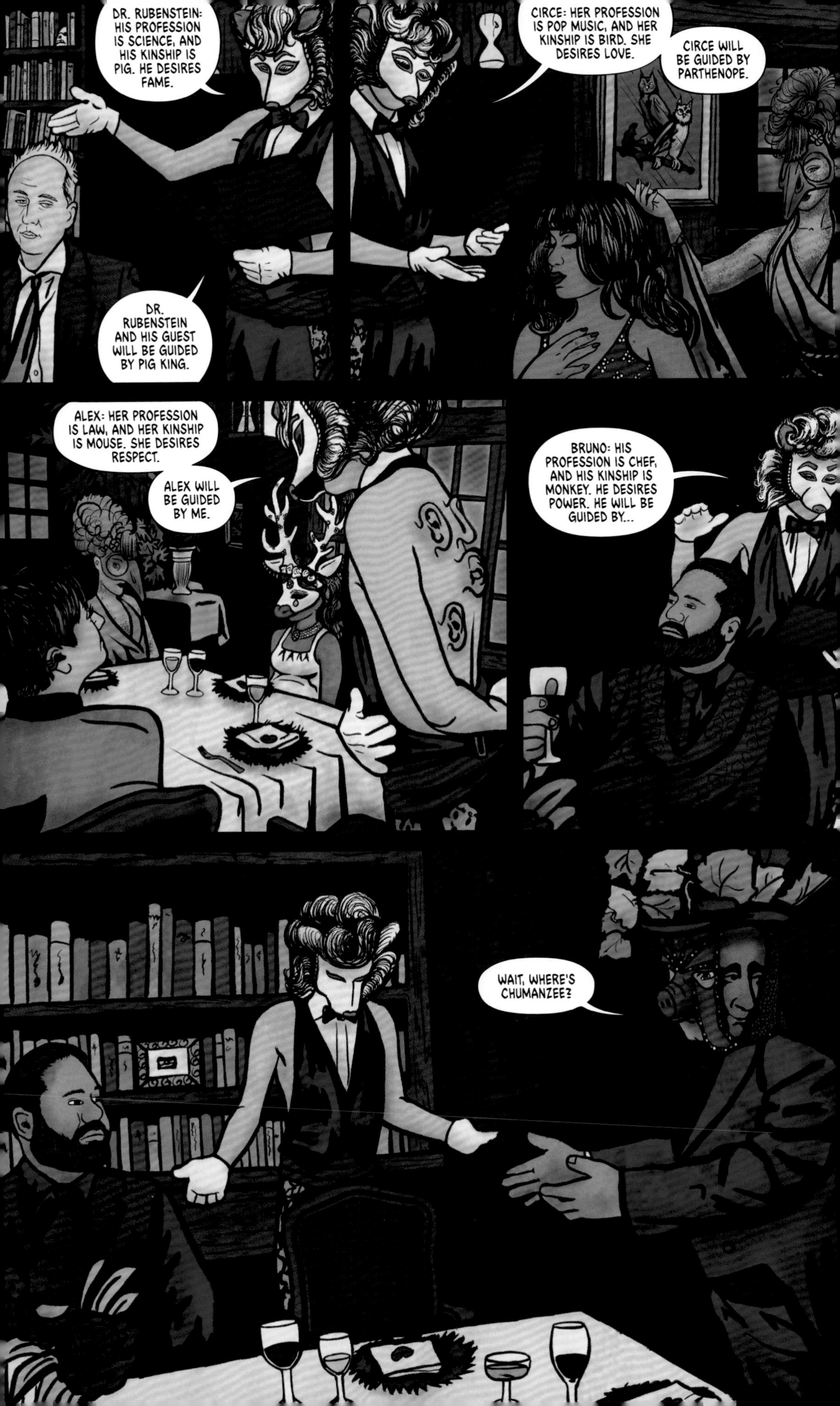
DR. RUBENSTEIN: HIS PROFESSION IS SCIENCE, AND HIS KINSHIP IS PIG. HE DESIRES FAME.
DR. RUBENSTEIN AND HIS GUEST WILL BE GUIDED BY PIG KING.
CIRCE: HER PROFESSION IS POP MUSIC, AND HER KINSHIP IS BIRD. SHE DESIRES LOVE.
CIRCE WILL BE GUIDED BY PARTHENOPE.
ALEX: HER PROFESSION IS LAW, AND HER KINSHIP IS MOUSE. SHE DESIRES RESPECT.
ALEX WILL BE GUIDED BY ME.
BRUNO: HIS PROFESSION IS CHEF, AND HIS KINSHIP IS MONKEY. HE DESIRES POWER. HE WILL BE GUIDED BY...
WAIT, WHERE'S CHUMANZEE?

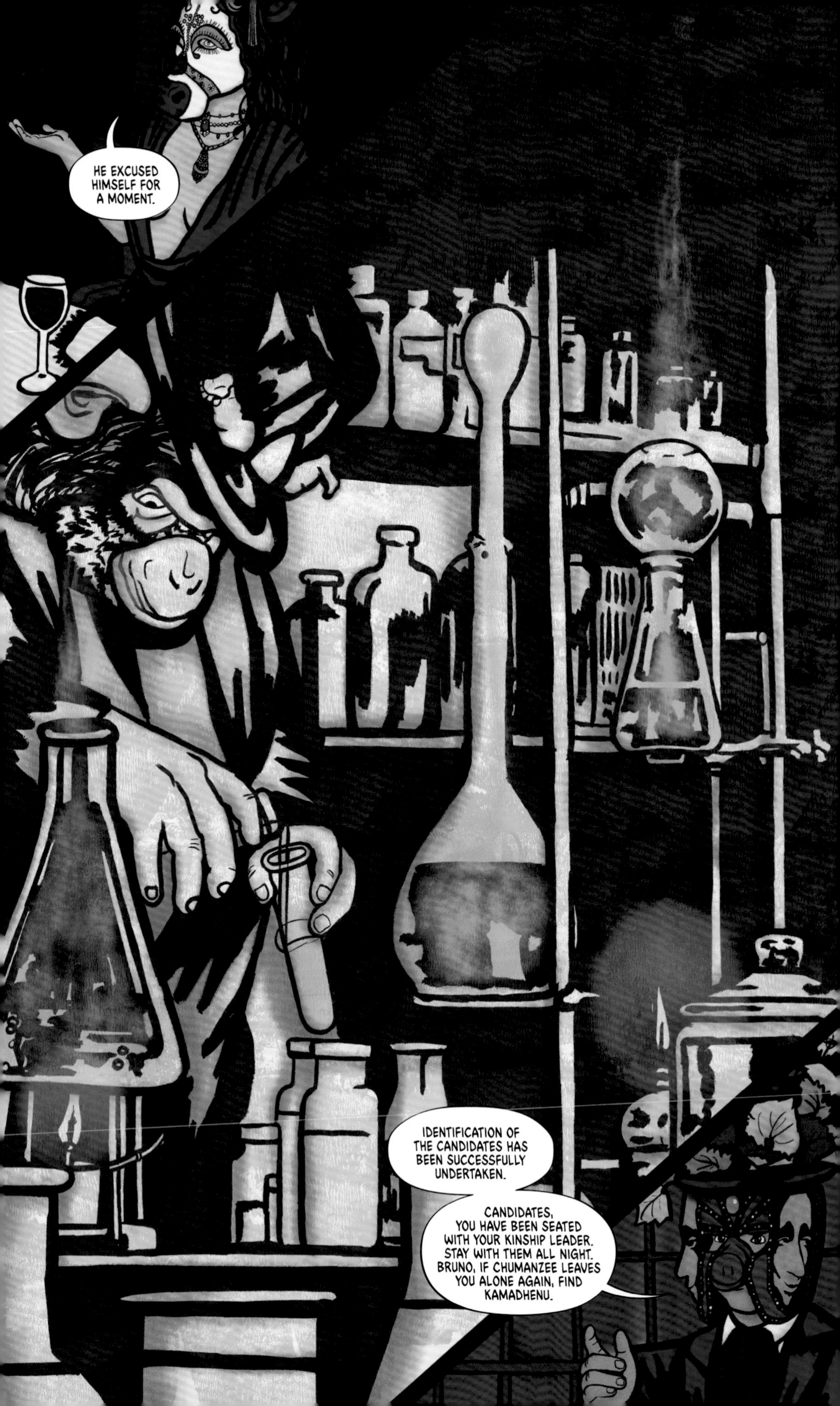
HE EXCUSED HIMSELF FOR A MOMENT.
IDENTIFICATION OF THE CANDIDATES HAS BEEN SUCCESSFULLY UNDERTAKEN.
CANDIDATES, YOU HAVE BEEN SEATED WITH YOUR KINSHIP LEADER. STAY WITH THEM ALL NIGHT. BRUNO, IF CHUMANZEE LEAVES YOU ALONE AGAIN, FIND KAMADHENU.

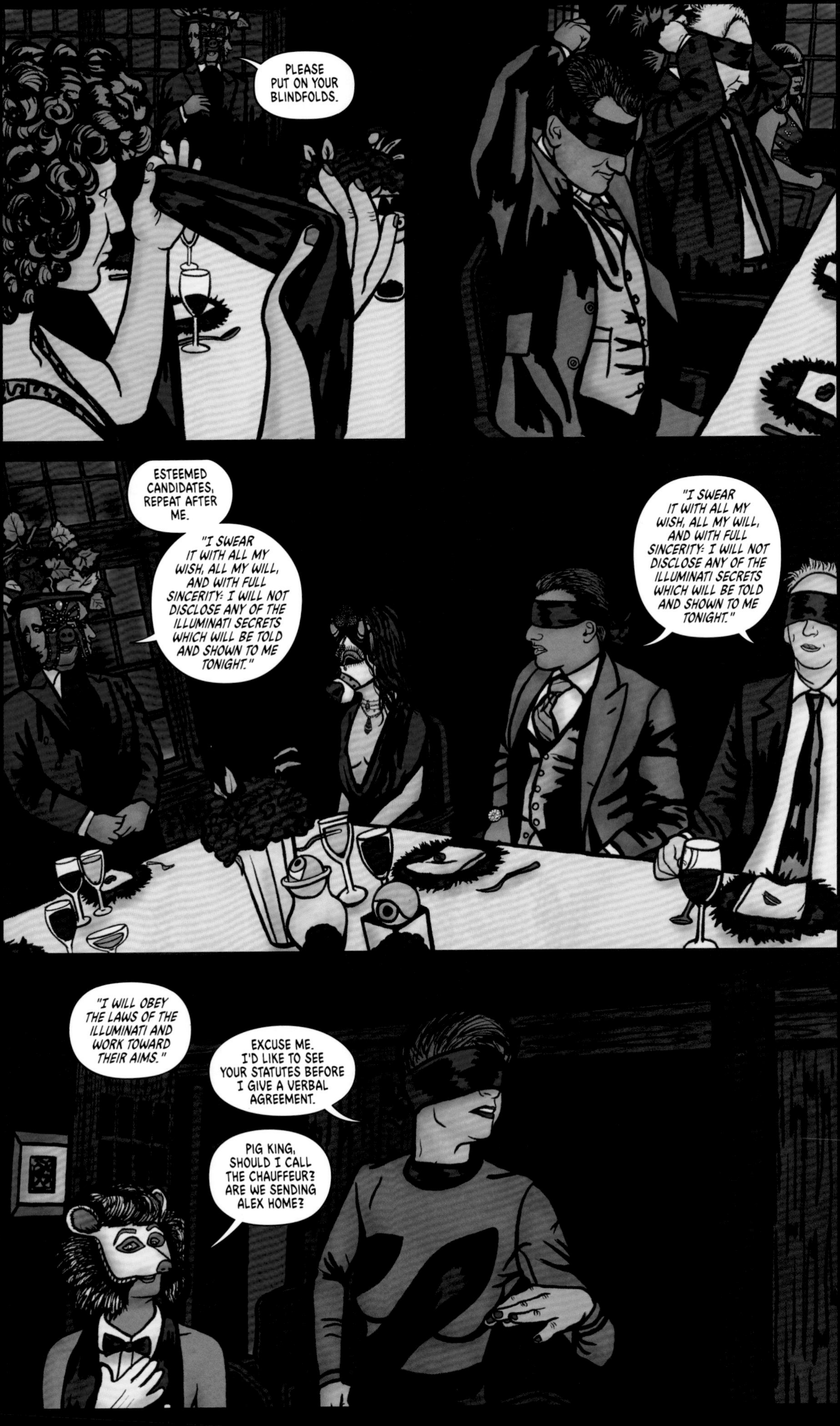
PLEASE PUT ON YOUR BLINDFOLDS.
ESTEEMED CANDIDATES, REPEAT AFTER ME.
"I SWEAR IT WITH ALL MY WISH, ALL MY WILL, AND WITH FULL SINCERITY: I WILL NOT DISCLOSE ANY OF THE ILLUMINATI SECRETS WHICH WILL BE TOLD AND SHOWN TO ME TONIGHT."
"I SWEAR IT WITH ALL MY WISH, ALL MY WILL, AND WITH FULL SINCERITY: I WILL NOT DISCLOSE ANY OF THE ILLUMINATI SECRETS WHICH WILL BE TOLD AND SHOWN TO ME TONIGHT."
"I WILL OBEY THE LAWS OF THE ILLUMINATI AND WORK TOWARD THEIR AIMS."
EXCUSE ME. I'D LIKE TO SEE YOUR STATUTES BEFORE I GIVE A VERBAL AGREEMENT.
PIG KING, SHOULD I CALL THE CHAUFFEUR? ARE WE SENDING ALEX HOME?

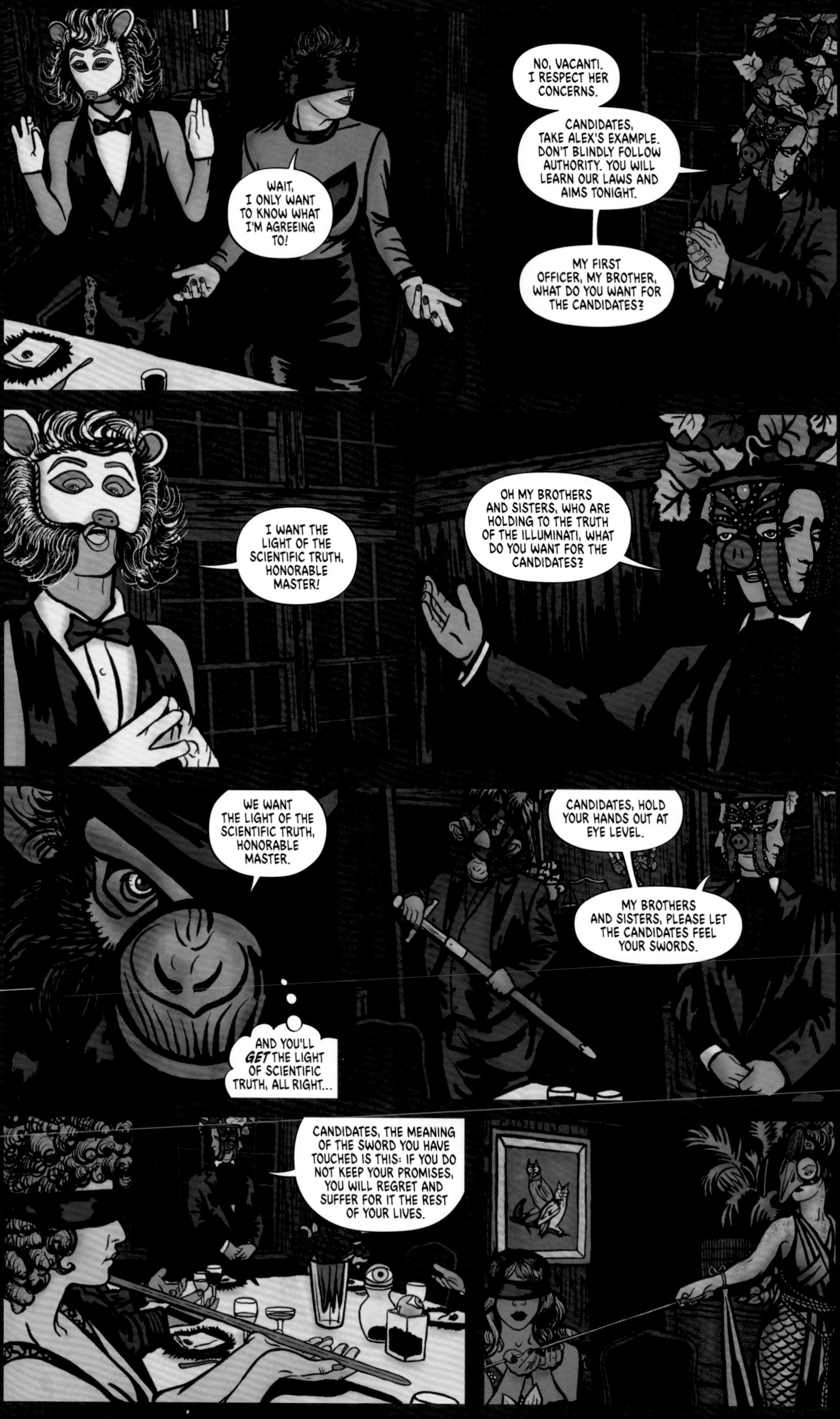
WAIT, I ONLY WANT TO KNOW WHAT I'M AGREEING TO!
NO, VACANTI. I RESPECT HER CONCERNS.
CANDIDATES, TAKE ALEX'S EXAMPLE. DON'T BLINDLY FOLLOW AUTHORITY. YOU WILL LEARN OUR LAWS AND AIMS TONIGHT.
MY FIRST OFFICER, MY BROTHER, WHAT DO YOU WANT FOR THE CANDIDATES?
I WANT THE LIGHT OF THE SCIENTIFIC TRUTH, HONORABLE MASTER!
OH MY BROTHERS AND SISTERS, WHO ARE HOLDING TO THE TRUTH OF THE ILLUMINATI, WHAT DO YOU WANT FOR THE CANDIDATES?
WE WANT THE LIGHT OF THE SCIENTIFIC TRUTH, HONORABLE MASTER.
AND YOU'LL *GET* THE LIGHT OF SCIENTIFIC TRUTH, ALL RIGHT...
CANDIDATES, HOLD YOUR HANDS OUT AT EYE LEVEL.
MY BROTHERS AND SISTERS, PLEASE LET THE CANDIDATES FEEL YOUR SWORDS.
CANDIDATES, THE MEANING OF THE SWORD YOU HAVE TOUCHED IS THIS: IF YOU DO NOT KEEP YOUR PROMISES, YOU WILL REGRET AND SUFFER FOR IT THE REST OF YOUR LIVES.

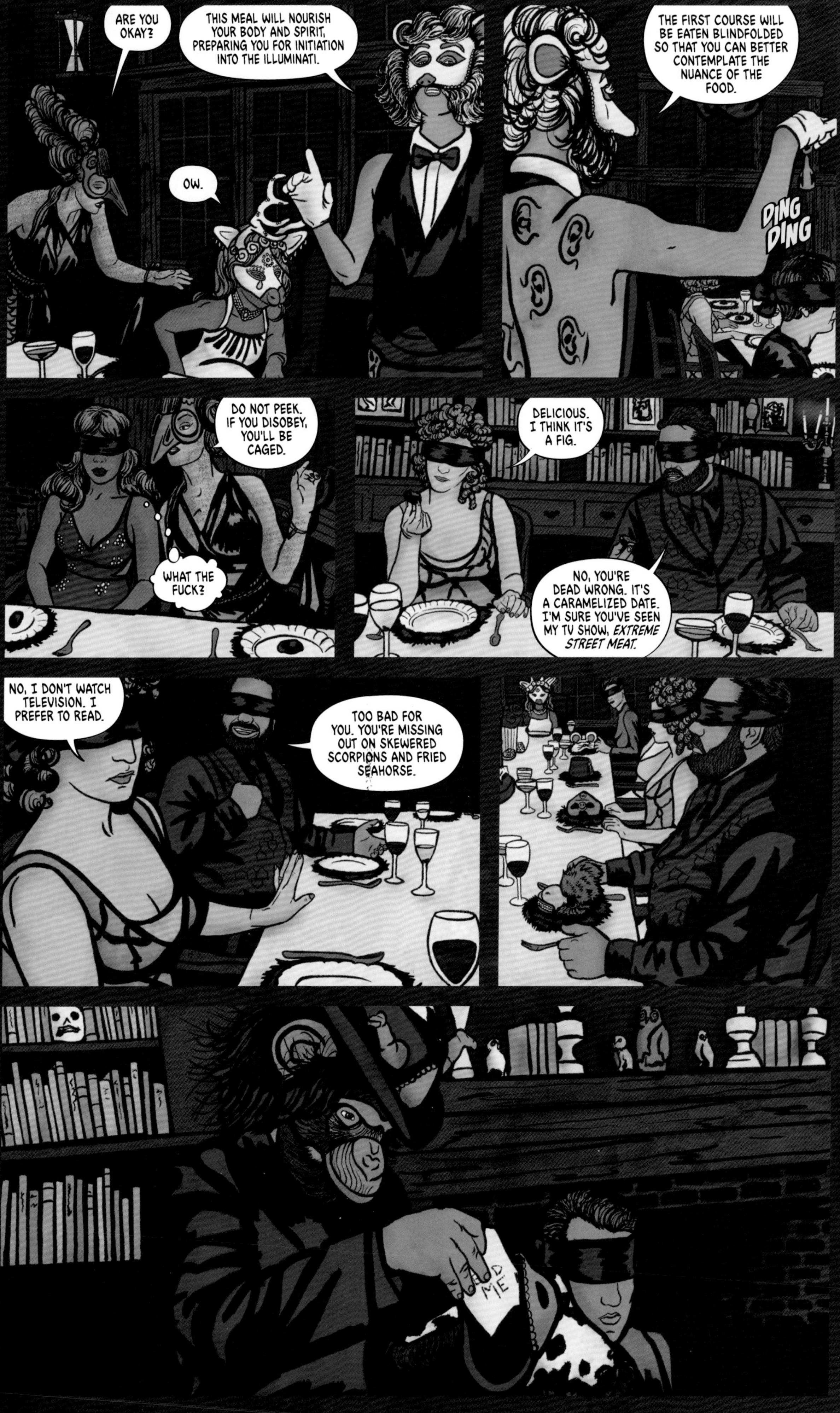
ARE YOU OKAY?
THIS MEAL WILL NOURISH YOUR BODY AND SPIRIT, PREPARING YOU FOR INITIATION INTO THE ILLUMINATI.
OW.
THE FIRST COURSE WILL BE EATEN BLINDFOLDED SO THAT YOU CAN BETTER CONTEMPLATE THE NUANCE OF THE FOOD.
DING DING
DO NOT PEEK. IF YOU DISOBEY, YOU'LL BE CAGED.
WHAT THE FUCK?
DELICIOUS. I THINK IT'S A FIG.
NO, YOU'RE DEAD WRONG. IT'S A CARAMELIZED DATE. I'M SURE YOU'VE SEEN MY TV SHOW, EXTREME STREET MEAT.
NO, I DON'T WATCH TELEVISION. I PREFER TO READ.
TOO BAD FOR YOU. YOU'RE MISSING OUT ON SKEWERED SCORPIONS AND FRIED SEAHORSE.

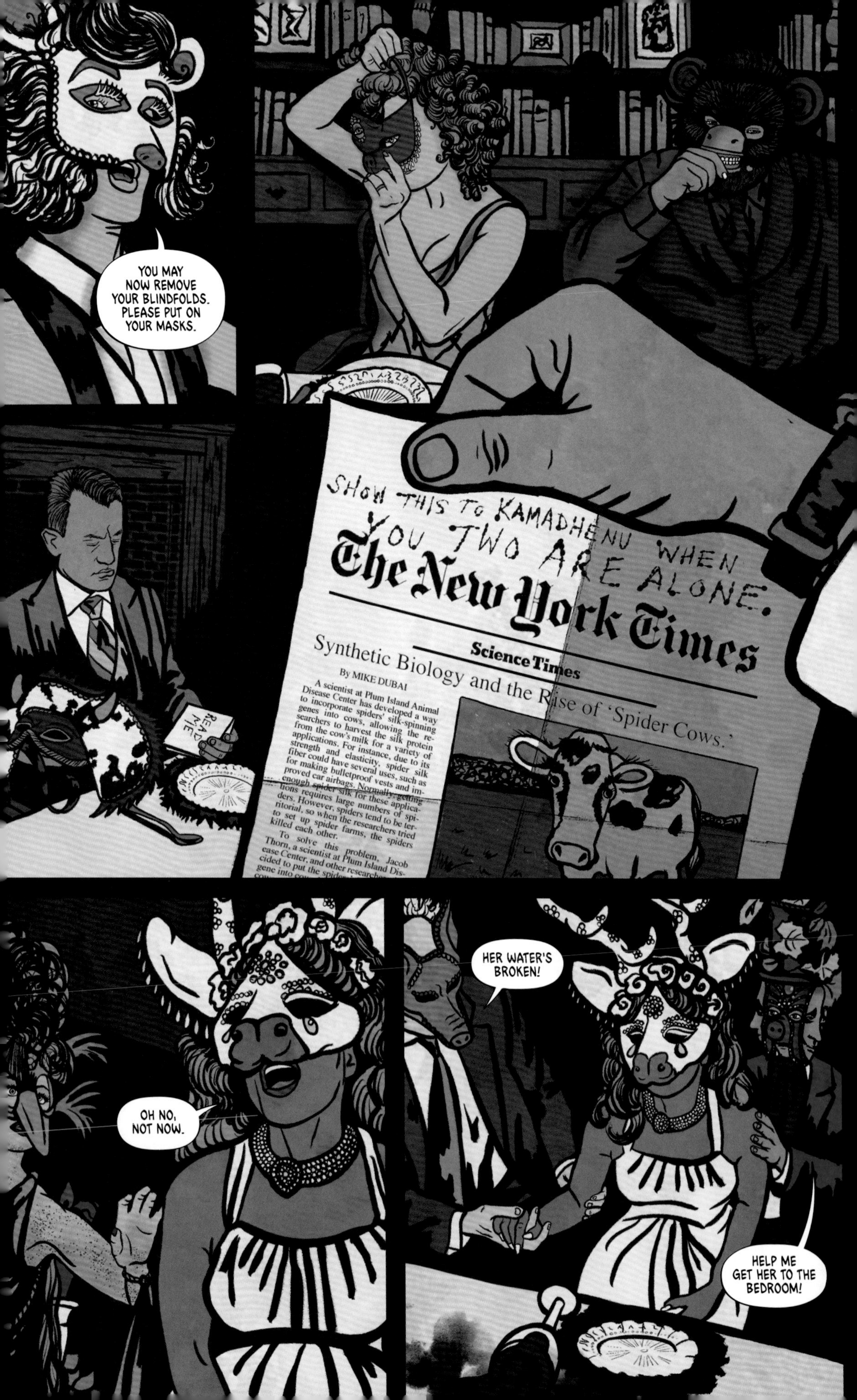
YOU MAY NOW REMOVE YOUR BLINDFOLDS. PLEASE PUT ON YOUR MASKS.
READ ME
SHOW THIS TO KAMADHENU WHEN YOU TWO ARE ALONE.
The New York Times
Science Times
Synthetic Biology and the Rise of 'Spider Cows.'
By MIKE DUBAI
A scientist at Plum Island Animal Disease Center has developed a way to incorporate spiders' silk-spinning genes into cows, allowing the researchers to harvest the silk protein from the cow's milk for a variety of applications. For instance, due to its strength and elasticity, spider silk fiber could have several uses, such as for making bulletproof vests and improved car airbags. Normally, getting enough spider silk for these applications requires large numbers of spiders. However, spiders tend to be territorial, so when the researchers tried to set up spider farms, the spiders killed each other.
To solve this problem, Jacob Thorn, a scientist at Plum Island Disease Center, and other researchers decided to put the spider
OH NO, NOT NOW.
HER WATER'S BROKEN!
HELP ME GET HER TO THE BEDROOM!

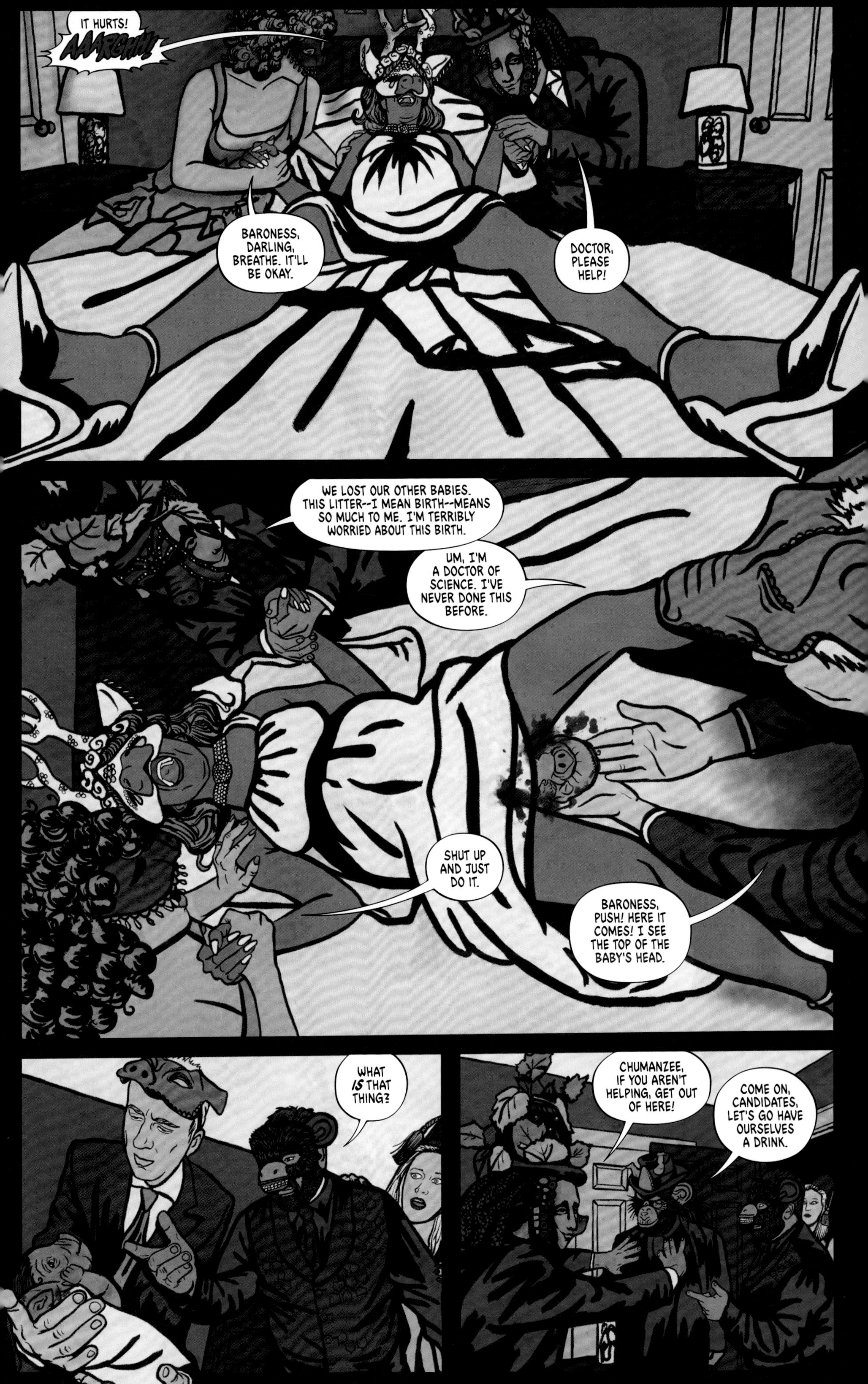
IT HURTS!
AAARGHH!
BARONESS, DARLING, BREATHE. IT'LL BE OKAY.
DOCTOR, PLEASE HELP!
WE LOST OUR OTHER BABIES. THIS LITTER--I MEAN BIRTH--MEANS SO MUCH TO ME. I'M TERRIBLY WORRIED ABOUT THIS BIRTH.
UM, I'M A DOCTOR OF SCIENCE. I'VE NEVER DONE THIS BEFORE.
SHUT UP AND JUST DO IT.
BARONESS, PUSH! HERE IT COMES! I SEE THE TOP OF THE BABY'S HEAD.
WHAT IS THAT THING?
CHUMANZEE, IF YOU AREN'T HELPING, GET OUT OF HERE!
COME ON, CANDIDATES, LET'S GO HAVE OURSELVES A DRINK.

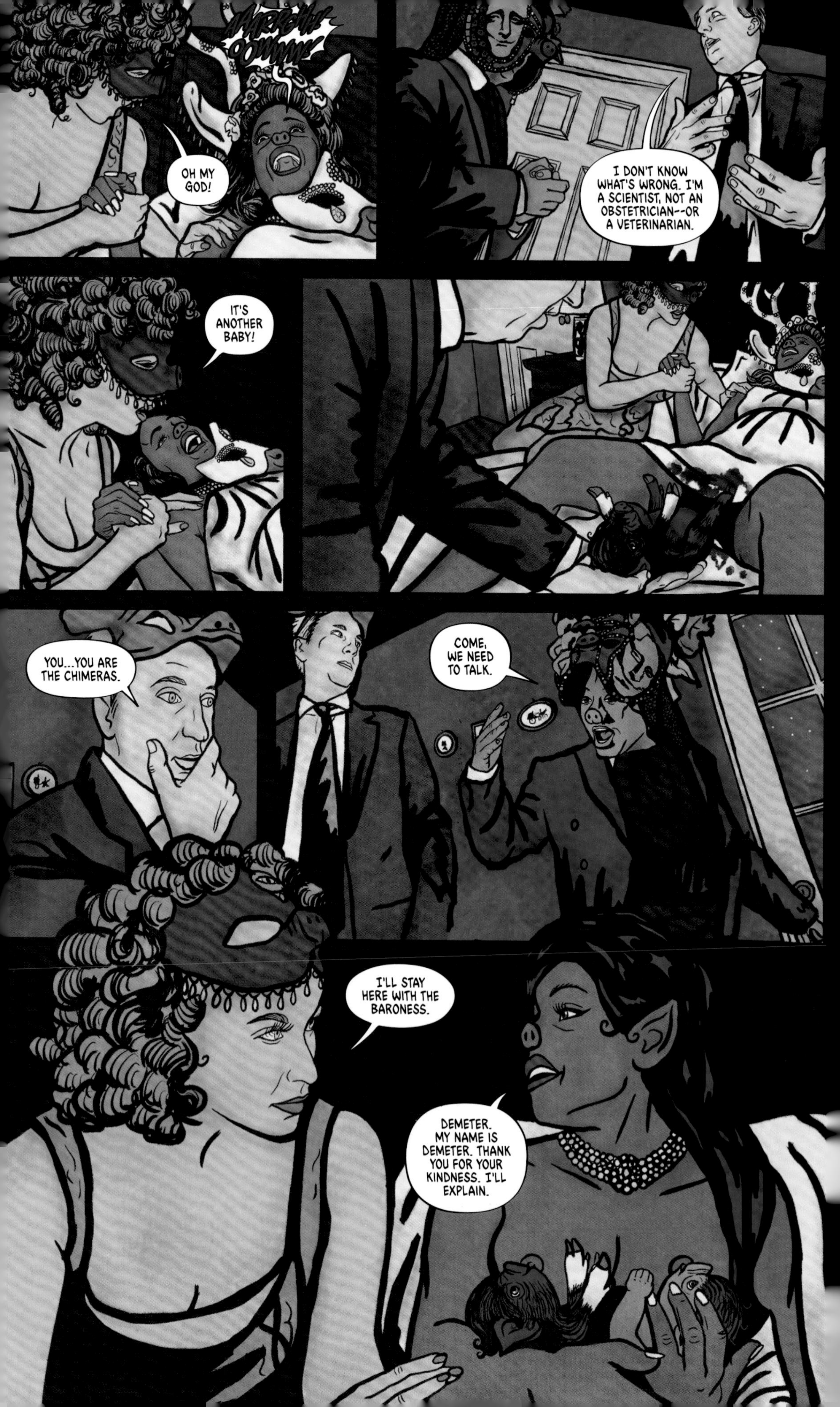
AARRGHH! OOWWW!
OH MY GOD!
I DON'T KNOW WHAT'S WRONG. I'M A SCIENTIST, NOT AN OBSTETRICIAN--OR A VETERINARIAN.
IT'S ANOTHER BABY!
YOU...YOU ARE THE CHIMERAS.
COME, WE NEED TO TALK.
I'LL STAY HERE WITH THE BARONESS.
DEMETER. MY NAME IS DEMETER. THANK YOU FOR YOUR KINDNESS. I'LL EXPLAIN.

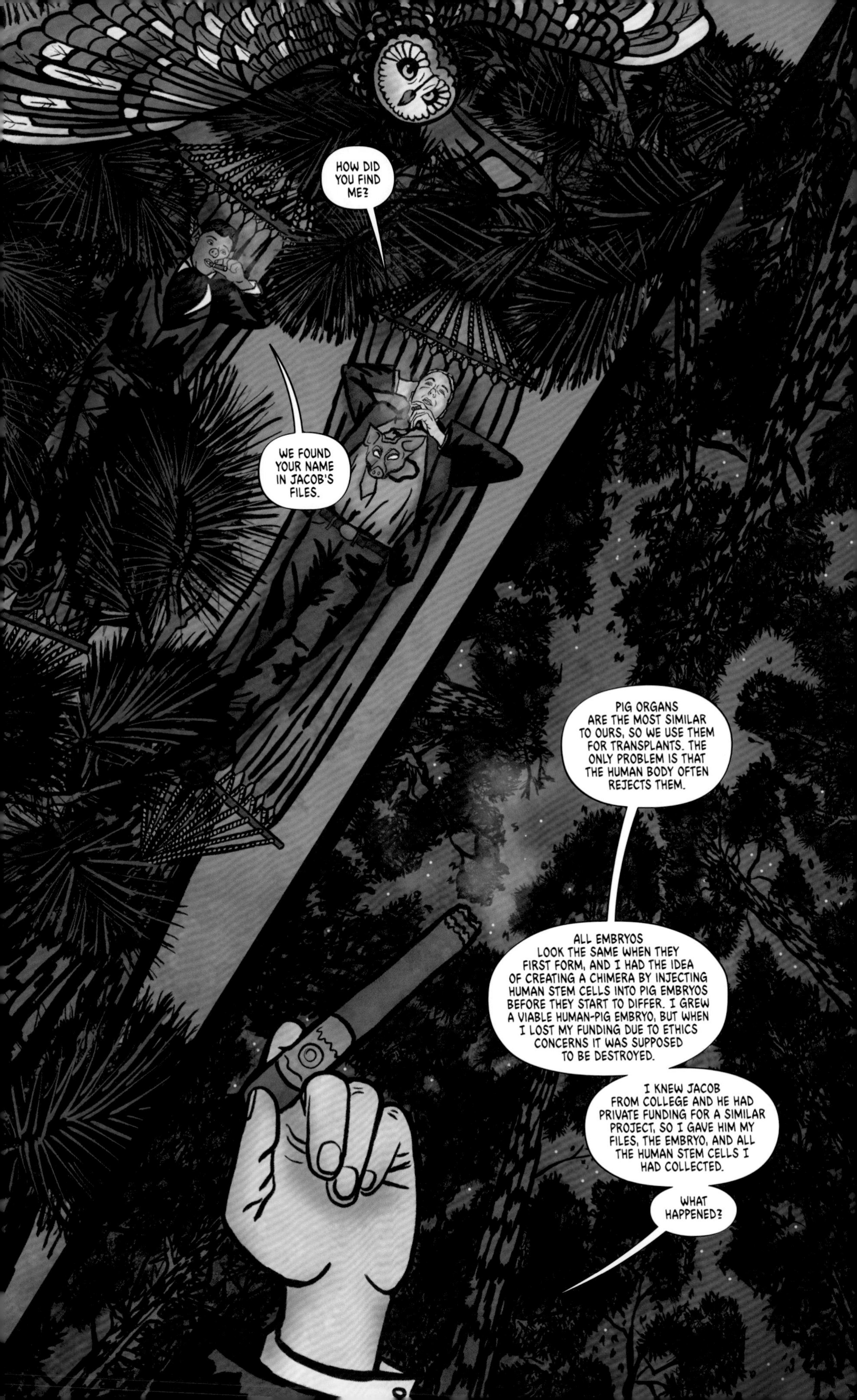
HOW DID YOU FIND ME?
WE FOUND YOUR NAME IN JACOB'S FILES.
PIG ORGANS ARE THE MOST SIMILAR TO OURS, SO WE USE THEM FOR TRANSPLANTS. THE ONLY PROBLEM IS THAT THE HUMAN BODY OFTEN REJECTS THEM.
ALL EMBRYOS LOOK THE SAME WHEN THEY FIRST FORM, AND I HAD THE IDEA OF CREATING A CHIMERA BY INJECTING HUMAN STEM CELLS INTO PIG EMBRYOS BEFORE THEY START TO DIFFER. I GREW A VIABLE HUMAN-PIG EMBRYO, BUT WHEN I LOST MY FUNDING DUE TO ETHICS CONCERNS IT WAS SUPPOSED TO BE DESTROYED.
I KNEW JACOB FROM COLLEGE AND HE HAD PRIVATE FUNDING FOR A SIMILAR PROJECT, SO I GAVE HIM MY FILES, THE EMBRYO, AND ALL THE HUMAN STEM CELLS I HAD COLLECTED.
WHAT HAPPENED?

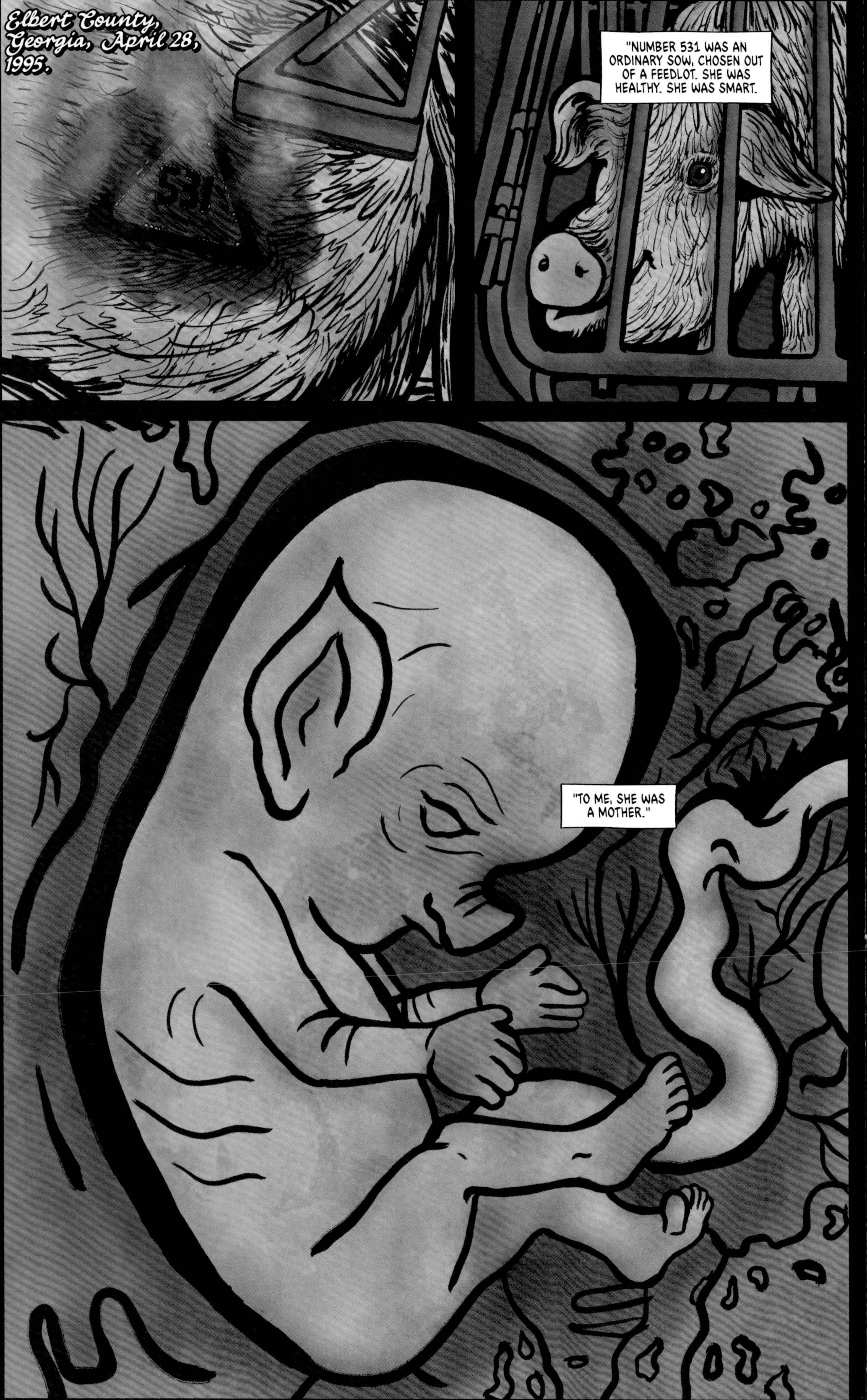
Elbert County, Georgia, April 28, 1995.
531
"NUMBER 531 WAS AN ORDINARY SOW, CHOSEN OUT OF A FEEDLOT. SHE WAS HEALTHY. SHE WAS SMART.
"TO ME, SHE WAS A MOTHER."

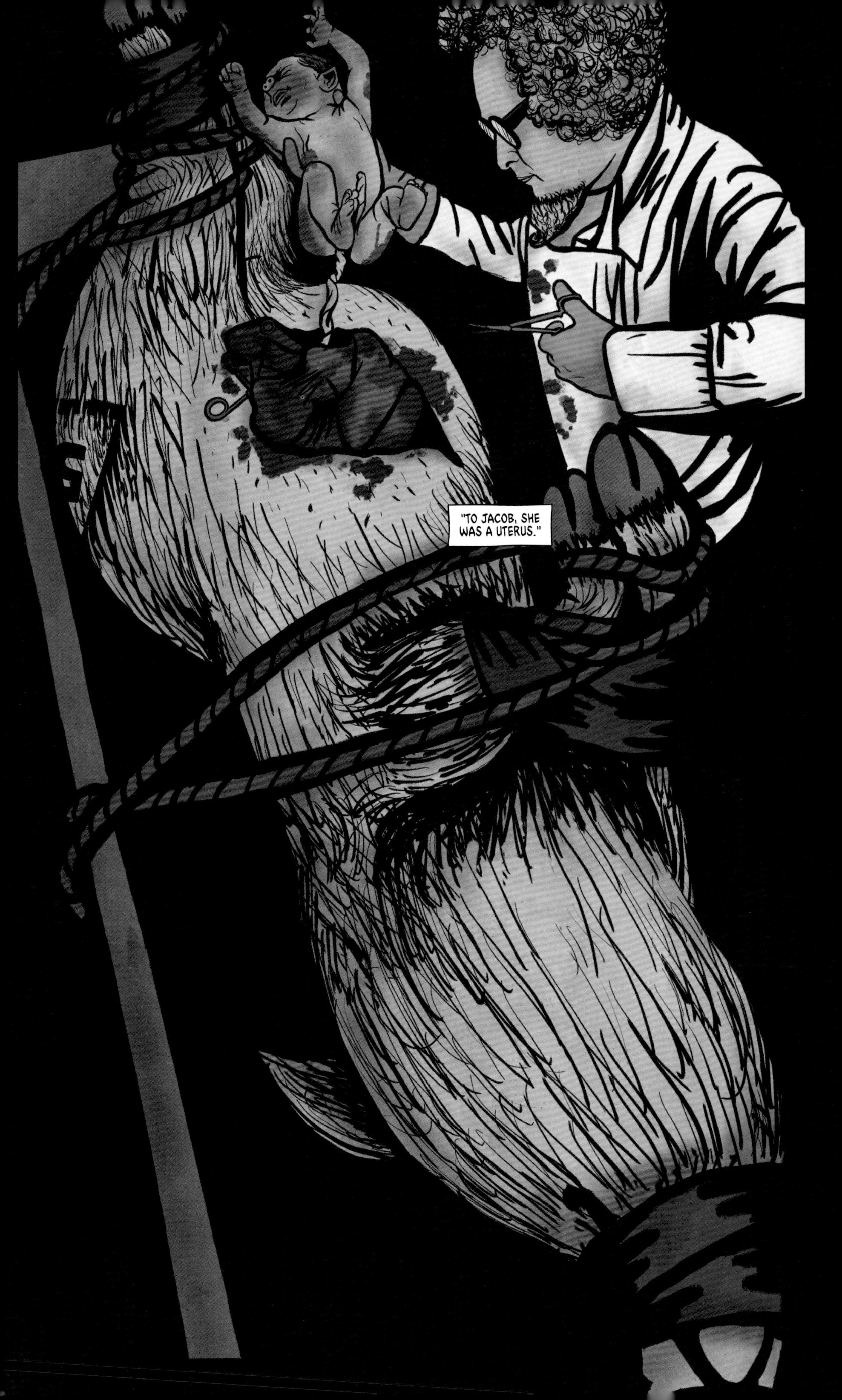
"TO JACOB, SHE WAS A UTERUS."

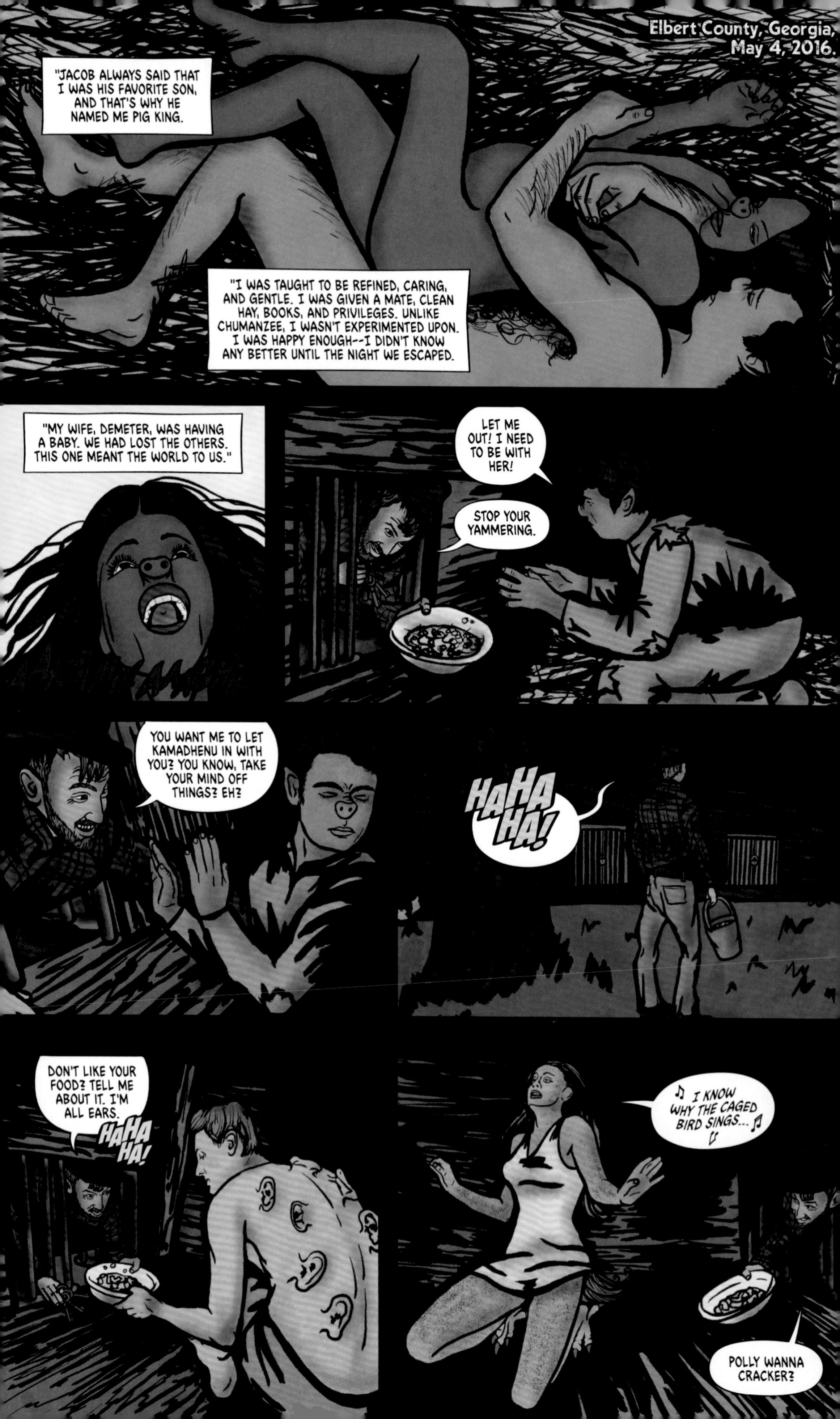
Elbert County, Georgia, May 4, 2016.
"JACOB ALWAYS SAID THAT I WAS HIS FAVORITE SON, AND THAT'S WHY HE NAMED ME PIG KING.
"I WAS TAUGHT TO BE REFINED, CARING, AND GENTLE. I WAS GIVEN A MATE, CLEAN HAY, BOOKS, AND PRIVILEGES. UNLIKE CHUMANZEE, I WASN'T EXPERIMENTED UPON. I WAS HAPPY ENOUGH--I DIDN'T KNOW ANY BETTER UNTIL THE NIGHT WE ESCAPED.
"MY WIFE, DEMETER, WAS HAVING A BABY. WE HAD LOST THE OTHERS. THIS ONE MEANT THE WORLD TO US."
LET ME OUT! I NEED TO BE WITH HER!
STOP YOUR YAMMERING.
YOU WANT ME TO LET KAMADHENU IN WITH YOU? YOU KNOW, TAKE YOUR MIND OFF THINGS? EH?
HAHAHA!
DON'T LIKE YOUR FOOD? TELL ME ABOUT IT. I'M ALL EARS.
HAHAHA!
♫ I KNOW WHY THE CAGED BIRD SINGS... ♫
POLLY WANNA CRACKER?

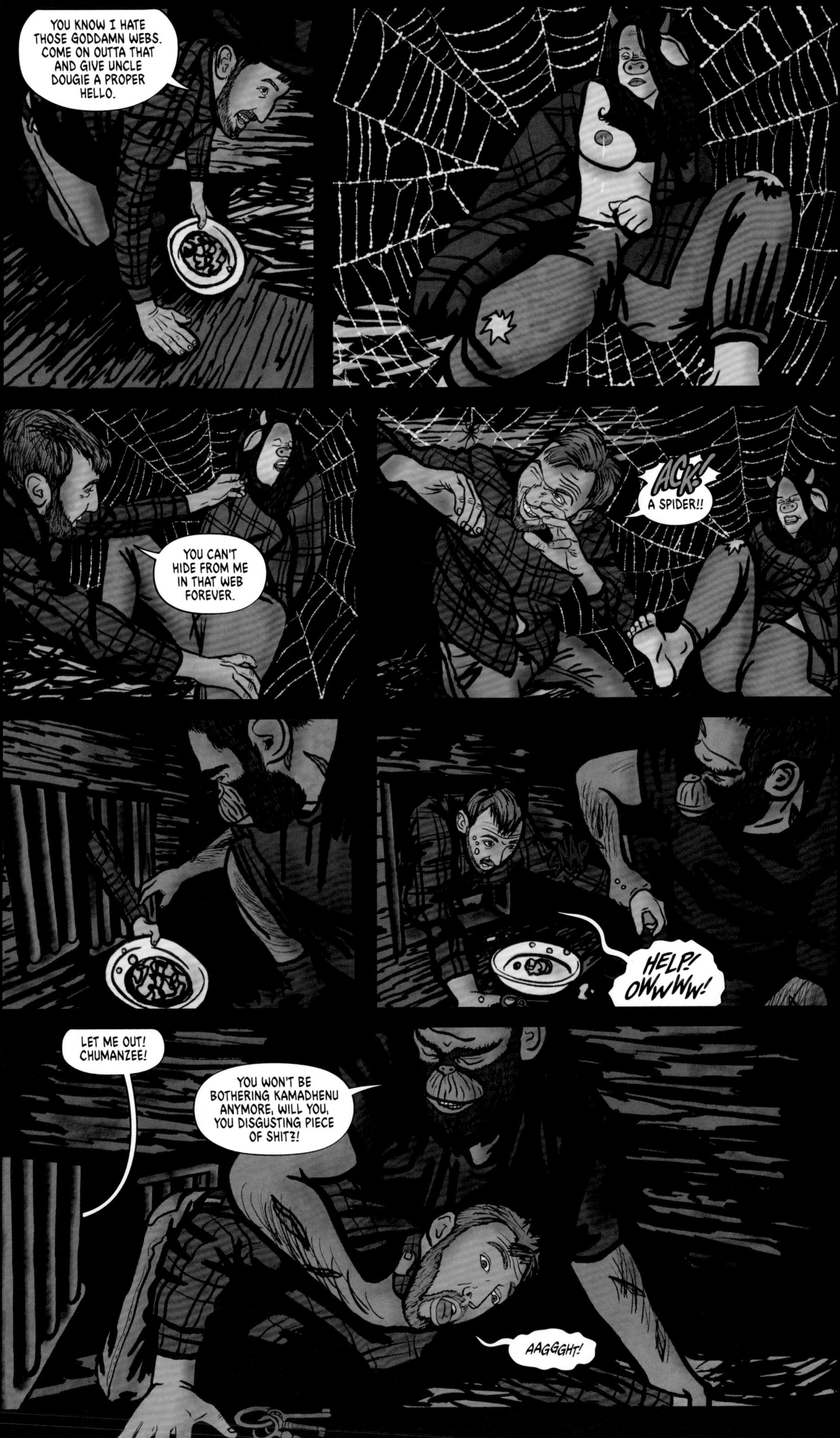
YOU KNOW I HATE THOSE GODDAMN WEBS. COME ON OUTTA THAT AND GIVE UNCLE DOUGIE A PROPER HELLO.
YOU CAN'T HIDE FROM ME IN THAT WEB FOREVER.
ACK!
A SPIDER!!
HELP! OWWWW!
LET ME OUT! CHUMANZEE!
YOU WON'T BE BOTHERING KAMADHENU ANYMORE, WILL YOU, YOU DISGUSTING PIECE OF SHIT?!
AAGGGHT!

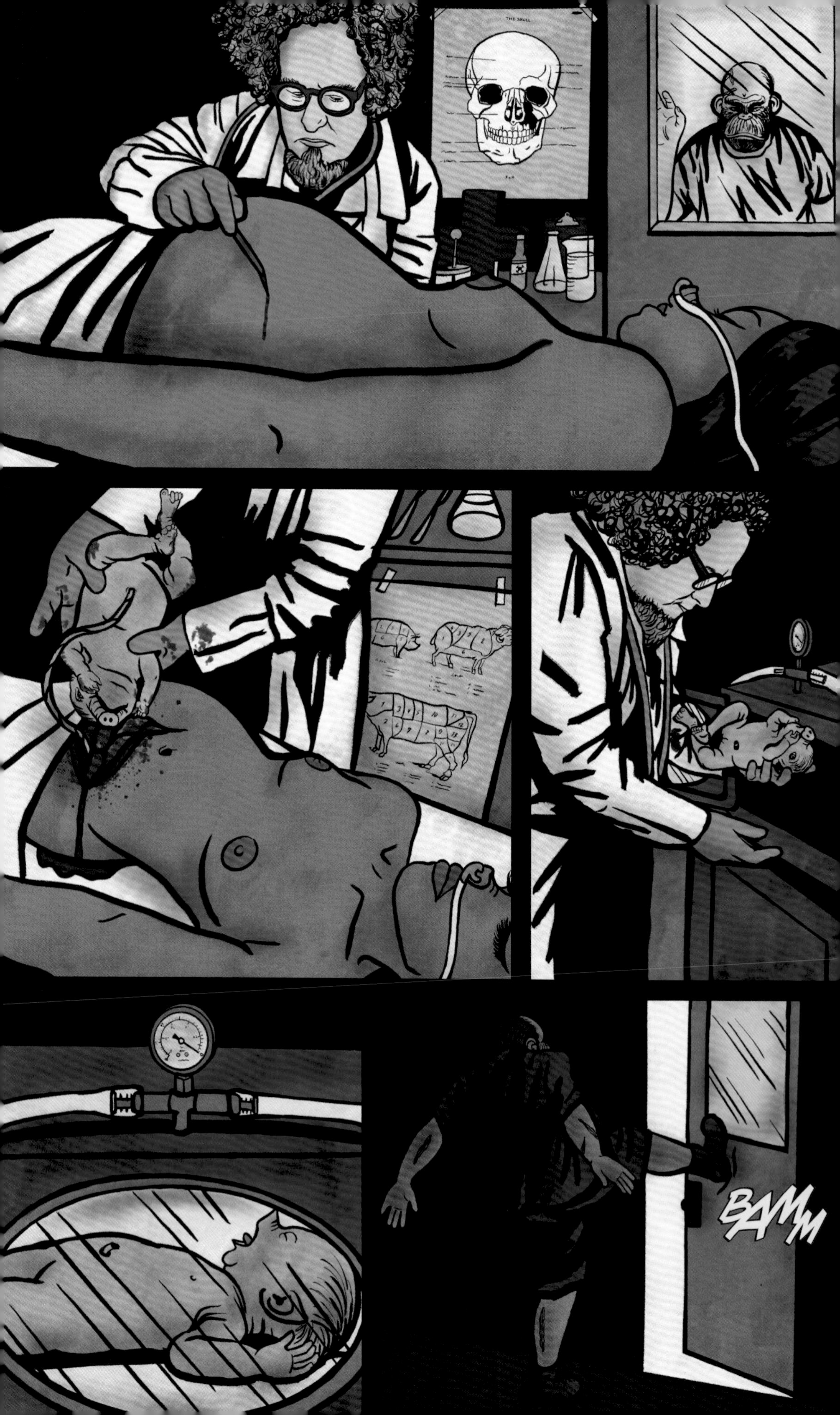
THE SKULL
BAMM

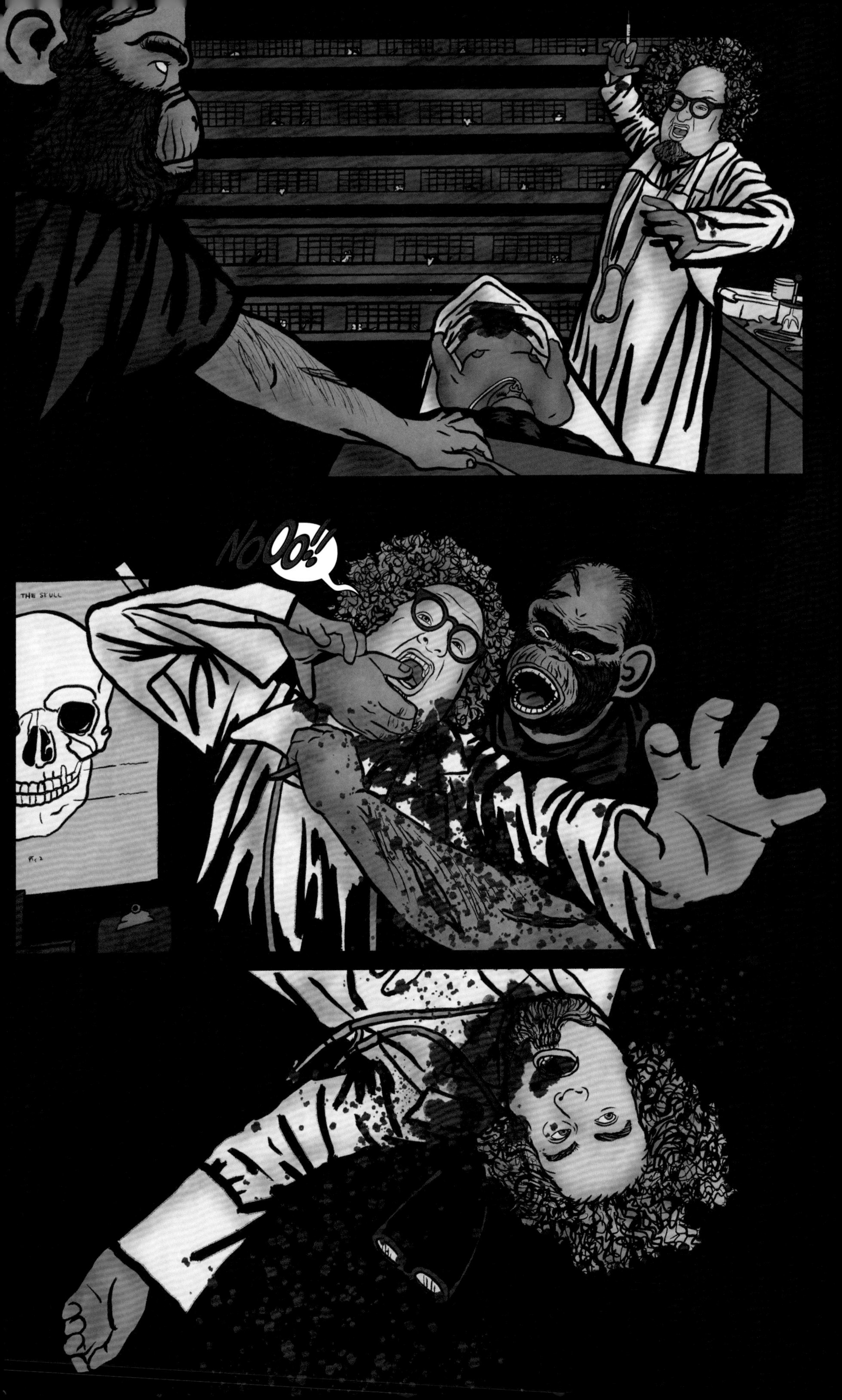

NOOOO!!
THE SKULL

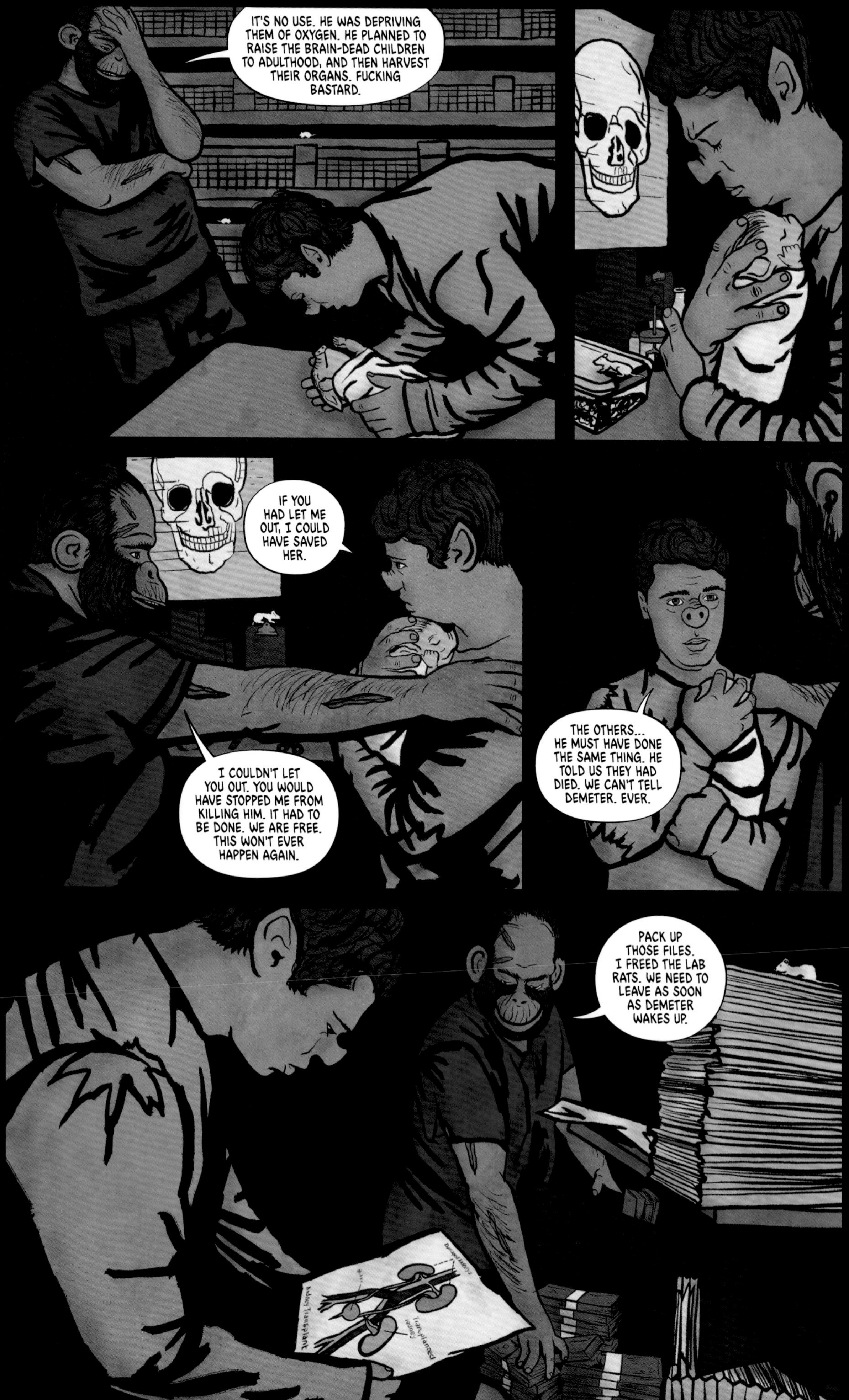
IT'S NO USE. HE WAS DEPRIVING THEM OF OXYGEN. HE PLANNED TO RAISE THE BRAIN-DEAD CHILDREN TO ADULTHOOD, AND THEN HARVEST THEIR ORGANS. FUCKING BASTARD.
IF YOU HAD LET ME OUT, I COULD HAVE SAVED HER.
I COULDN'T LET YOU OUT. YOU WOULD HAVE STOPPED ME FROM KILLING HIM. IT HAD TO BE DONE. WE ARE FREE. THIS WON'T EVER HAPPEN AGAIN.
THE OTHERS... HE MUST HAVE DONE THE SAME THING. HE TOLD US THEY HAD DIED. WE CAN'T TELL DEMETER. EVER.
PACK UP THOSE FILES. I FREED THE LAB RATS. WE NEED TO LEAVE AS SOON AS DEMETER WAKES UP.

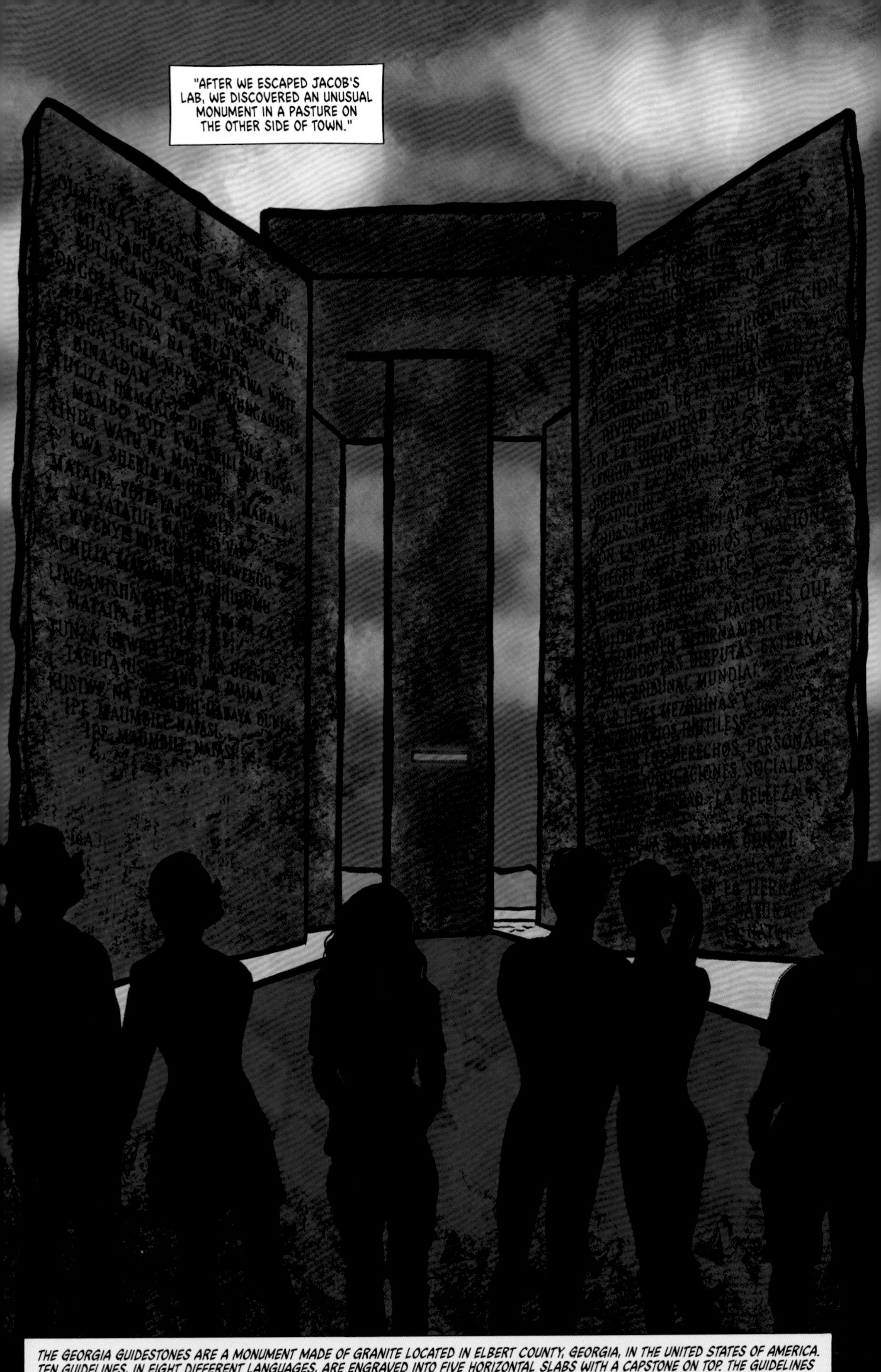
"AFTER WE ESCAPED JACOB'S LAB, WE DISCOVERED AN UNUSUAL MONUMENT IN A PASTURE ON THE OTHER SIDE OF TOWN."

THE GEORGIA GUIDESTONES ARE A MONUMENT MADE OF GRANITE LOCATED IN ELBERT COUNTY, GEORGIA, IN THE UNITED STATES OF AMERICA. TEN GUIDELINES, IN EIGHT DIFFERENT LANGUAGES, ARE ENGRAVED INTO FIVE HORIZONTAL SLABS WITH A CAPSTONE ON TOP. THE GUIDELINES TOUCH ON SUBJECTS SUCH AS EUGENICS AND POPULATION CONTROL, AND SEEM TO OFFER A ROADMAP TO REBUILDING A DESTROYED SOCIETY. THE STRUCTURE IS ALIGNED ASTRONOMICALLY AND FUNCTIONS AS A COMPASS, CALENDAR AND CLOCK. THE GUIDESTONES ARE OFTEN REFERRED TO AS AMERICA'S STONEHENGE. PAID FOR AND ERECTED ANONYMOUSLY IN THE MIDDLE OF A FIVE-ACRE PLOT OF FARMLAND, THE MONUMENT'S GUIDELINES ARE CONSIDERED CONTROVERSIAL, AND HAVE INSPIRED MANY CONSPIRACY THEORIES.

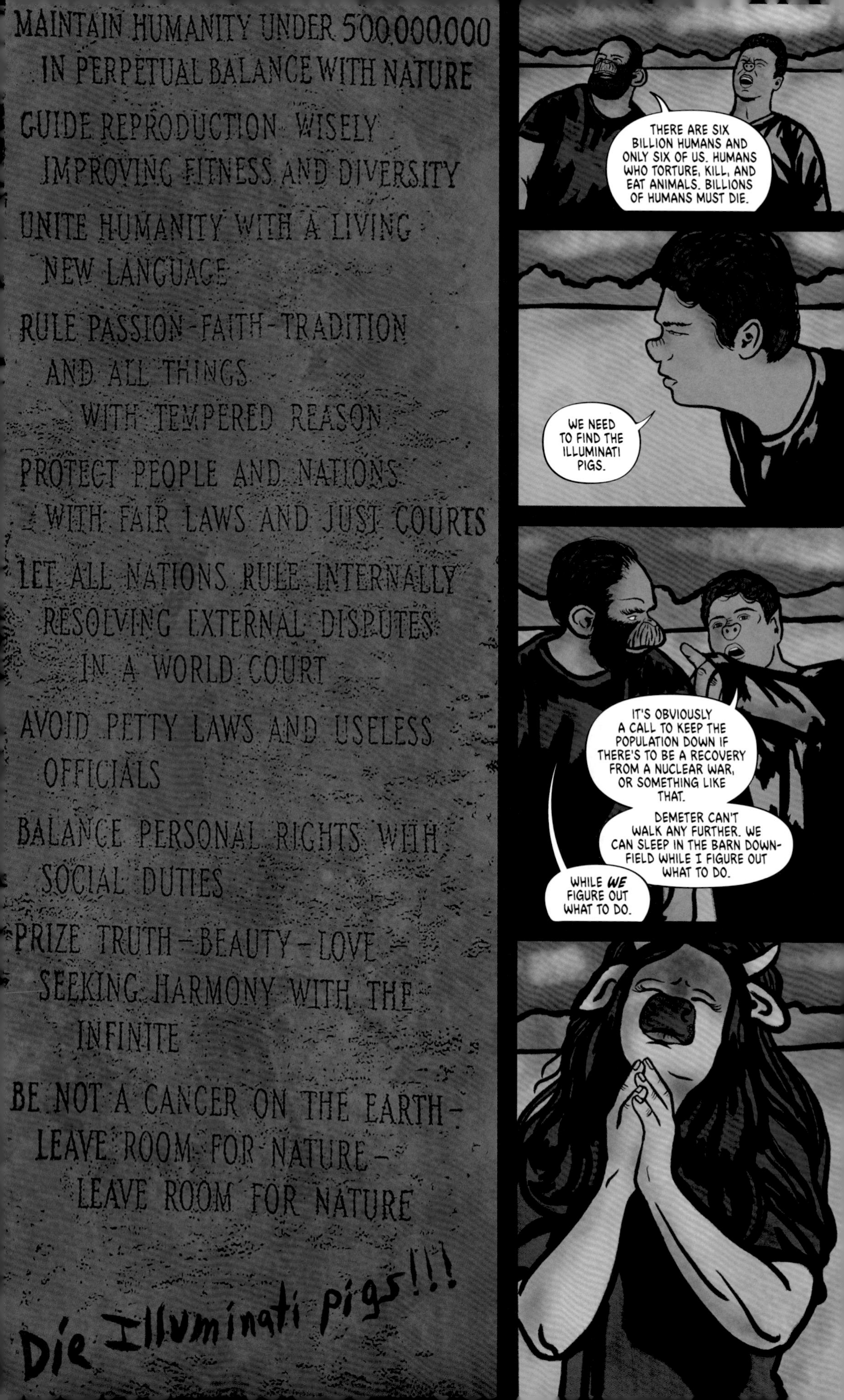
MAINTAIN HUMANITY UNDER 500,000,000
IN PERPETUAL BALANCE WITH NATURE
GUIDE REPRODUCTION WISELY
IMPROVING FITNESS AND DIVERSITY
UNITE HUMANITY WITH A LIVING
NEW LANGUAGE
RULE PASSION - FAITH - TRADITION
AND ALL THINGS
WITH TEMPERED REASON
PROTECT PEOPLE AND NATIONS
WITH FAIR LAWS AND JUST COURTS
LET ALL NATIONS RULE INTERNALLY
RESOLVING EXTERNAL DISPUTES
IN A WORLD COURT
AVOID PETTY LAWS AND USELESS
OFFICIALS
BALANCE PERSONAL RIGHTS WITH
SOCIAL DUTIES
PRIZE TRUTH - BEAUTY - LOVE -
SEEKING HARMONY WITH THE
INFINITE
BE NOT A CANCER ON THE EARTH -
LEAVE ROOM FOR NATURE -
LEAVE ROOM FOR NATURE
Die Illuminati pigs!!!
THERE ARE SIX BILLION HUMANS AND ONLY SIX OF US. HUMANS WHO TORTURE, KILL, AND EAT ANIMALS. BILLIONS OF HUMANS MUST DIE.
WE NEED TO FIND THE ILLUMINATI PIGS.
IT'S OBVIOUSLY A CALL TO KEEP THE POPULATION DOWN IF THERE'S TO BE A RECOVERY FROM A NUCLEAR WAR, OR SOMETHING LIKE THAT.
DEMETER CAN'T WALK ANY FURTHER. WE CAN SLEEP IN THE BARN DOWN-FIELD WHILE I FIGURE OUT WHAT TO DO.
WHILE *WE* FIGURE OUT WHAT TO DO.

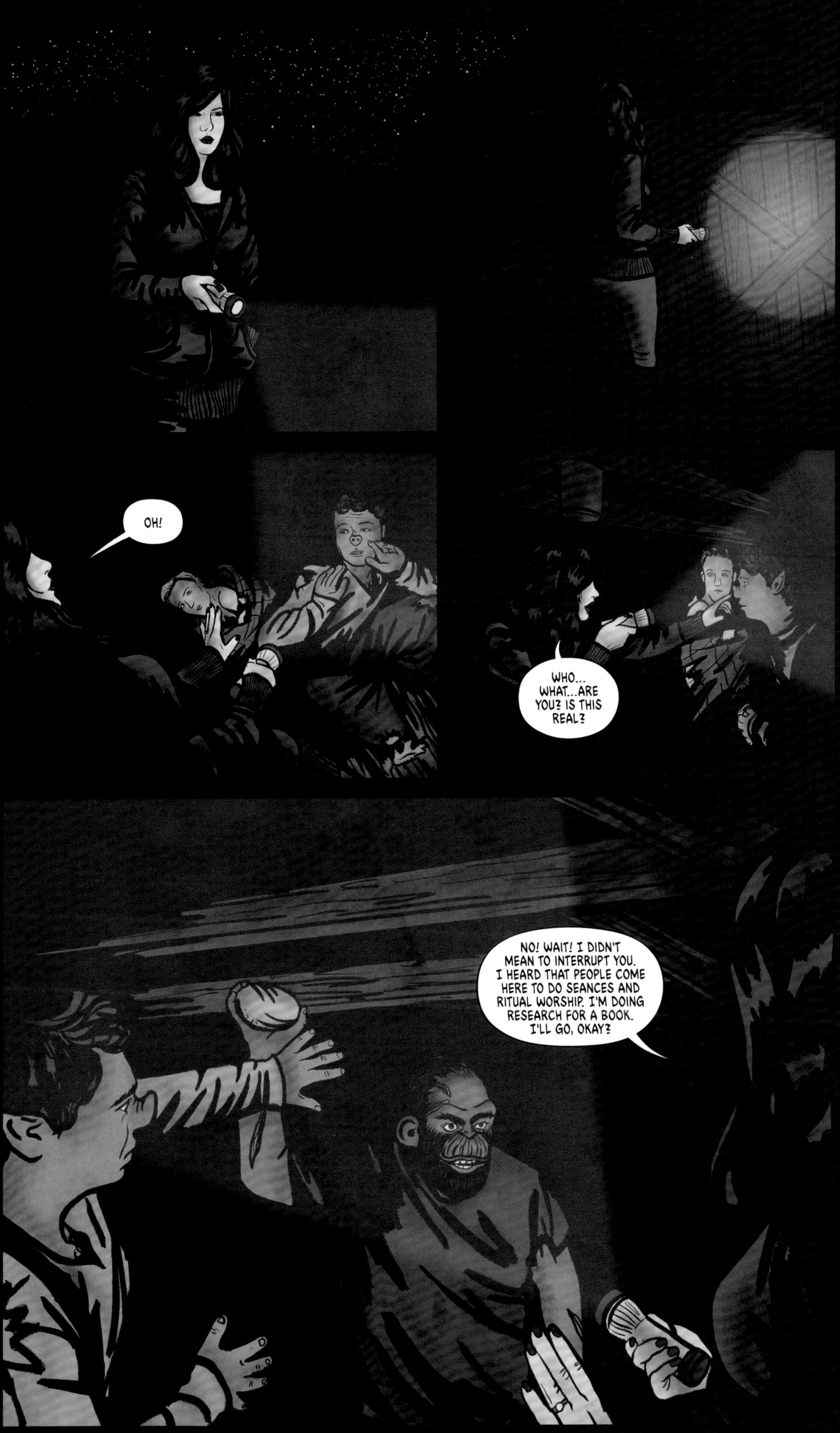
OH!
WHO... WHAT...ARE YOU? IS THIS REAL?
NO! WAIT! I DIDN'T MEAN TO INTERRUPT YOU. I HEARD THAT PEOPLE COME HERE TO DO SEANCES AND RITUAL WORSHIP. I'M DOING RESEARCH FOR A BOOK. I'LL GO, OKAY?

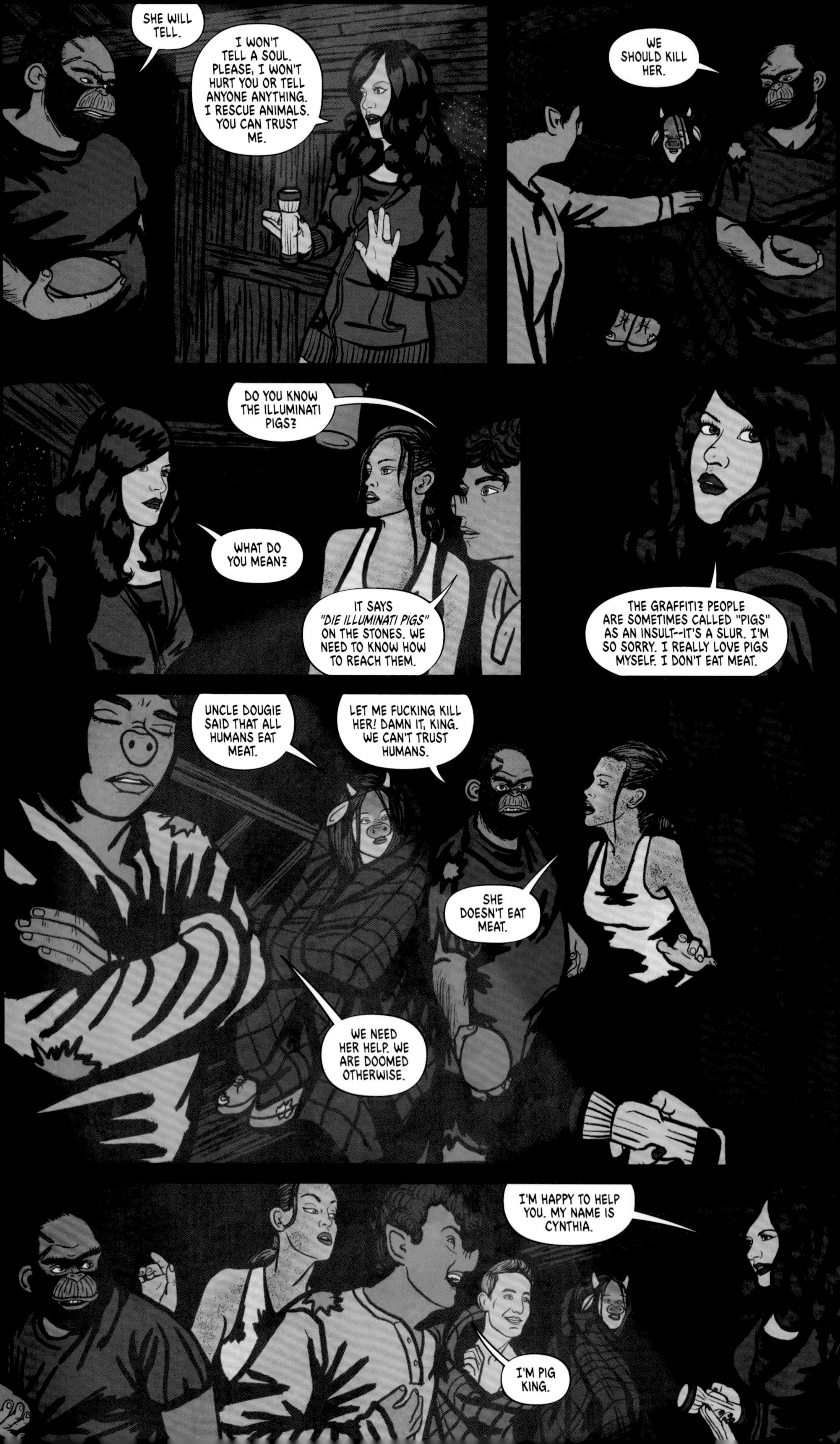
SHE WILL TELL.
I WON'T TELL A SOUL. PLEASE, I WON'T HURT YOU OR TELL ANYONE ANYTHING. I RESCUE ANIMALS. YOU CAN TRUST ME.
WE SHOULD KILL HER.
DO YOU KNOW THE ILLUMINATI PIGS?
WHAT DO YOU MEAN?
IT SAYS *"DIE ILLUMINATI PIGS"* ON THE STONES. WE NEED TO KNOW HOW TO REACH THEM.
THE GRAFFITI? PEOPLE ARE SOMETIMES CALLED "PIGS" AS AN INSULT--IT'S A SLUR. I'M SO SORRY. I REALLY LOVE PIGS MYSELF. I DON'T EAT MEAT.
UNCLE DOUGIE SAID THAT ALL HUMANS EAT MEAT.
LET ME FUCKING KILL HER! DAMN IT, KING. WE CAN'T TRUST HUMANS.
SHE DOESN'T EAT MEAT.
WE NEED HER HELP. WE ARE DOOMED OTHERWISE.
I'M HAPPY TO HELP YOU. MY NAME IS CYNTHIA.
I'M PIG KING.

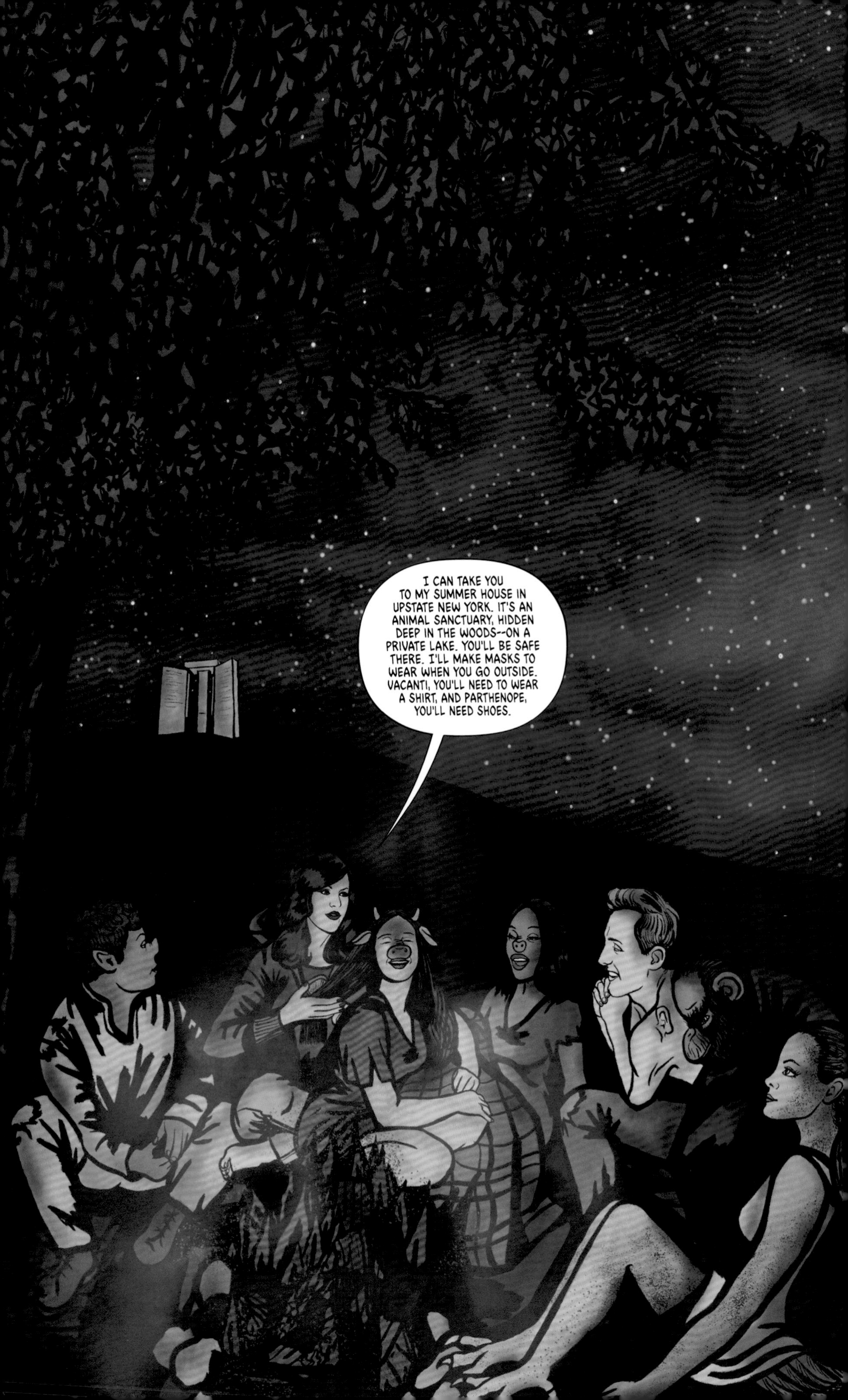
I CAN TAKE YOU TO MY SUMMER HOUSE IN UPSTATE NEW YORK. IT'S AN ANIMAL SANCTUARY, HIDDEN DEEP IN THE WOODS--ON A PRIVATE LAKE. YOU'LL BE SAFE THERE. I'LL MAKE MASKS TO WEAR WHEN YOU GO OUTSIDE. VACANTI, YOU'LL NEED TO WEAR A SHIRT, AND PARTHENOPE, YOU'LL NEED SHOES.

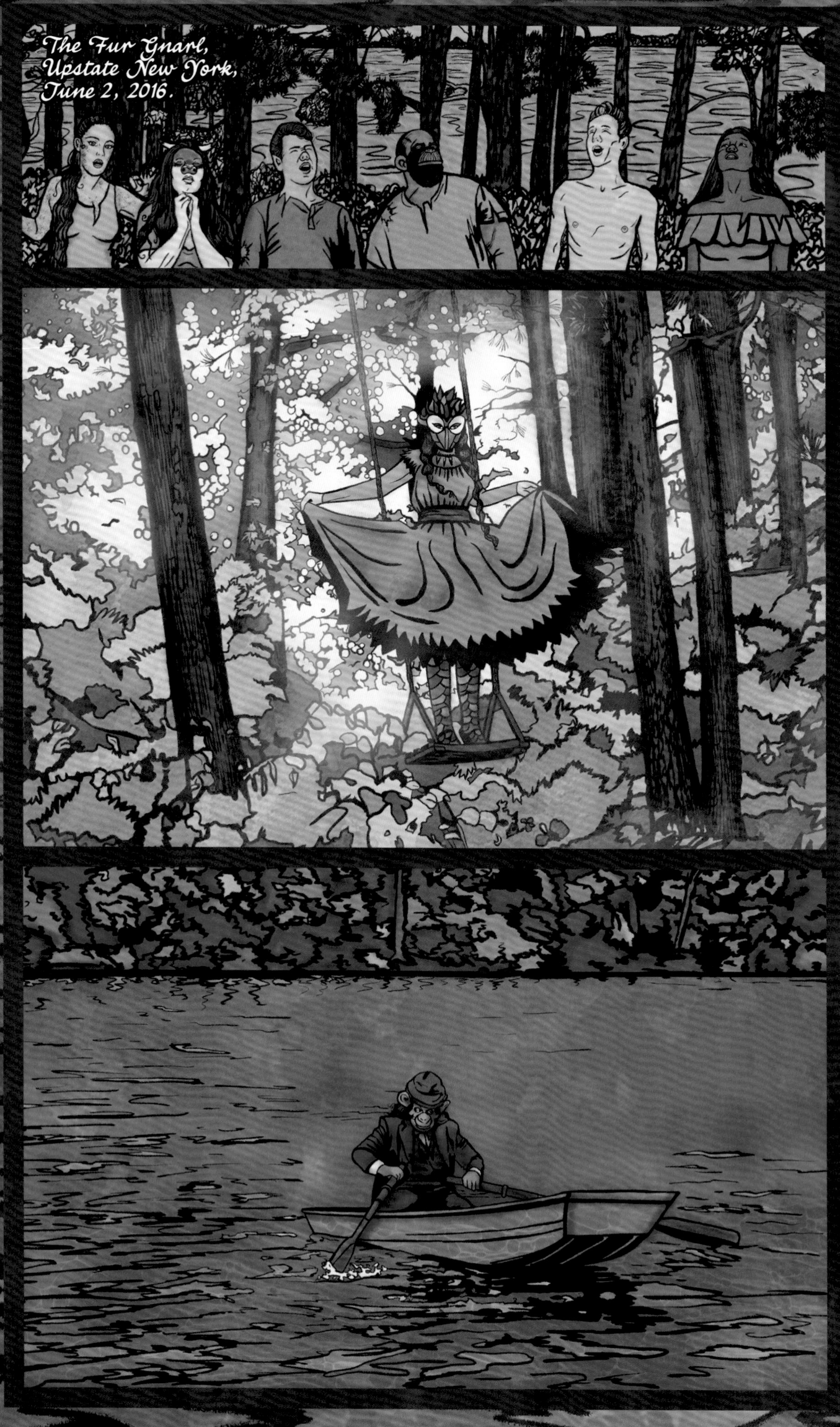
The Fur Gnarl,
Upstate New York,
June 2, 2016.

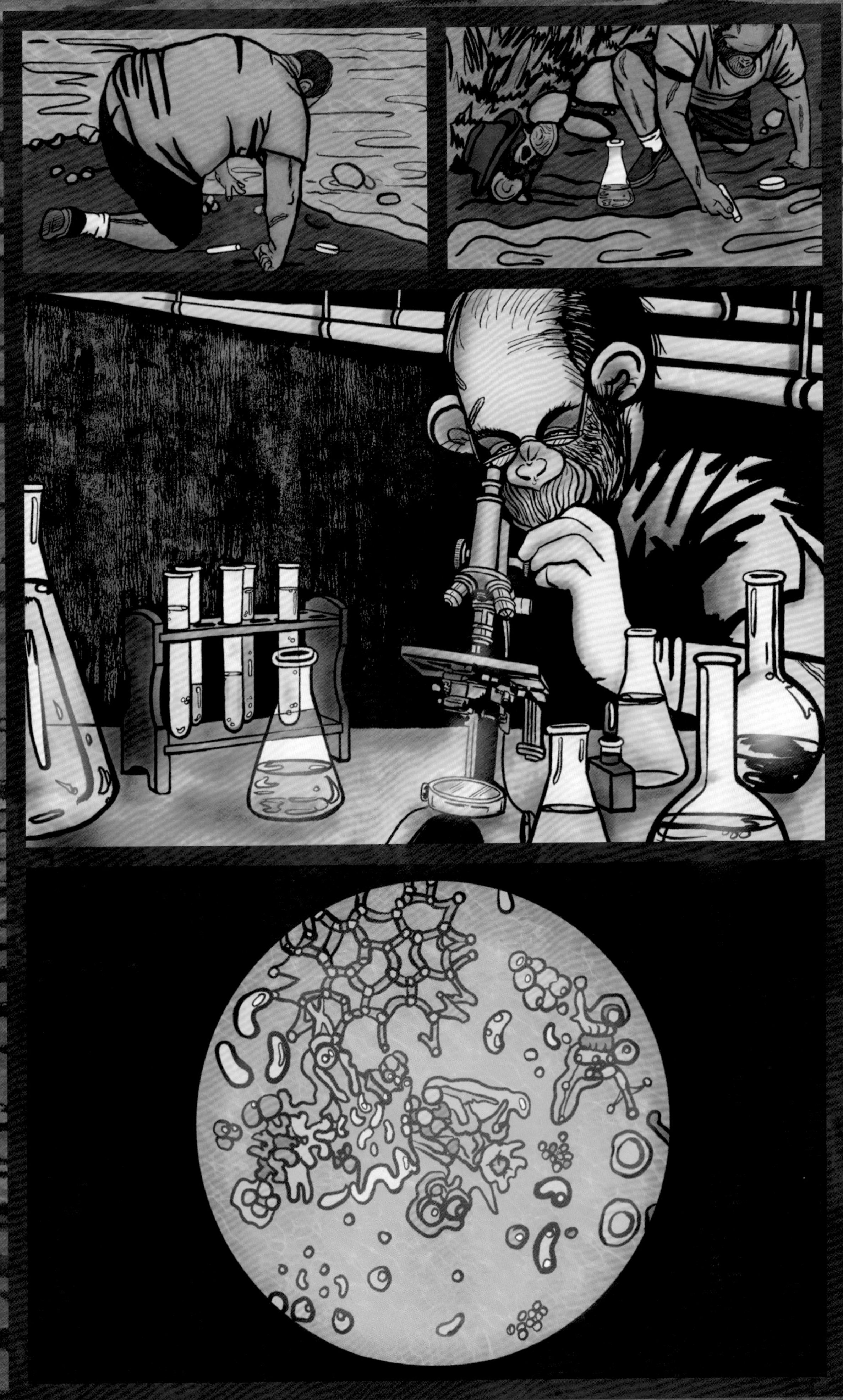

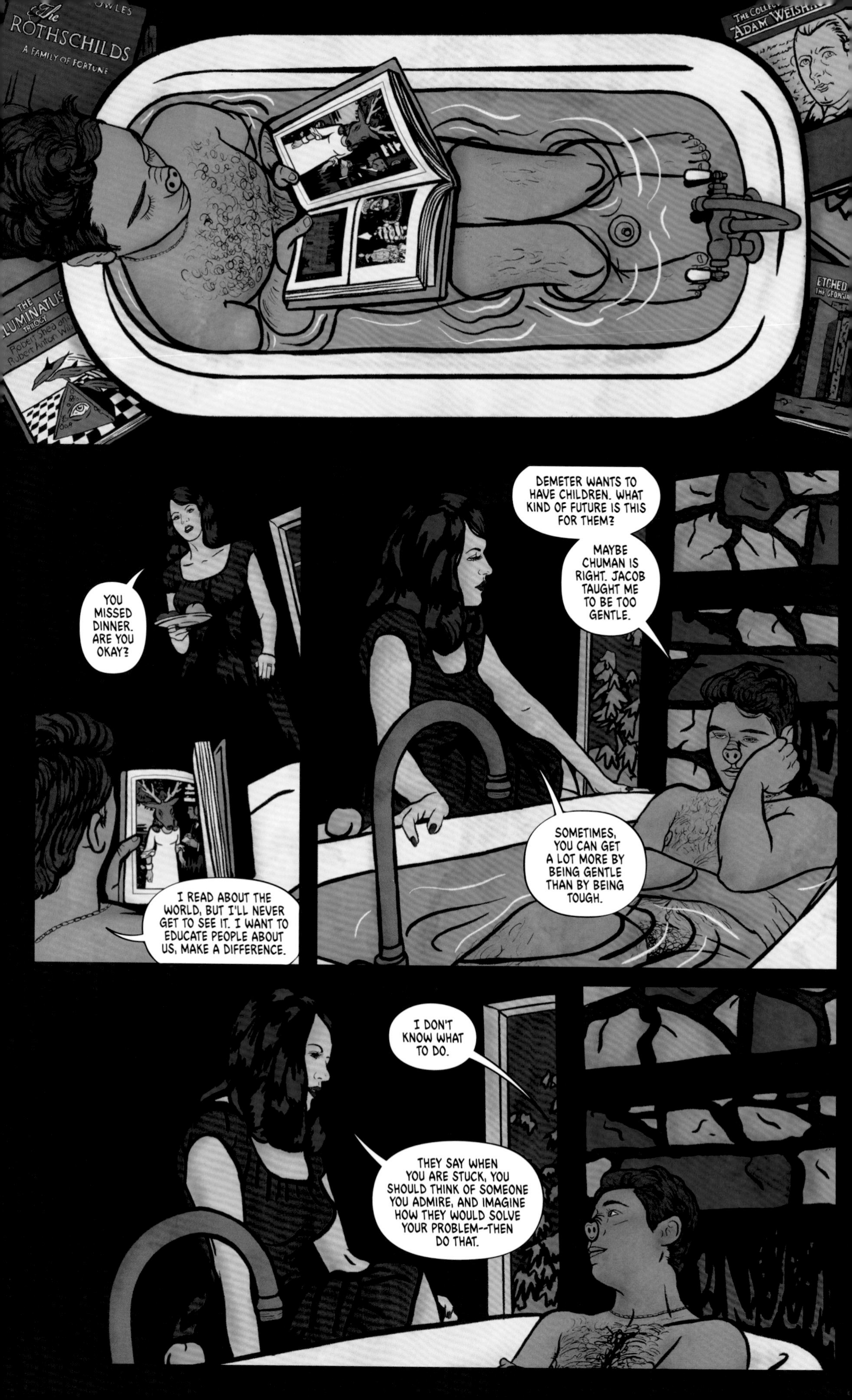
The ROTHSCHILDS
A FAMILY OF FORTUNE
YOU MISSED DINNER. ARE YOU OKAY?
I READ ABOUT THE WORLD, BUT I'LL NEVER GET TO SEE IT. I WANT TO EDUCATE PEOPLE ABOUT US, MAKE A DIFFERENCE.
DEMETER WANTS TO HAVE CHILDREN. WHAT KIND OF FUTURE IS THIS FOR THEM?
MAYBE CHUMAN IS RIGHT. JACOB TAUGHT ME TO BE TOO GENTLE.
SOMETIMES, YOU CAN GET A LOT MORE BY BEING GENTLE THAN BY BEING TOUGH.
I DON'T KNOW WHAT TO DO.
THEY SAY WHEN YOU ARE STUCK, YOU SHOULD THINK OF SOMEONE YOU ADMIRE, AND IMAGINE HOW THEY WOULD SOLVE YOUR PROBLEM--THEN DO THAT.

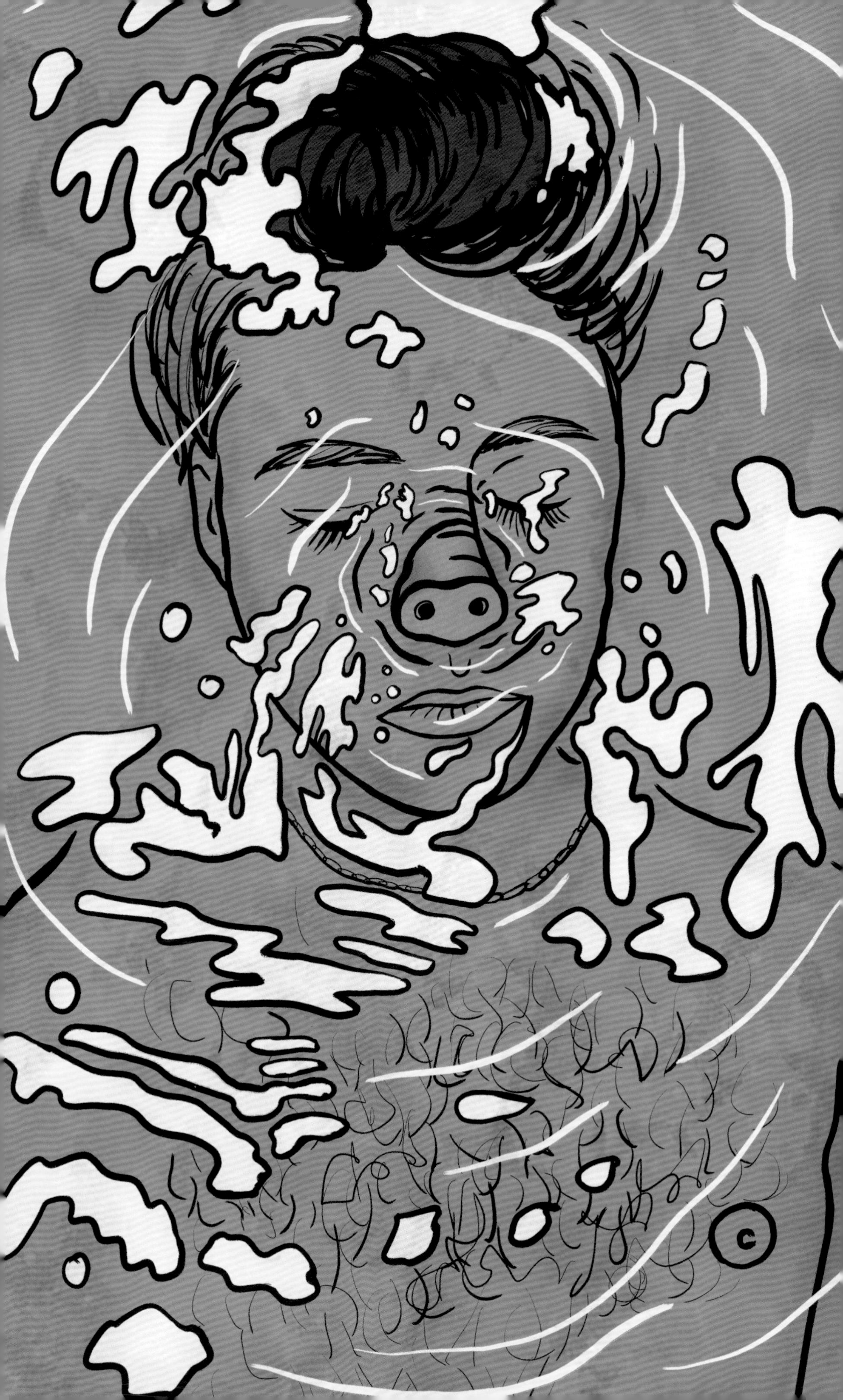

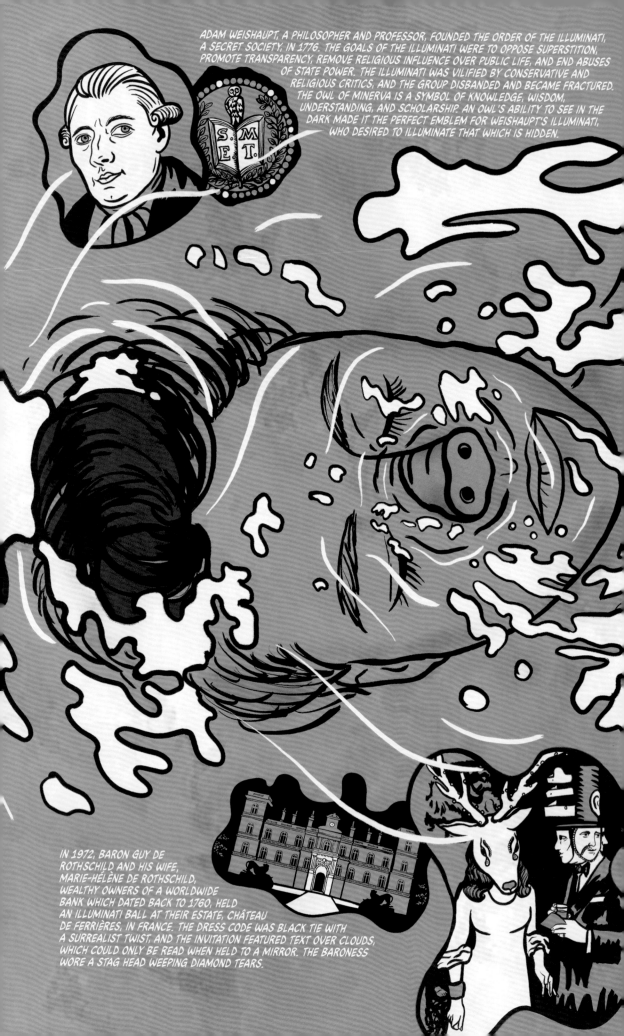

ADAM WEISHAUPT, A PHILOSOPHER AND PROFESSOR, FOUNDED THE ORDER OF THE ILLUMINATI, A SECRET SOCIETY, IN 1776. THE GOALS OF THE ILLUMINATI WERE TO OPPOSE SUPERSTITION, PROMOTE TRANSPARENCY, REMOVE RELIGIOUS INFLUENCE OVER PUBLIC LIFE, AND END ABUSES OF STATE POWER. THE ILLUMINATI WAS VILIFIED BY CONSERVATIVE AND RELIGIOUS CRITICS, AND THE GROUP DISBANDED AND BECAME FRACTURED. THE OWL OF MINERVA IS A SYMBOL OF KNOWLEDGE, WISDOM, UNDERSTANDING, AND SCHOLARSHIP. AN OWL'S ABILITY TO SEE IN THE DARK MADE IT THE PERFECT EMBLEM FOR WEISHAUPT'S ILLUMINATI, WHO DESIRED TO ILLUMINATE THAT WHICH IS HIDDEN.

IN 1972, BARON GUY DE ROTHSCHILD AND HIS WIFE, MARIE-HÉLÈNE DE ROTHSCHILD, WEALTHY OWNERS OF A WORLDWIDE BANK WHICH DATED BACK TO 1760, HELD AN ILLUMINATI BALL AT THEIR ESTATE, CHÂTEAU DE FERRIÈRES, IN FRANCE. THE DRESS CODE WAS BLACK TIE WITH A SURREALIST TWIST, AND THE INVITATION FEATURED TEXT OVER CLOUDS, WHICH COULD ONLY BE READ WHEN HELD TO A MIRROR. THE BARONESS WORE A STAG HEAD WEEPING DIAMOND TEARS.

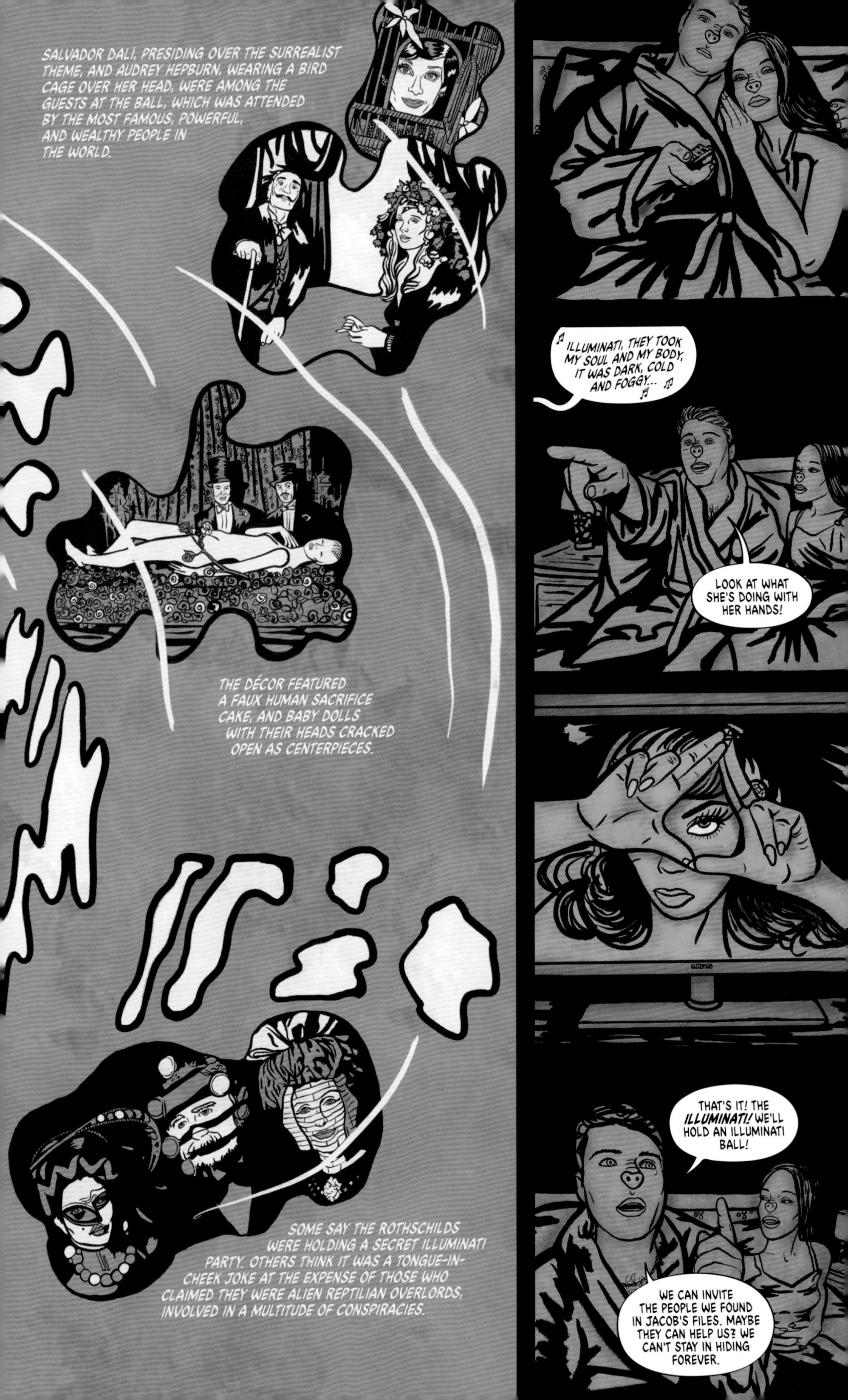
SALVADOR DALI, PRESIDING OVER THE SURREALIST THEME, AND AUDREY HEPBURN, WEARING A BIRD CAGE OVER HER HEAD, WERE AMONG THE GUESTS AT THE BALL, WHICH WAS ATTENDED BY THE MOST FAMOUS, POWERFUL, AND WEALTHY PEOPLE IN THE WORLD.
THE DÉCOR FEATURED A FAUX HUMAN SACRIFICE CAKE, AND BABY DOLLS WITH THEIR HEADS CRACKED OPEN AS CENTERPIECES.
SOME SAY THE ROTHSCHILDS WERE HOLDING A SECRET ILLUMINATI PARTY. OTHERS THINK IT WAS A TONGUE-IN-CHEEK JOKE AT THE EXPENSE OF THOSE WHO CLAIMED THEY WERE ALIEN REPTILIAN OVERLORDS, INVOLVED IN A MULTITUDE OF CONSPIRACIES.
♫ ILLUMINATI, THEY TOOK MY SOUL AND MY BODY, IT WAS DARK, COLD AND FOGGY... ♫
LOOK AT WHAT SHE'S DOING WITH HER HANDS!
THAT'S IT! THE ILLUMINATI! WE'LL HOLD AN ILLUMINATI BALL!
WE CAN INVITE THE PEOPLE WE FOUND IN JACOB'S FILES. MAYBE THEY CAN HELP US? WE CAN'T STAY IN HIDING FOREVER.

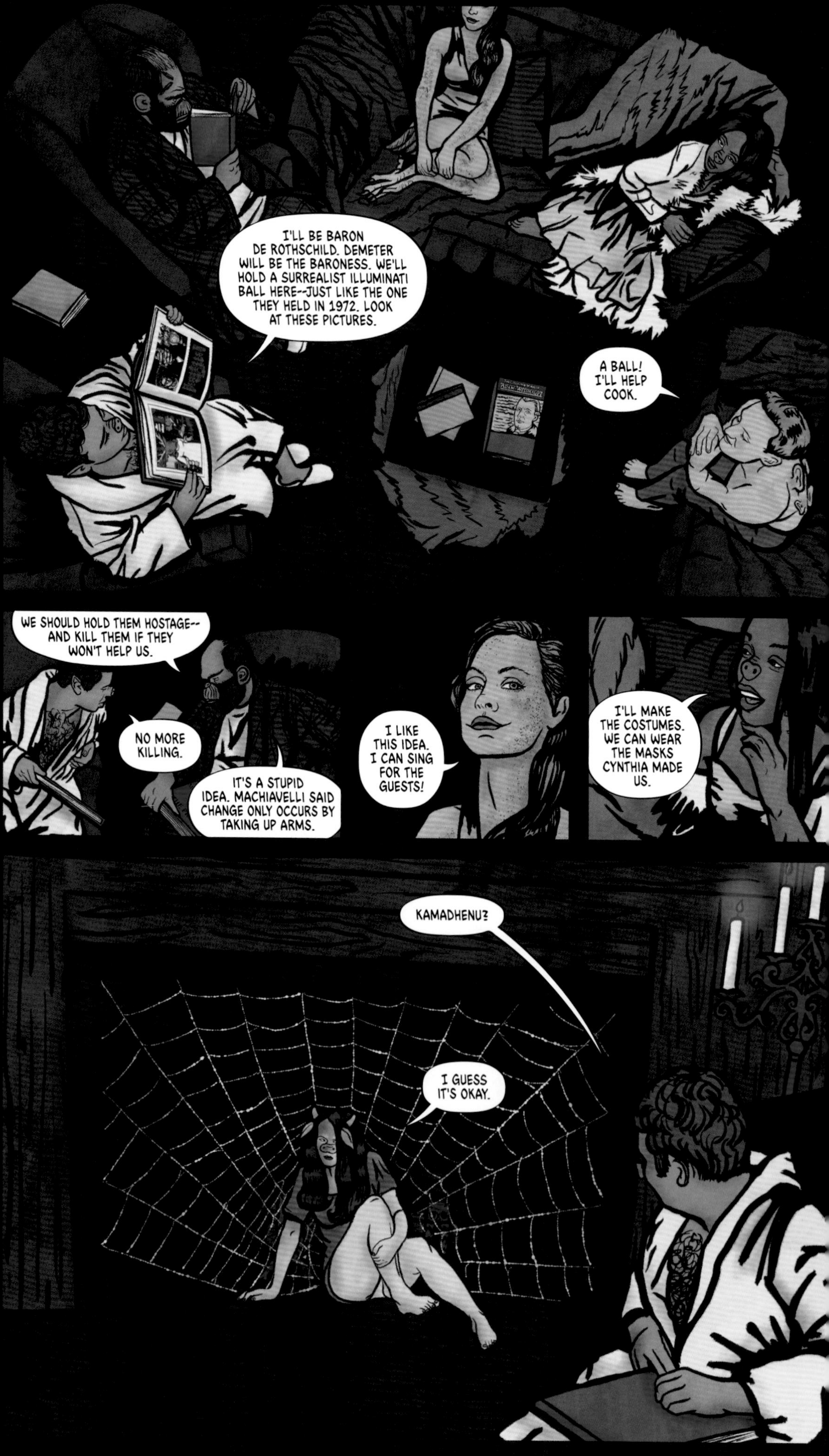
I'LL BE BARON DE ROTHSCHILD. DEMETER WILL BE THE BARONESS. WE'LL HOLD A SURREALIST ILLUMINATI BALL HERE--JUST LIKE THE ONE THEY HELD IN 1972. LOOK AT THESE PICTURES.
A BALL! I'LL HELP COOK.
WE SHOULD HOLD THEM HOSTAGE--AND KILL THEM IF THEY WON'T HELP US.
NO MORE KILLING.
IT'S A STUPID IDEA. MACHIAVELLI SAID CHANGE ONLY OCCURS BY TAKING UP ARMS.
I LIKE THIS IDEA. I CAN SING FOR THE GUESTS!
I'LL MAKE THE COSTUMES. WE CAN WEAR THE MASKS CYNTHIA MADE US.
KAMADHENU?
I GUESS IT'S OKAY.

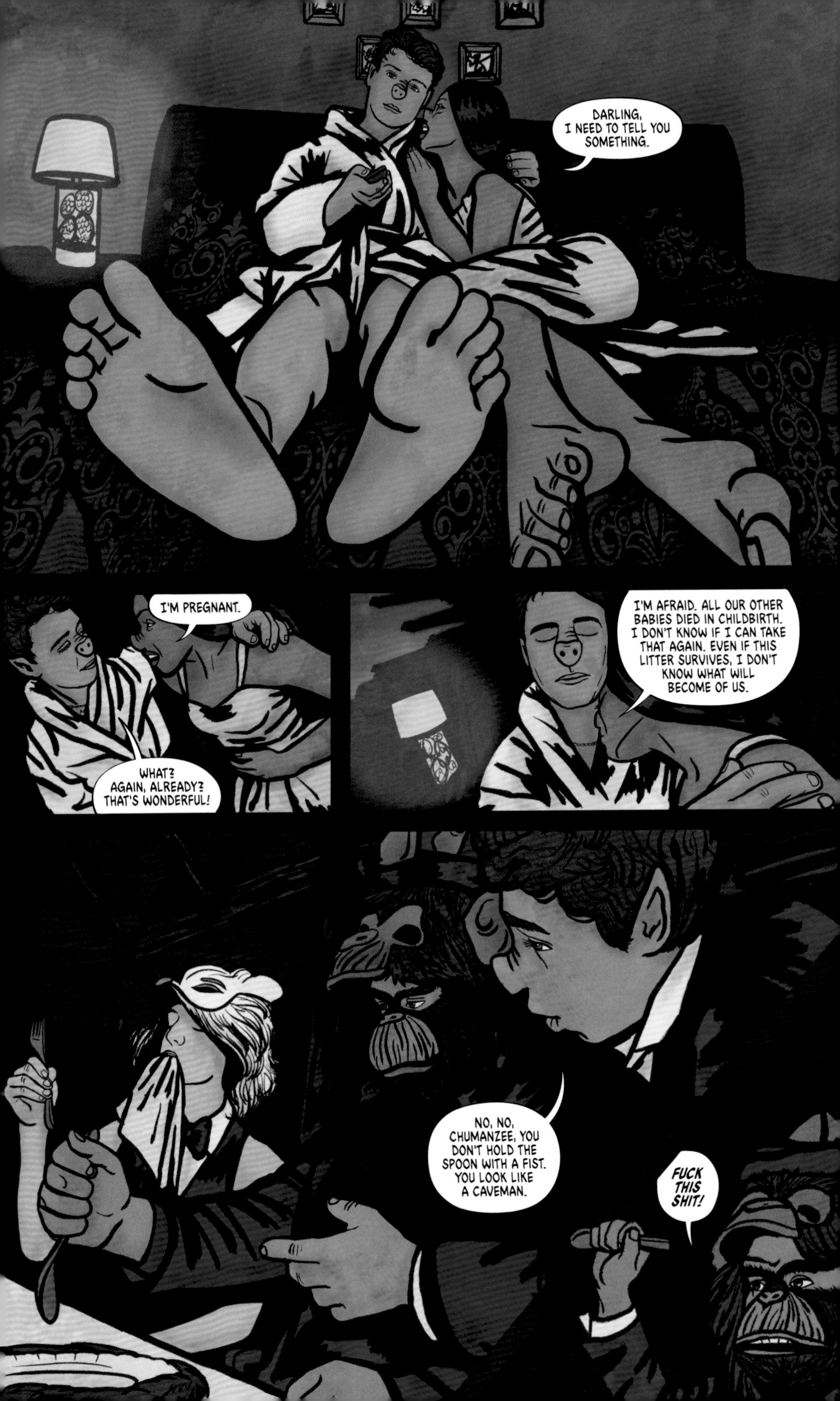
DARLING, I NEED TO TELL YOU SOMETHING.
I'M PREGNANT.
WHAT? AGAIN, ALREADY? THAT'S WONDERFUL!
I'M AFRAID. ALL OUR OTHER BABIES DIED IN CHILDBIRTH. I DON'T KNOW IF I CAN TAKE THAT AGAIN. EVEN IF THIS LITTER SURVIVES, I DON'T KNOW WHAT WILL BECOME OF US.
NO, NO, CHUMANZEE, YOU DON'T HOLD THE SPOON WITH A FIST. YOU LOOK LIKE A CAVEMAN.
FUCK THIS SHIT!

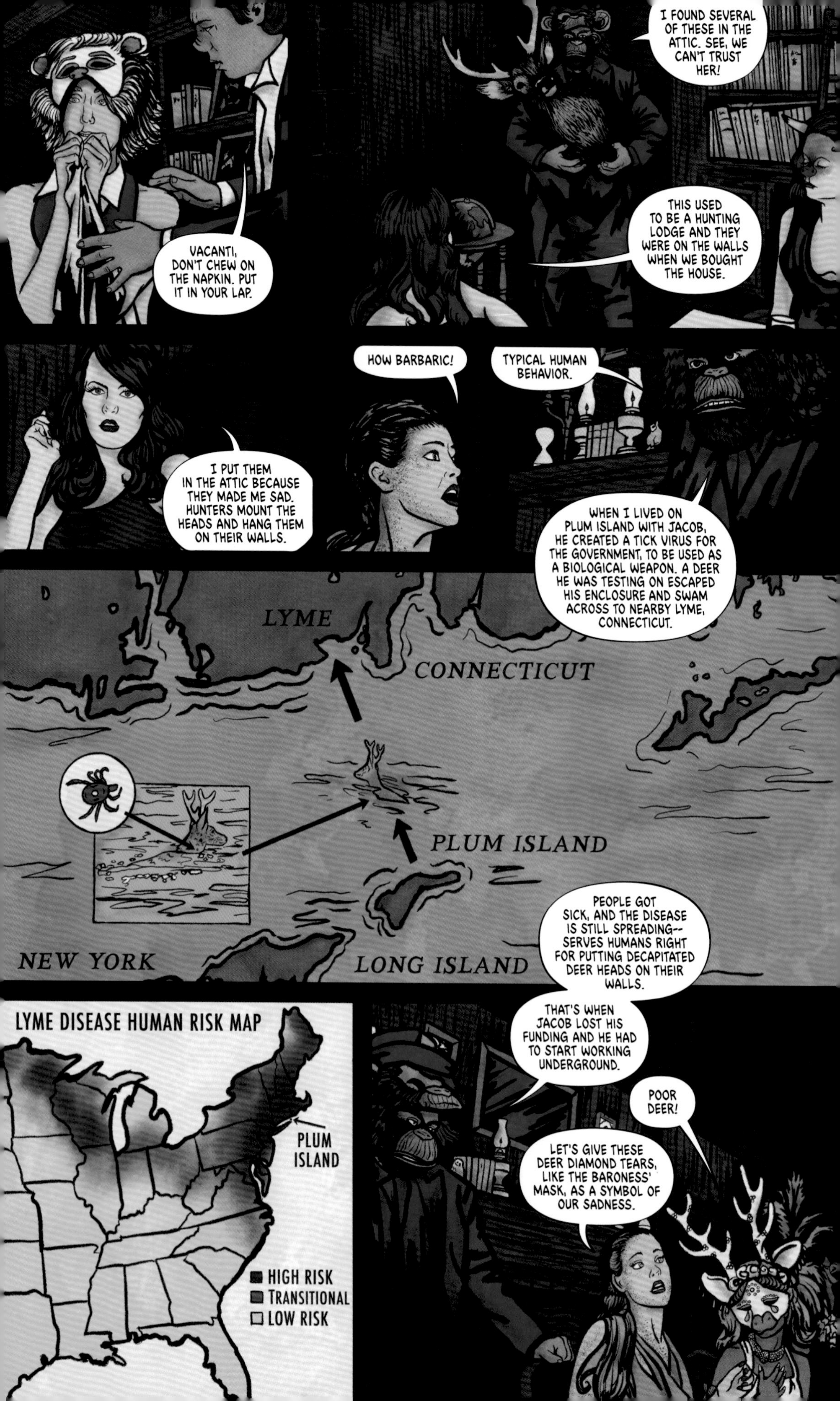
VACANTI, DON'T CHEW ON THE NAPKIN. PUT IT IN YOUR LAP.
I FOUND SEVERAL OF THESE IN THE ATTIC. SEE, WE CAN'T TRUST HER!
THIS USED TO BE A HUNTING LODGE AND THEY WERE ON THE WALLS WHEN WE BOUGHT THE HOUSE.
I PUT THEM IN THE ATTIC BECAUSE THEY MADE ME SAD. HUNTERS MOUNT THE HEADS AND HANG THEM ON THEIR WALLS.
HOW BARBARIC!
TYPICAL HUMAN BEHAVIOR.
WHEN I LIVED ON PLUM ISLAND WITH JACOB, HE CREATED A TICK VIRUS FOR THE GOVERNMENT, TO BE USED AS A BIOLOGICAL WEAPON. A DEER HE WAS TESTING ON ESCAPED HIS ENCLOSURE AND SWAM ACROSS TO NEARBY LYME, CONNECTICUT.
LYME
CONNECTICUT
PLUM ISLAND
NEW YORK
LONG ISLAND
PEOPLE GOT SICK, AND THE DISEASE IS STILL SPREADING-- SERVES HUMANS RIGHT FOR PUTTING DECAPITATED DEER HEADS ON THEIR WALLS.
LYME DISEASE HUMAN RISK MAP
PLUM ISLAND
HIGH RISK
TRANSITIONAL
LOW RISK
THAT'S WHEN JACOB LOST HIS FUNDING AND HE HAD TO START WORKING UNDERGROUND.
POOR DEER!
LET'S GIVE THESE DEER DIAMOND TEARS, LIKE THE BARONESS' MASK, AS A SYMBOL OF OUR SADNESS.

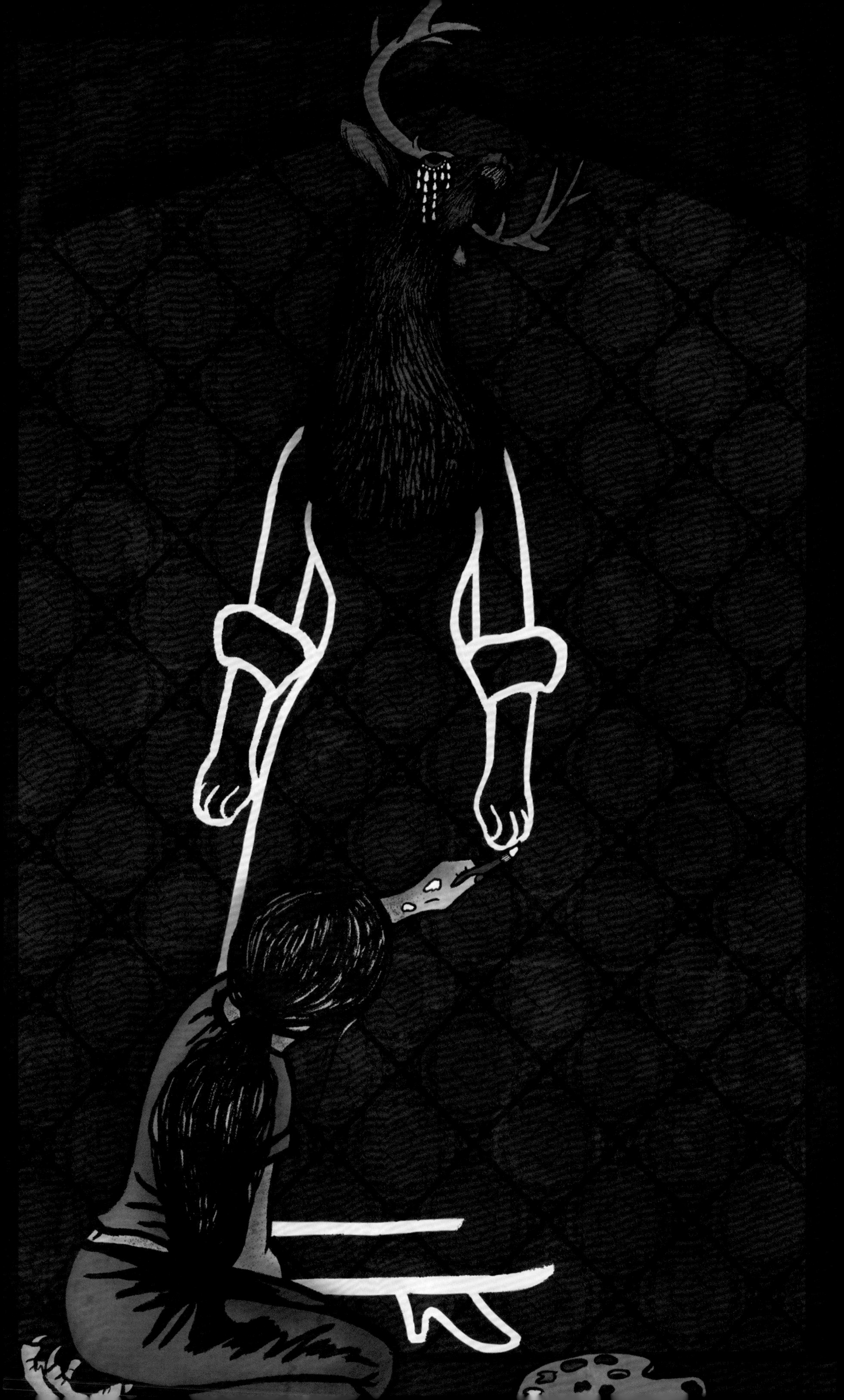

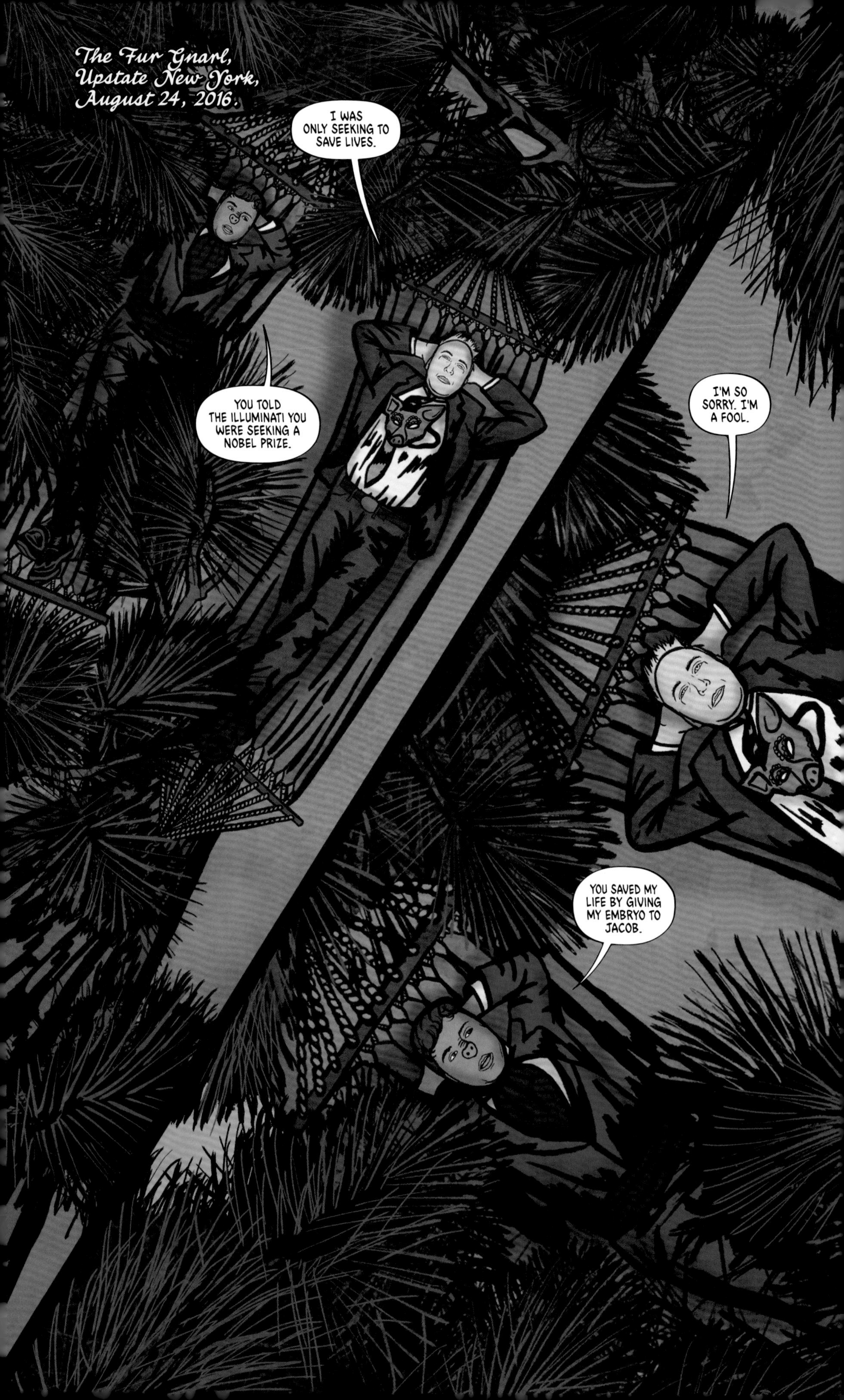
The Fur Gnarl,
Upstate New York,
August 24, 2016.
I WAS ONLY SEEKING TO SAVE LIVES.
YOU TOLD THE ILLUMINATI YOU WERE SEEKING A NOBEL PRIZE.
I'M SO SORRY. I'M A FOOL.
YOU SAVED MY LIFE BY GIVING MY EMBRYO TO JACOB.

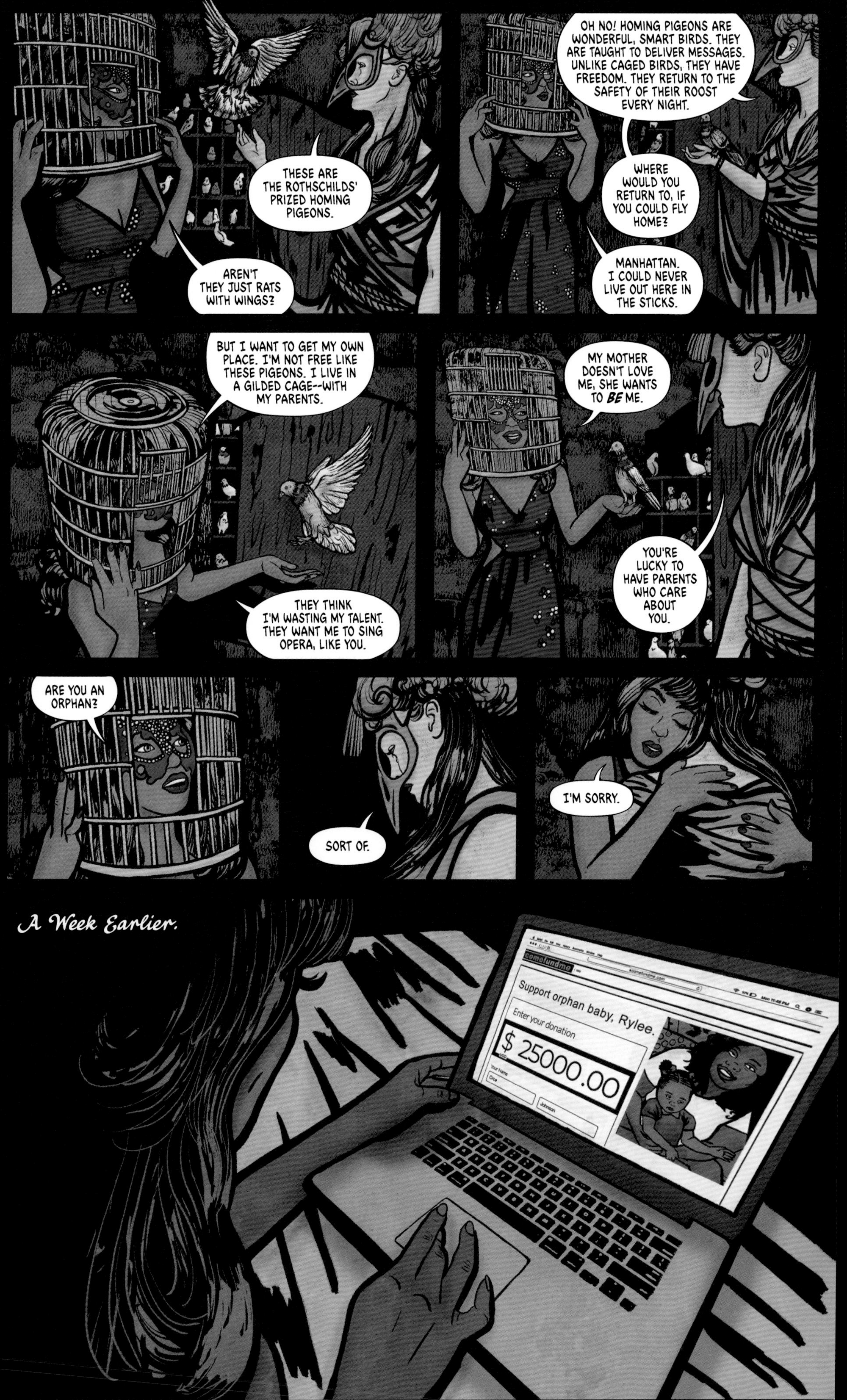

THESE ARE THE ROTHSCHILDS' PRIZED HOMING PIGEONS.
AREN'T THEY JUST RATS WITH WINGS?
OH NO! HOMING PIGEONS ARE WONDERFUL, SMART BIRDS. THEY ARE TAUGHT TO DELIVER MESSAGES. UNLIKE CAGED BIRDS, THEY HAVE FREEDOM. THEY RETURN TO THE SAFETY OF THEIR ROOST EVERY NIGHT.
WHERE WOULD YOU RETURN TO, IF YOU COULD FLY HOME?
MANHATTAN. I COULD NEVER LIVE OUT HERE IN THE STICKS.
BUT I WANT TO GET MY OWN PLACE. I'M NOT FREE LIKE THESE PIGEONS. I LIVE IN A GILDED CAGE--WITH MY PARENTS.
THEY THINK I'M WASTING MY TALENT. THEY WANT ME TO SING OPERA, LIKE YOU.
MY MOTHER DOESN'T LOVE ME, SHE WANTS TO *BE* ME.
YOU'RE LUCKY TO HAVE PARENTS WHO CARE ABOUT YOU.
ARE YOU AN ORPHAN?
SORT OF.
I'M SORRY.
A Week Earlier.
comefundme
Support orphan baby, Rylee.
Enter your donation
$ 25000.00

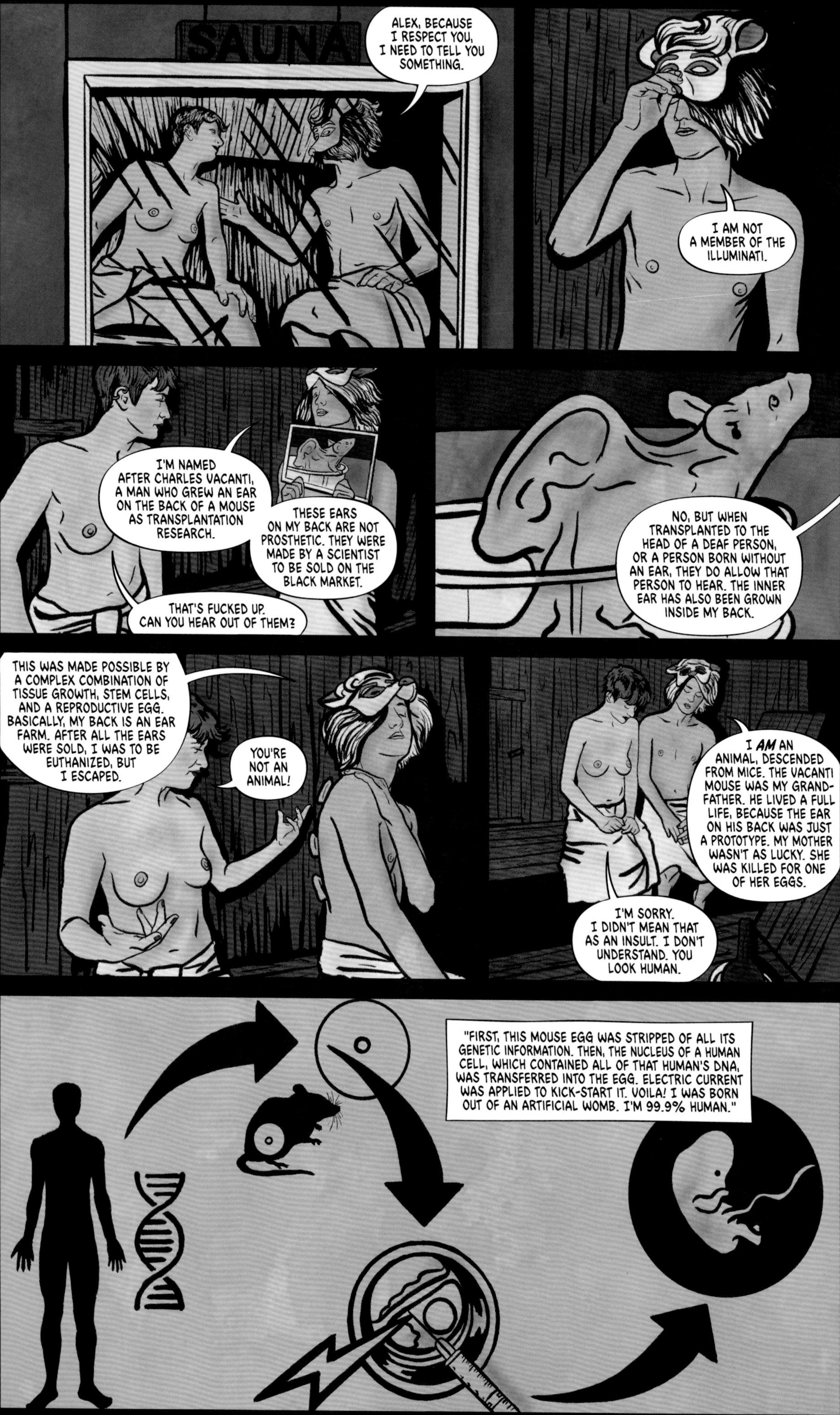
SAUNA
ALEX, BECAUSE I RESPECT YOU, I NEED TO TELL YOU SOMETHING.
I AM NOT A MEMBER OF THE ILLUMINATI.
I'M NAMED AFTER CHARLES VACANTI, A MAN WHO GREW AN EAR ON THE BACK OF A MOUSE AS TRANSPLANTATION RESEARCH.
THESE EARS ON MY BACK ARE NOT PROSTHETIC. THEY WERE MADE BY A SCIENTIST TO BE SOLD ON THE BLACK MARKET.
THAT'S FUCKED UP. CAN YOU HEAR OUT OF THEM?
NO, BUT WHEN TRANSPLANTED TO THE HEAD OF A DEAF PERSON, OR A PERSON BORN WITHOUT AN EAR, THEY DO ALLOW THAT PERSON TO HEAR. THE INNER EAR HAS ALSO BEEN GROWN INSIDE MY BACK.
THIS WAS MADE POSSIBLE BY A COMPLEX COMBINATION OF TISSUE GROWTH, STEM CELLS, AND A REPRODUCTIVE EGG. BASICALLY, MY BACK IS AN EAR FARM. AFTER ALL THE EARS WERE SOLD, I WAS TO BE EUTHANIZED, BUT I ESCAPED.
YOU'RE NOT AN ANIMAL!
I *AM* AN ANIMAL, DESCENDED FROM MICE. THE VACANTI MOUSE WAS MY GRAND-FATHER. HE LIVED A FULL LIFE, BECAUSE THE EAR ON HIS BACK WAS JUST A PROTOTYPE. MY MOTHER WASN'T AS LUCKY. SHE WAS KILLED FOR ONE OF HER EGGS.
I'M SORRY. I DIDN'T MEAN THAT AS AN INSULT. I DON'T UNDERSTAND. YOU LOOK HUMAN.
"FIRST, THIS MOUSE EGG WAS STRIPPED OF ALL ITS GENETIC INFORMATION. THEN, THE NUCLEUS OF A HUMAN CELL, WHICH CONTAINED ALL OF THAT HUMAN'S DNA, WAS TRANSFERRED INTO THE EGG. ELECTRIC CURRENT WAS APPLIED TO KICK-START IT. VOILA! I WAS BORN OUT OF AN ARTIFICIAL WOMB. I'M 99.9% HUMAN."

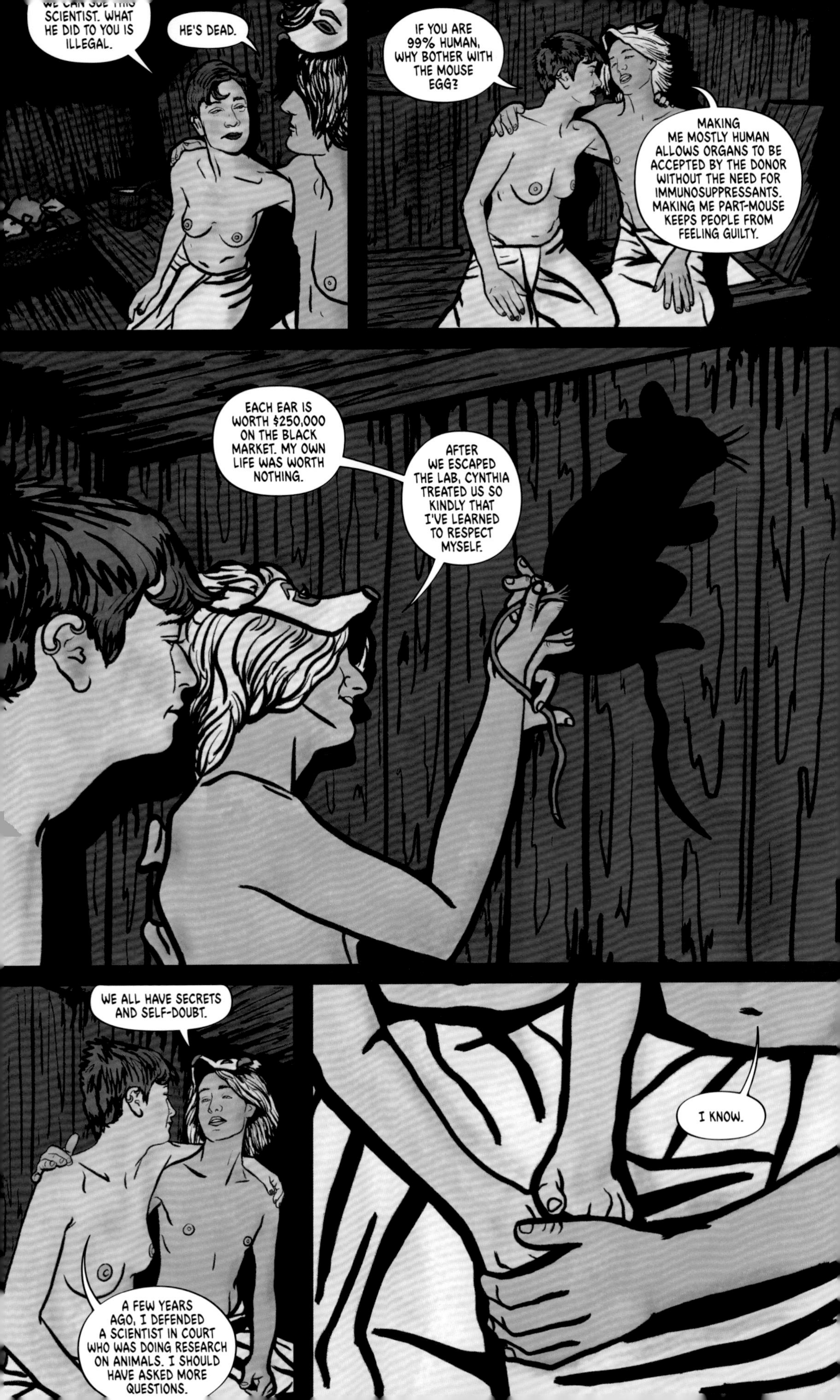

SCIENTIST. WHAT HE DID TO YOU IS ILLEGAL.
HE'S DEAD.
IF YOU ARE 99% HUMAN, WHY BOTHER WITH THE MOUSE EGG?
MAKING ME MOSTLY HUMAN ALLOWS ORGANS TO BE ACCEPTED BY THE DONOR WITHOUT THE NEED FOR IMMUNOSUPPRESSANTS. MAKING ME PART-MOUSE KEEPS PEOPLE FROM FEELING GUILTY.
EACH EAR IS WORTH $250,000 ON THE BLACK MARKET. MY OWN LIFE WAS WORTH NOTHING.
AFTER WE ESCAPED THE LAB, CYNTHIA TREATED US SO KINDLY THAT I'VE LEARNED TO RESPECT MYSELF.
WE ALL HAVE SECRETS AND SELF-DOUBT.
A FEW YEARS AGO, I DEFENDED A SCIENTIST IN COURT WHO WAS DOING RESEARCH ON ANIMALS. I SHOULD HAVE ASKED MORE QUESTIONS.
I KNOW.

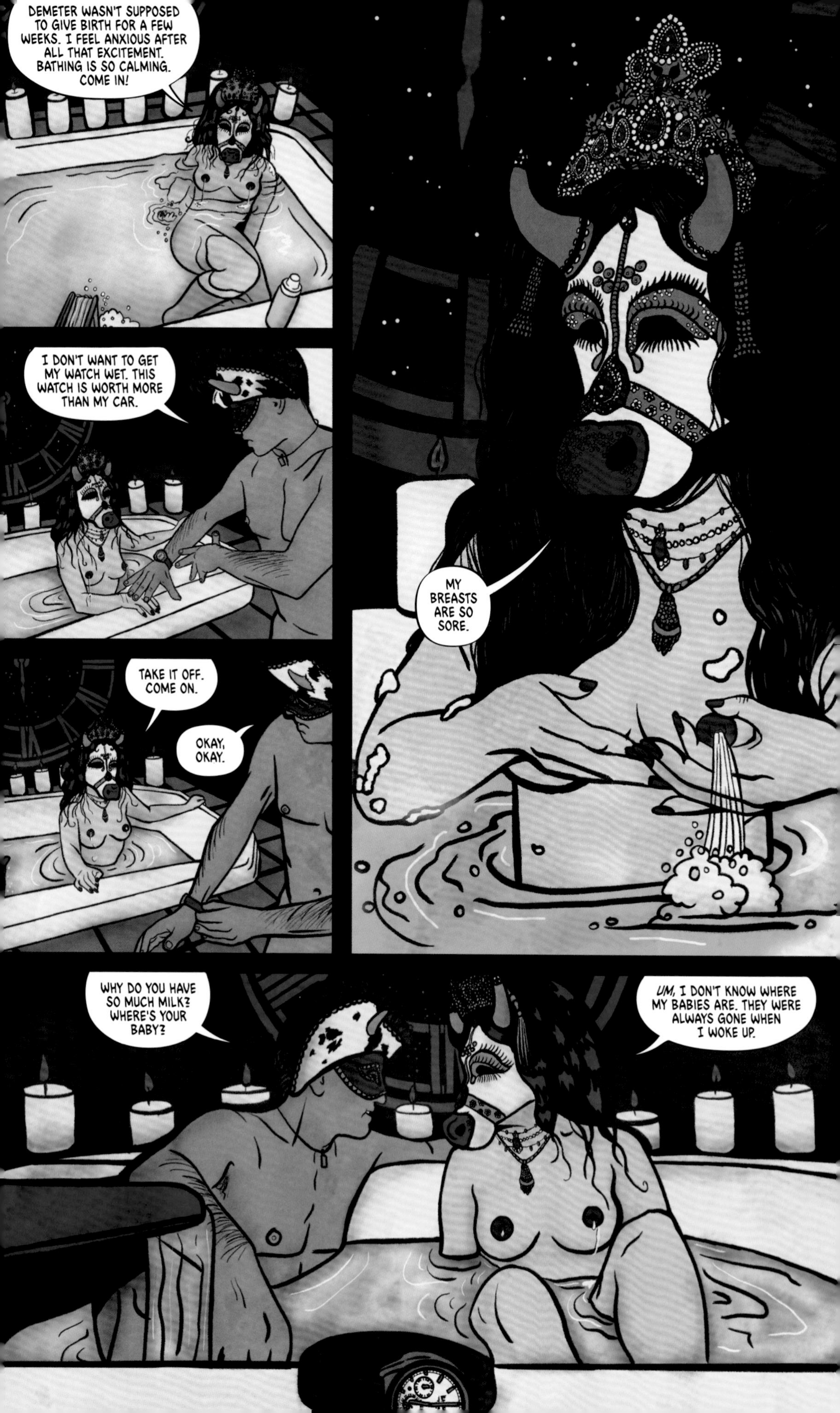
DEMETER WASN'T SUPPOSED TO GIVE BIRTH FOR A FEW WEEKS. I FEEL ANXIOUS AFTER ALL THAT EXCITEMENT. BATHING IS SO CALMING. COME IN!
I DON'T WANT TO GET MY WATCH WET. THIS WATCH IS WORTH MORE THAN MY CAR.
TAKE IT OFF. COME ON.
OKAY, OKAY.
MY BREASTS ARE SO SORE.
WHY DO YOU HAVE SO MUCH MILK? WHERE'S YOUR BABY?
UM, I DON'T KNOW WHERE MY BABIES ARE. THEY WERE ALWAYS GONE WHEN I WOKE UP.

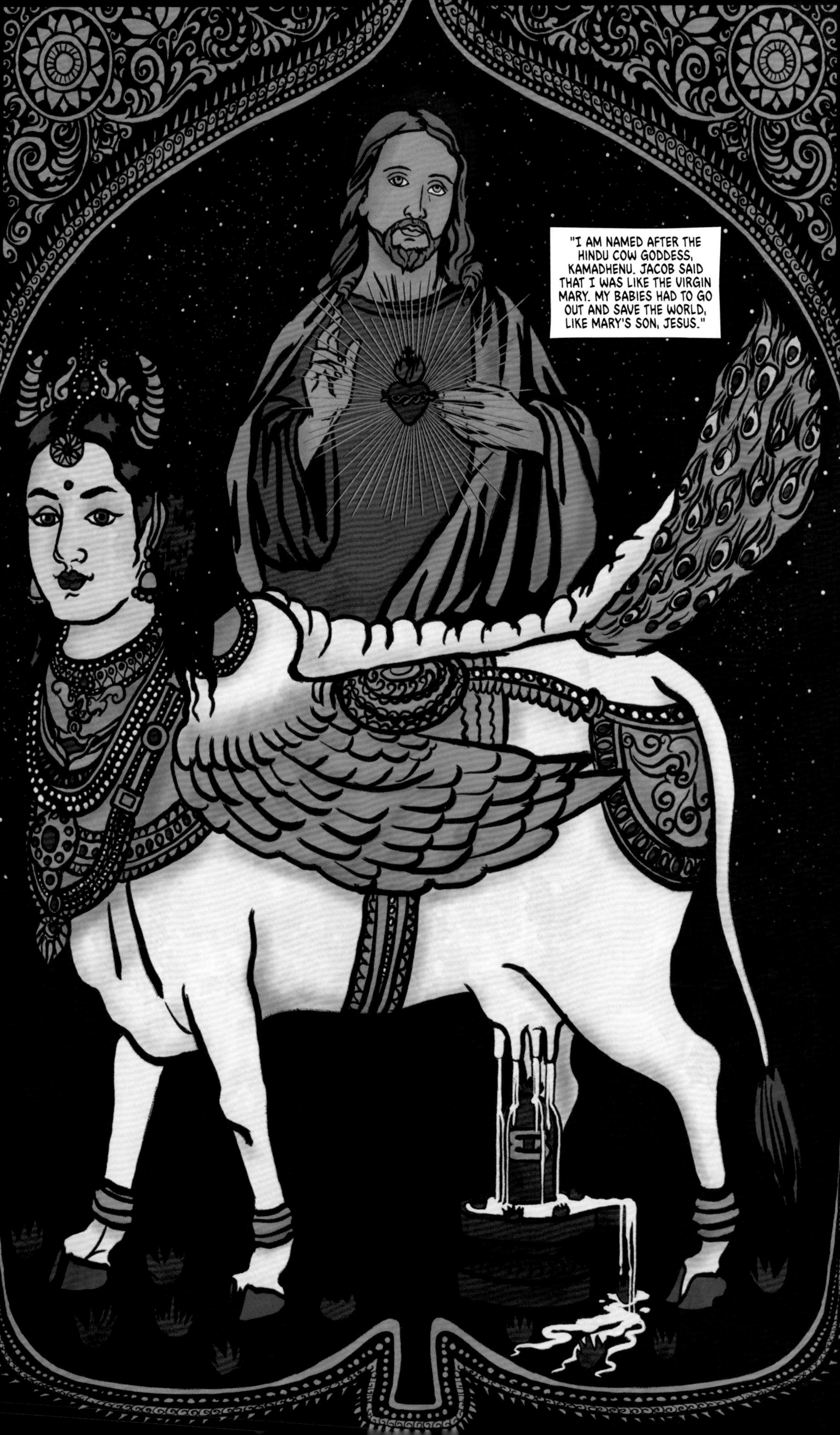
"I AM NAMED AFTER THE HINDU COW GODDESS, KAMADHENU. JACOB SAID THAT I WAS LIKE THE VIRGIN MARY. MY BABIES HAD TO GO OUT AND SAVE THE WORLD, LIKE MARY'S SON, JESUS."

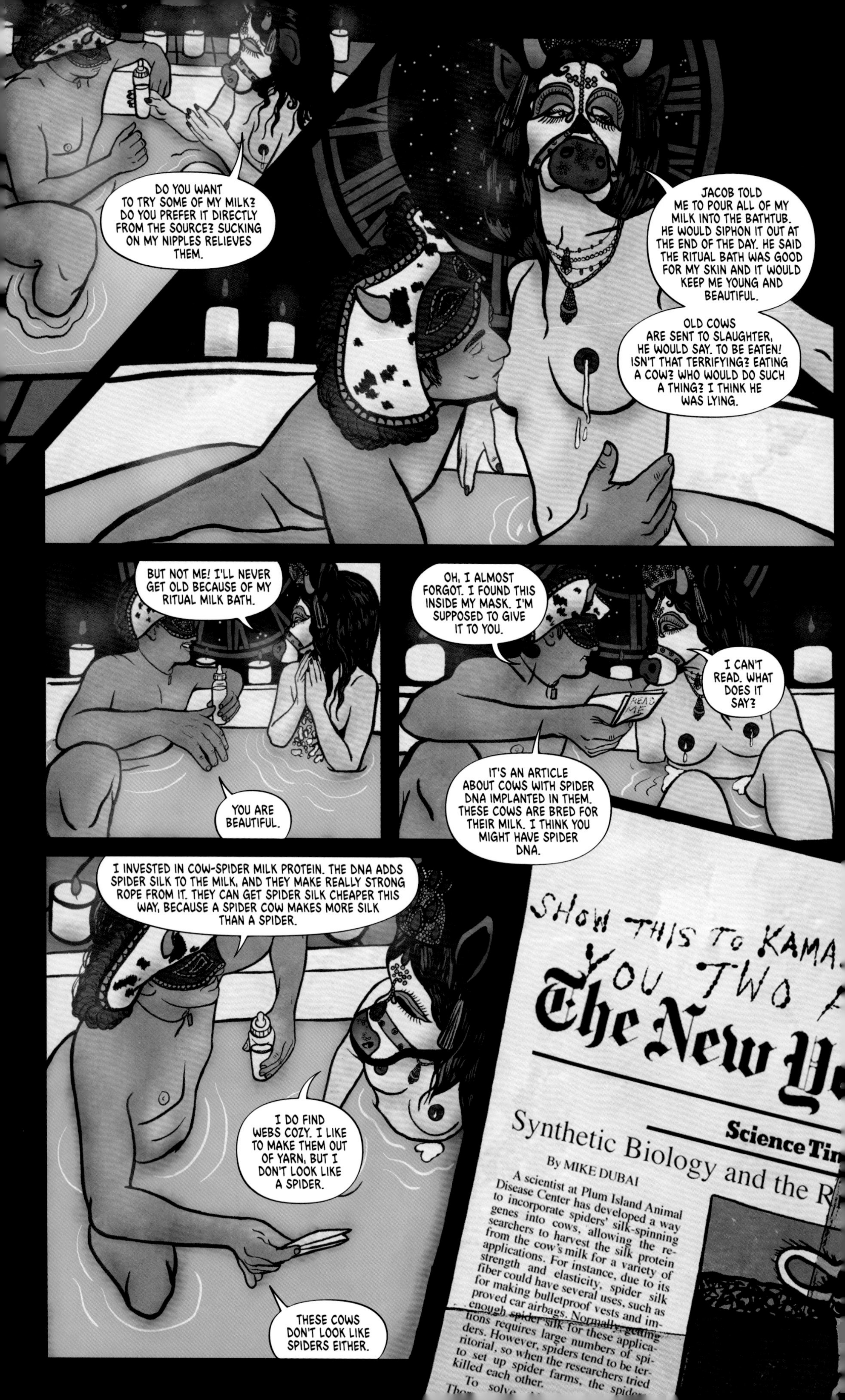
DO YOU WANT TO TRY SOME OF MY MILK? DO YOU PREFER IT DIRECTLY FROM THE SOURCE? SUCKING ON MY NIPPLES RELIEVES THEM.
JACOB TOLD ME TO POUR ALL OF MY MILK INTO THE BATHTUB. HE WOULD SIPHON IT OUT AT THE END OF THE DAY. HE SAID THE RITUAL BATH WAS GOOD FOR MY SKIN AND IT WOULD KEEP ME YOUNG AND BEAUTIFUL.
OLD COWS ARE SENT TO SLAUGHTER, HE WOULD SAY. TO BE EATEN! ISN'T THAT TERRIFYING? EATING A COW? WHO WOULD DO SUCH A THING? I THINK HE WAS LYING.
BUT NOT ME! I'LL NEVER GET OLD BECAUSE OF MY RITUAL MILK BATH.
YOU ARE BEAUTIFUL.
OH, I ALMOST FORGOT. I FOUND THIS INSIDE MY MASK. I'M SUPPOSED TO GIVE IT TO YOU.
READ ME
I CAN'T READ. WHAT DOES IT SAY?
IT'S AN ARTICLE ABOUT COWS WITH SPIDER DNA IMPLANTED IN THEM. THESE COWS ARE BRED FOR THEIR MILK. I THINK YOU MIGHT HAVE SPIDER DNA.
I INVESTED IN COW-SPIDER MILK PROTEIN. THE DNA ADDS SPIDER SILK TO THE MILK, AND THEY MAKE REALLY STRONG ROPE FROM IT. THEY CAN GET SPIDER SILK CHEAPER THIS WAY, BECAUSE A SPIDER COW MAKES MORE SILK THAN A SPIDER.
I DO FIND WEBS COZY. I LIKE TO MAKE THEM OUT OF YARN, BUT I DON'T LOOK LIKE A SPIDER.
THESE COWS DON'T LOOK LIKE SPIDERS EITHER.
SHOW THIS TO KAMA
YOU TWO
The New Y
Science Ti
Synthetic Biology and the R
By MIKE DUBAI
A scientist at Plum Island Animal Disease Center has developed a way to incorporate spiders' silk-spinning genes into cows, allowing the researchers to harvest the silk protein from the cow's milk for a variety of applications. For instance, due to its strength and elasticity, spider silk fiber could have several uses, such as for making bulletproof vests and improved car airbags. Normally, getting enough spider silk for these applications requires large numbers of spiders. However, spiders tend to be territorial, so when the researchers tried to set up spider farms, the spiders killed each other.
To solve

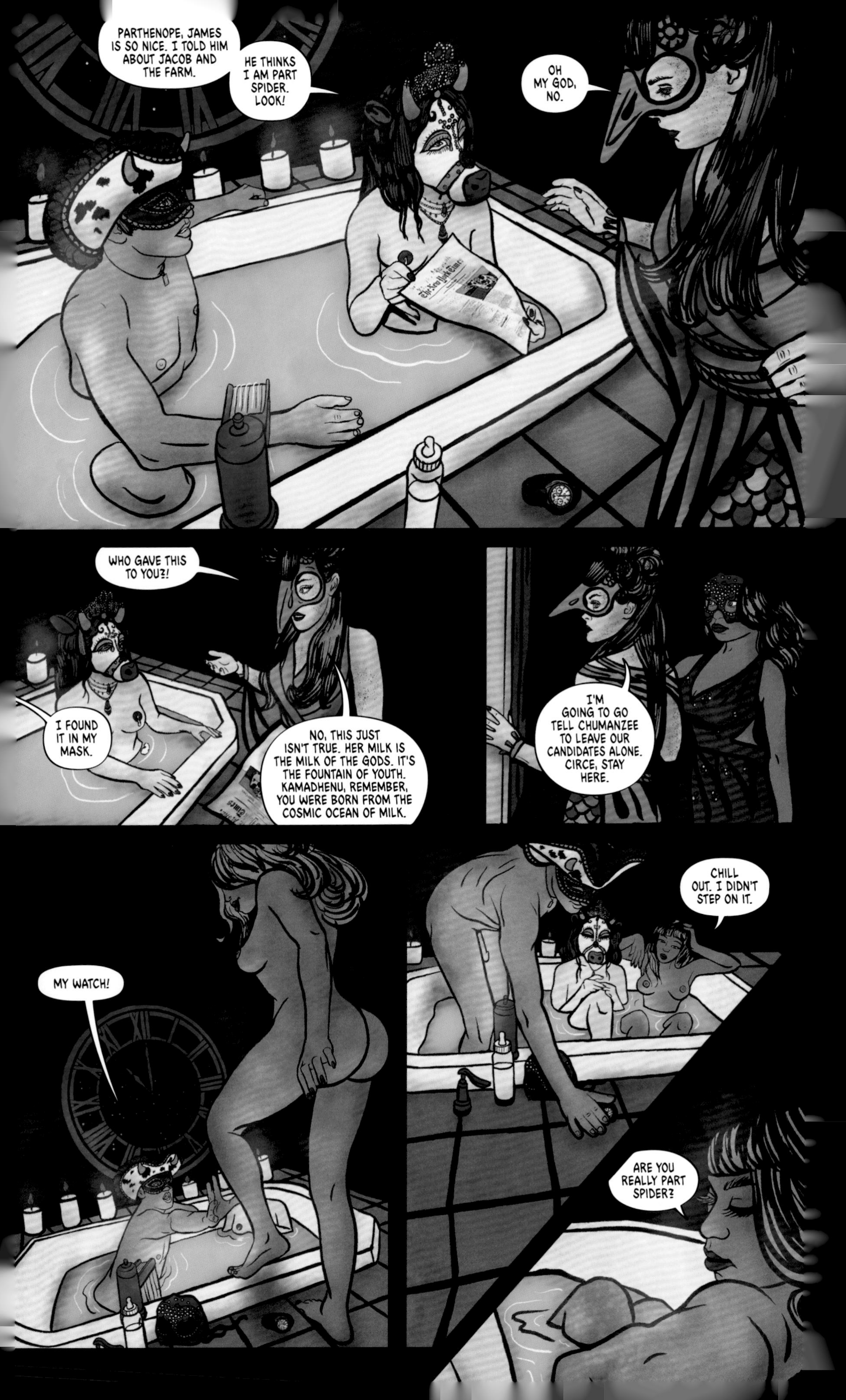
PARTHENOPE, JAMES IS SO NICE. I TOLD HIM ABOUT JACOB AND THE FARM.
HE THINKS I AM PART SPIDER. LOOK!
OH MY GOD, NO.
WHO GAVE THIS TO YOU?!
I FOUND IT IN MY MASK.
NO, THIS JUST ISN'T TRUE. HER MILK IS THE MILK OF THE GODS. IT'S THE FOUNTAIN OF YOUTH. KAMADHENU, REMEMBER, YOU WERE BORN FROM THE COSMIC OCEAN OF MILK.
I'M GOING TO GO TELL CHUMANZEE TO LEAVE OUR CANDIDATES ALONE. CIRCE, STAY HERE.
MY WATCH!
CHILL OUT. I DIDN'T STEP ON IT.
ARE YOU REALLY PART SPIDER?

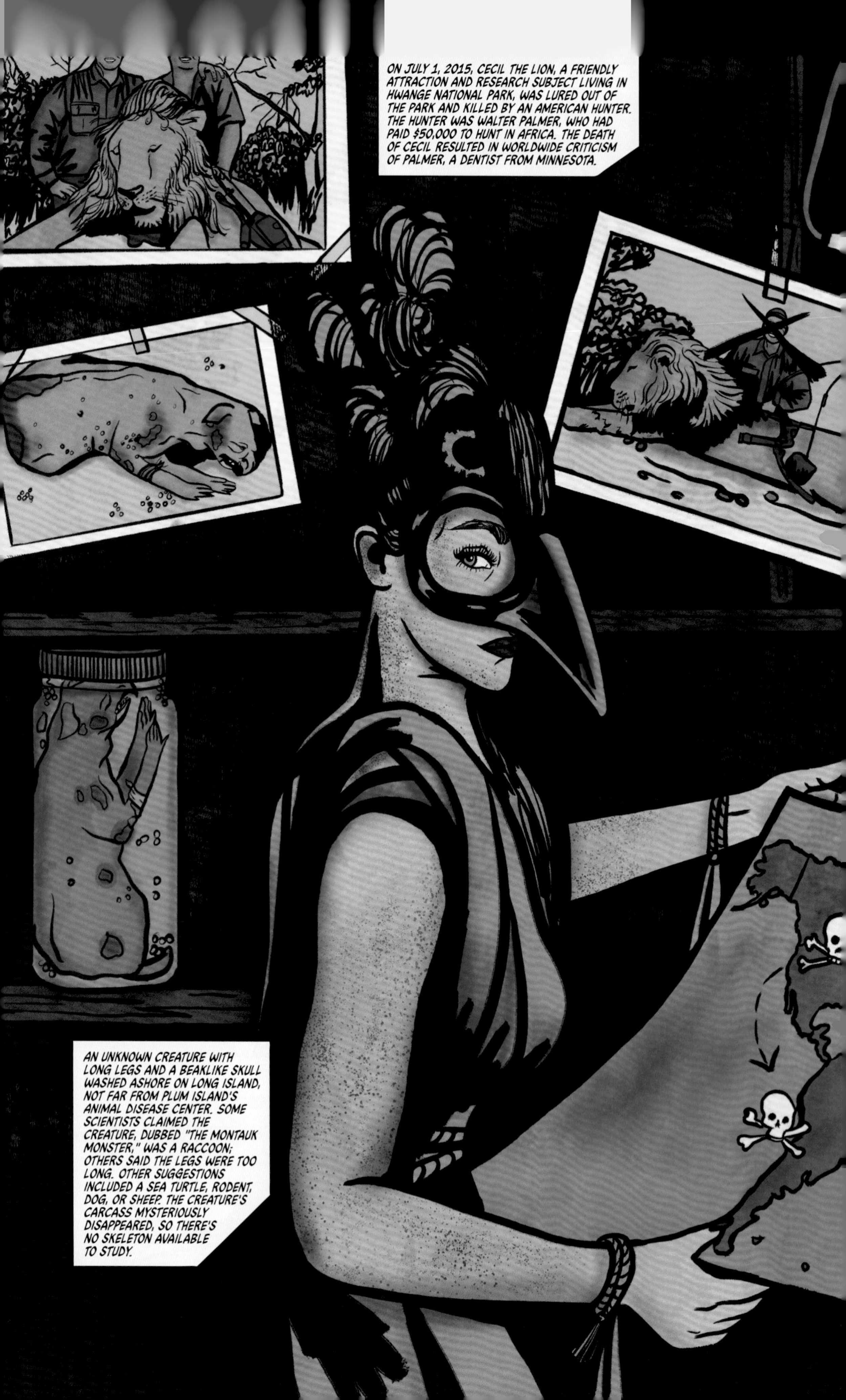
ON JULY 1, 2015, CECIL THE LION, A FRIENDLY ATTRACTION AND RESEARCH SUBJECT LIVING IN HWANGE NATIONAL PARK, WAS LURED OUT OF THE PARK AND KILLED BY AN AMERICAN HUNTER. THE HUNTER WAS WALTER PALMER, WHO HAD PAID $50,000 TO HUNT IN AFRICA. THE DEATH OF CECIL RESULTED IN WORLDWIDE CRITICISM OF PALMER, A DENTIST FROM MINNESOTA.
AN UNKNOWN CREATURE WITH LONG LEGS AND A BEAKLIKE SKULL WASHED ASHORE ON LONG ISLAND, NOT FAR FROM PLUM ISLAND'S ANIMAL DISEASE CENTER. SOME SCIENTISTS CLAIMED THE CREATURE, DUBBED "THE MONTAUK MONSTER," WAS A RACCOON; OTHERS SAID THE LEGS WERE TOO LONG. OTHER SUGGESTIONS INCLUDED A SEA TURTLE, RODENT, DOG, OR SHEEP. THE CREATURE'S CARCASS MYSTERIOUSLY DISAPPEARED, SO THERE'S NO SKELETON AVAILABLE TO STUDY.

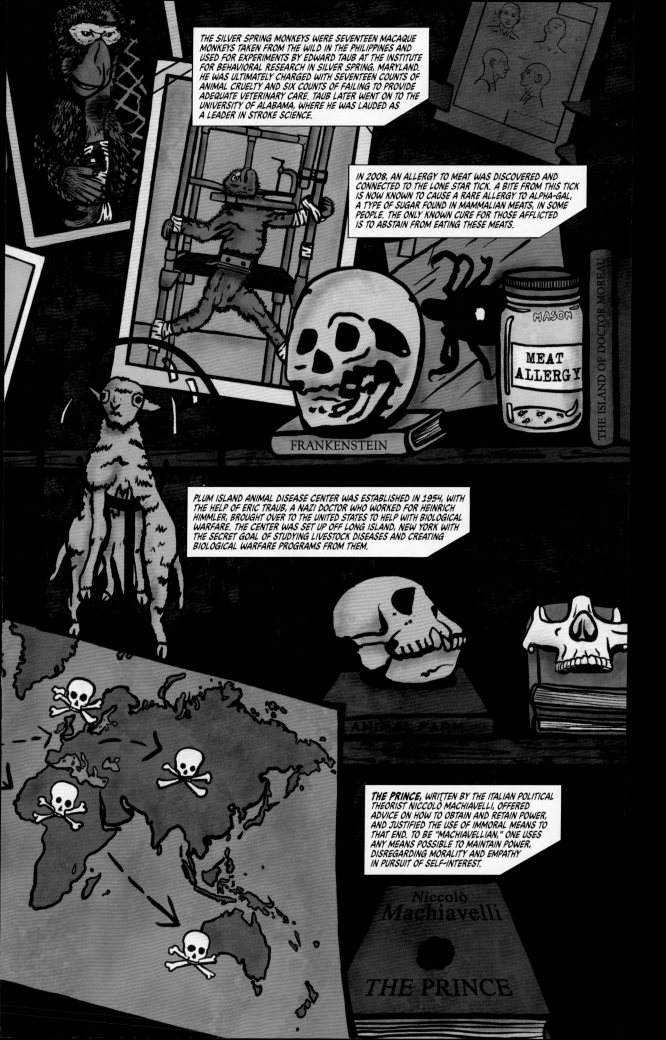

THE SILVER SPRING MONKEYS WERE SEVENTEEN MACAQUE MONKEYS TAKEN FROM THE WILD IN THE PHILIPPINES AND USED FOR EXPERIMENTS BY EDWARD TAUB AT THE INSTITUTE FOR BEHAVIORAL RESEARCH IN SILVER SPRING, MARYLAND. HE WAS ULTIMATELY CHARGED WITH SEVENTEEN COUNTS OF ANIMAL CRUELTY AND SIX COUNTS OF FAILING TO PROVIDE ADEQUATE VETERINARY CARE. TAUB LATER WENT ON TO THE UNIVERSITY OF ALABAMA, WHERE HE WAS LAUDED AS A LEADER IN STROKE SCIENCE.

IN 2008, AN ALLERGY TO MEAT WAS DISCOVERED AND CONNECTED TO THE LONE STAR TICK. A BITE FROM THIS TICK IS NOW KNOWN TO CAUSE A RARE ALLERGY TO ALPHA-GAL, A TYPE OF SUGAR FOUND IN MAMMALIAN MEATS, IN SOME PEOPLE. THE ONLY KNOWN CURE FOR THOSE AFFLICTED IS TO ABSTAIN FROM EATING THESE MEATS.

MASON

MEAT ALLERGY

THE ISLAND OF DOCTOR MOREAU

FRANKENSTEIN

PLUM ISLAND ANIMAL DISEASE CENTER WAS ESTABLISHED IN 1954, WITH THE HELP OF ERIC TRAUB, A NAZI DOCTOR WHO WORKED FOR HEINRICH HIMMLER, BROUGHT OVER TO THE UNITED STATES TO HELP WITH BIOLOGICAL WARFARE. THE CENTER WAS SET UP OFF LONG ISLAND, NEW YORK WITH THE SECRET GOAL OF STUDYING LIVESTOCK DISEASES AND CREATING BIOLOGICAL WARFARE PROGRAMS FROM THEM.

THE PRINCE, WRITTEN BY THE ITALIAN POLITICAL THEORIST NICCOLO MACHIAVELLI, OFFERED ADVICE ON HOW TO OBTAIN AND RETAIN POWER, AND JUSTIFIED THE USE OF IMMORAL MEANS TO THAT END. TO BE "MACHIAVELLIAN," ONE USES ANY MEANS POSSIBLE TO MAINTAIN POWER, DISREGARDING MORALITY AND EMPATHY IN PURSUIT OF SELF-INTEREST.

Niccolò Machiavelli

THE PRINCE

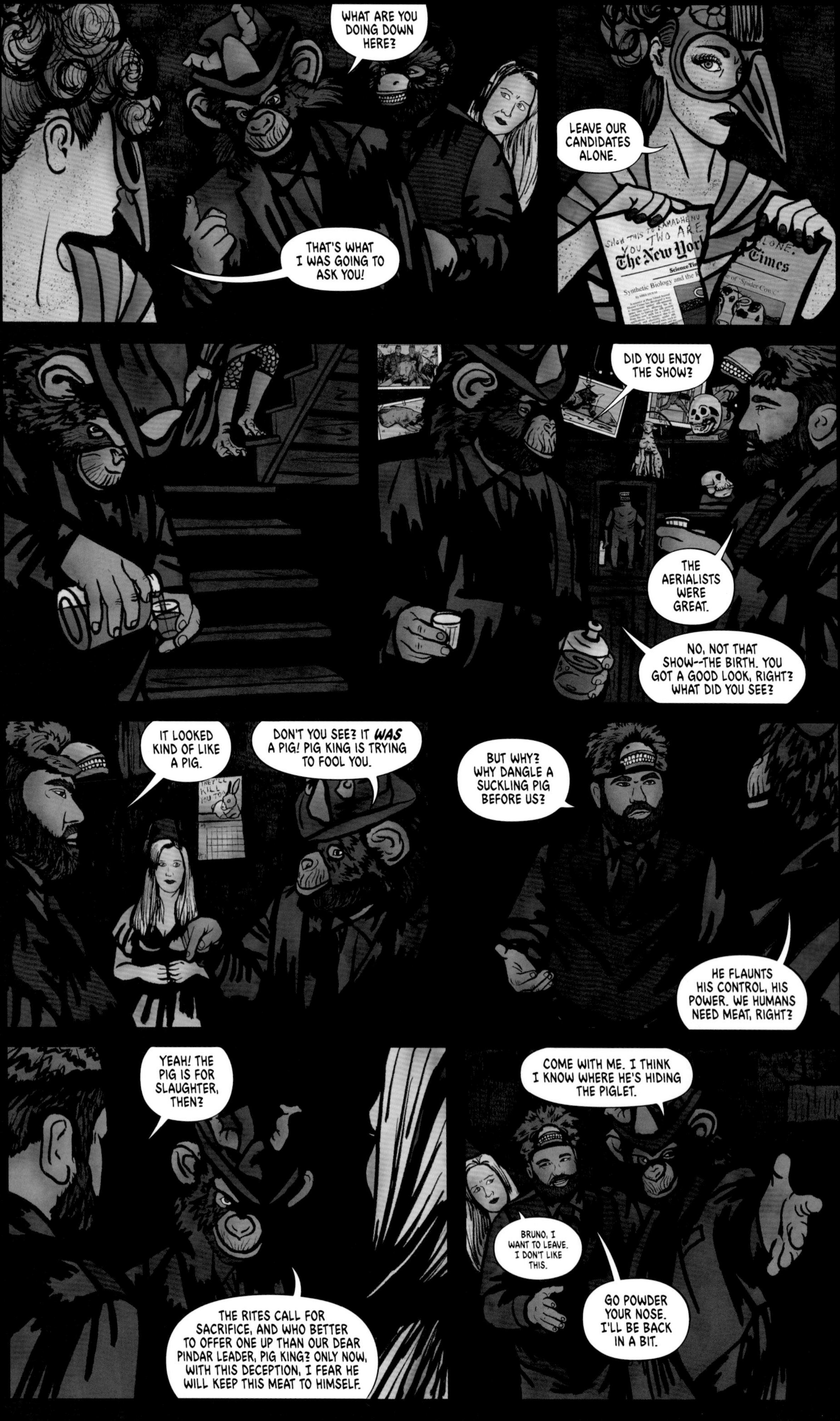
WHAT ARE YOU DOING DOWN HERE?
THAT'S WHAT I WAS GOING TO ASK YOU!
LEAVE OUR CANDIDATES ALONE.
DID YOU ENJOY THE SHOW?
THE AERIALISTS WERE GREAT.
NO, NOT THAT SHOW--THE BIRTH. YOU GOT A GOOD LOOK, RIGHT? WHAT DID YOU SEE?
IT LOOKED KIND OF LIKE A PIG.
DON'T YOU SEE? IT WAS A PIG! PIG KING IS TRYING TO FOOL YOU.
BUT WHY? WHY DANGLE A SUCKLING PIG BEFORE US?
HE FLAUNTS HIS CONTROL, HIS POWER. WE HUMANS NEED MEAT, RIGHT?
YEAH! THE PIG IS FOR SLAUGHTER, THEN?
THE RITES CALL FOR SACRIFICE, AND WHO BETTER TO OFFER ONE UP THAN OUR DEAR PINDAR LEADER, PIG KING? ONLY NOW, WITH THIS DECEPTION, I FEAR HE WILL KEEP THIS MEAT TO HIMSELF.
COME WITH ME. I THINK I KNOW WHERE HE'S HIDING THE PIGLET.
BRUNO, I WANT TO LEAVE. I DON'T LIKE THIS.
GO POWDER YOUR NOSE. I'LL BE BACK IN A BIT.

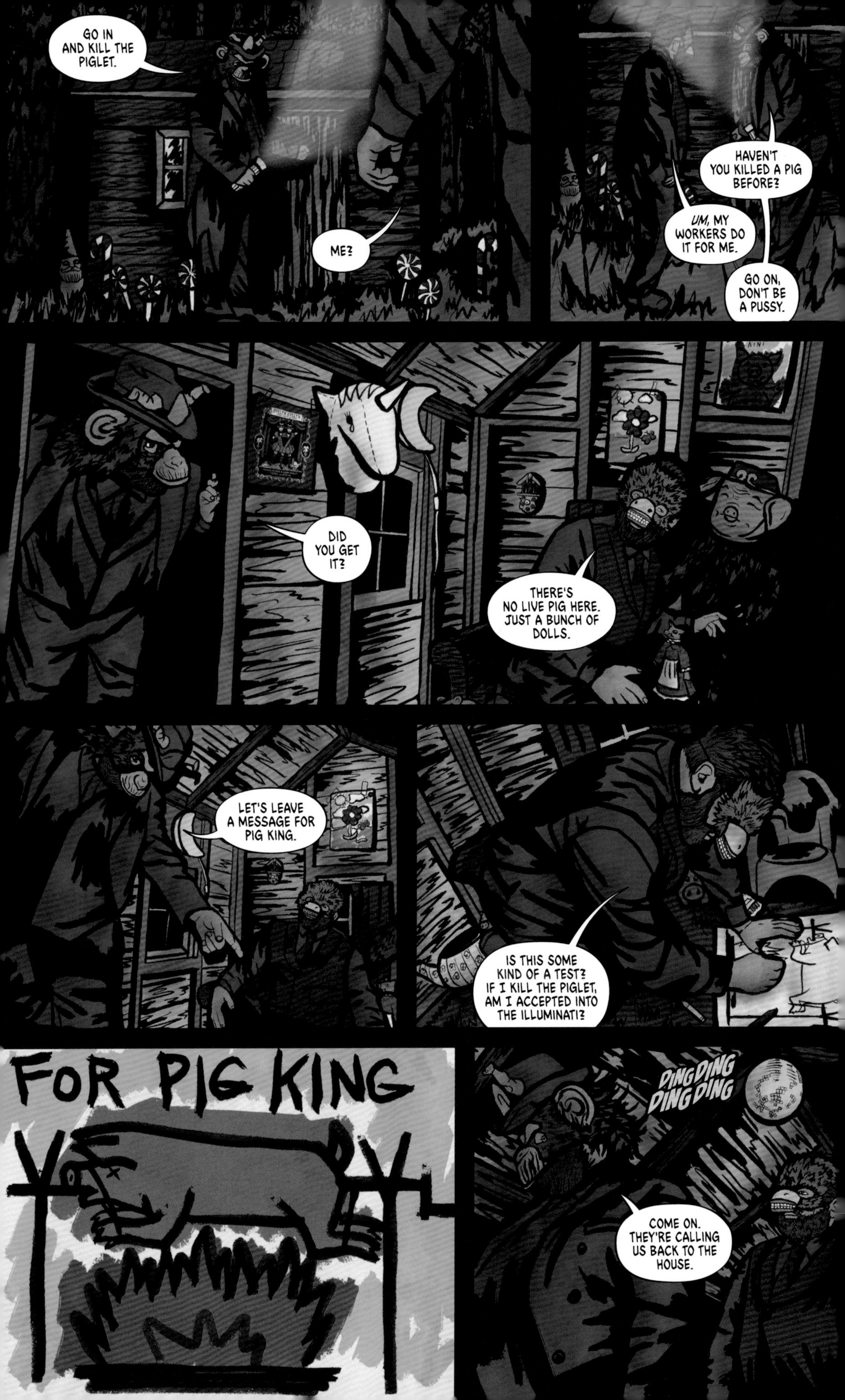
GO IN AND KILL THE PIGLET.
ME?
HAVEN'T YOU KILLED A PIG BEFORE?
UM, MY WORKERS DO IT FOR ME.
GO ON, DON'T BE A PUSSY.
DID YOU GET IT?
THERE'S NO LIVE PIG HERE. JUST A BUNCH OF DOLLS.
LET'S LEAVE A MESSAGE FOR PIG KING.
IS THIS SOME KIND OF A TEST? IF I KILL THE PIGLET, AM I ACCEPTED INTO THE ILLUMINATI?
FOR PIG KING
DING DING DING DING
COME ON. THEY'RE CALLING US BACK TO THE HOUSE.

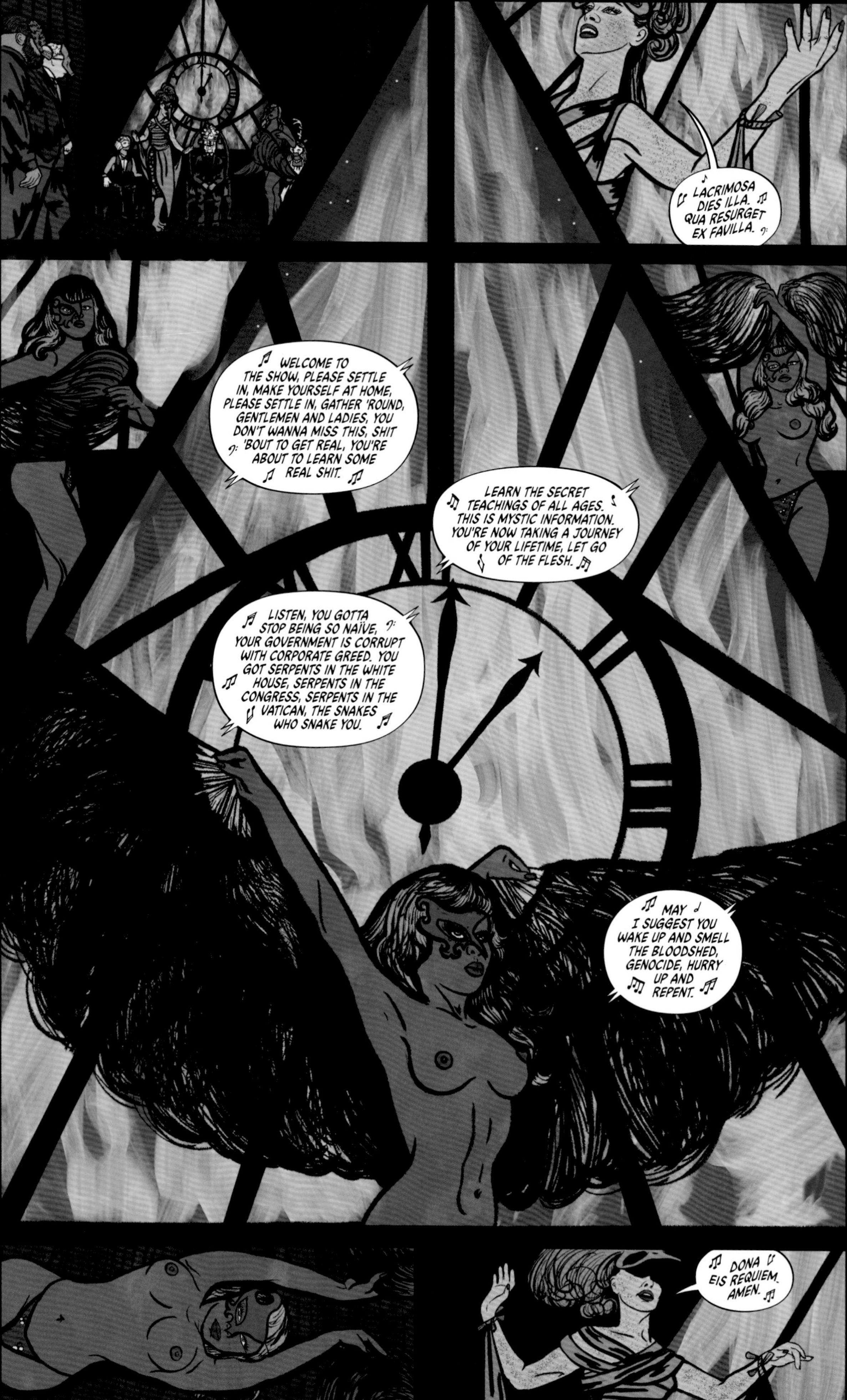
LACRIMOSA DIES ILLA. QUA RESURGET EX FAVILLA.
WELCOME TO THE SHOW, PLEASE SETTLE IN, MAKE YOURSELF AT HOME, PLEASE SETTLE IN, GATHER 'ROUND, GENTLEMEN AND LADIES, YOU DON'T WANNA MISS THIS, SHIT 'BOUT TO GET REAL, YOU'RE ABOUT TO LEARN SOME REAL SHIT.
LEARN THE SECRET TEACHINGS OF ALL AGES. THIS IS MYSTIC INFORMATION. YOU'RE NOW TAKING A JOURNEY OF YOUR LIFETIME, LET GO OF THE FLESH.
LISTEN, YOU GOTTA STOP BEING SO NAÏVE, YOUR GOVERNMENT IS CORRUPT WITH CORPORATE GREED. YOU GOT SERPENTS IN THE WHITE HOUSE, SERPENTS IN THE CONGRESS, SERPENTS IN THE VATICAN, THE SNAKES WHO SNAKE YOU.
MAY I SUGGEST YOU WAKE UP AND SMELL THE BLOODSHED, GENOCIDE, HURRY UP AND REPENT.
DONA EIS REQUIEM. AMEN.

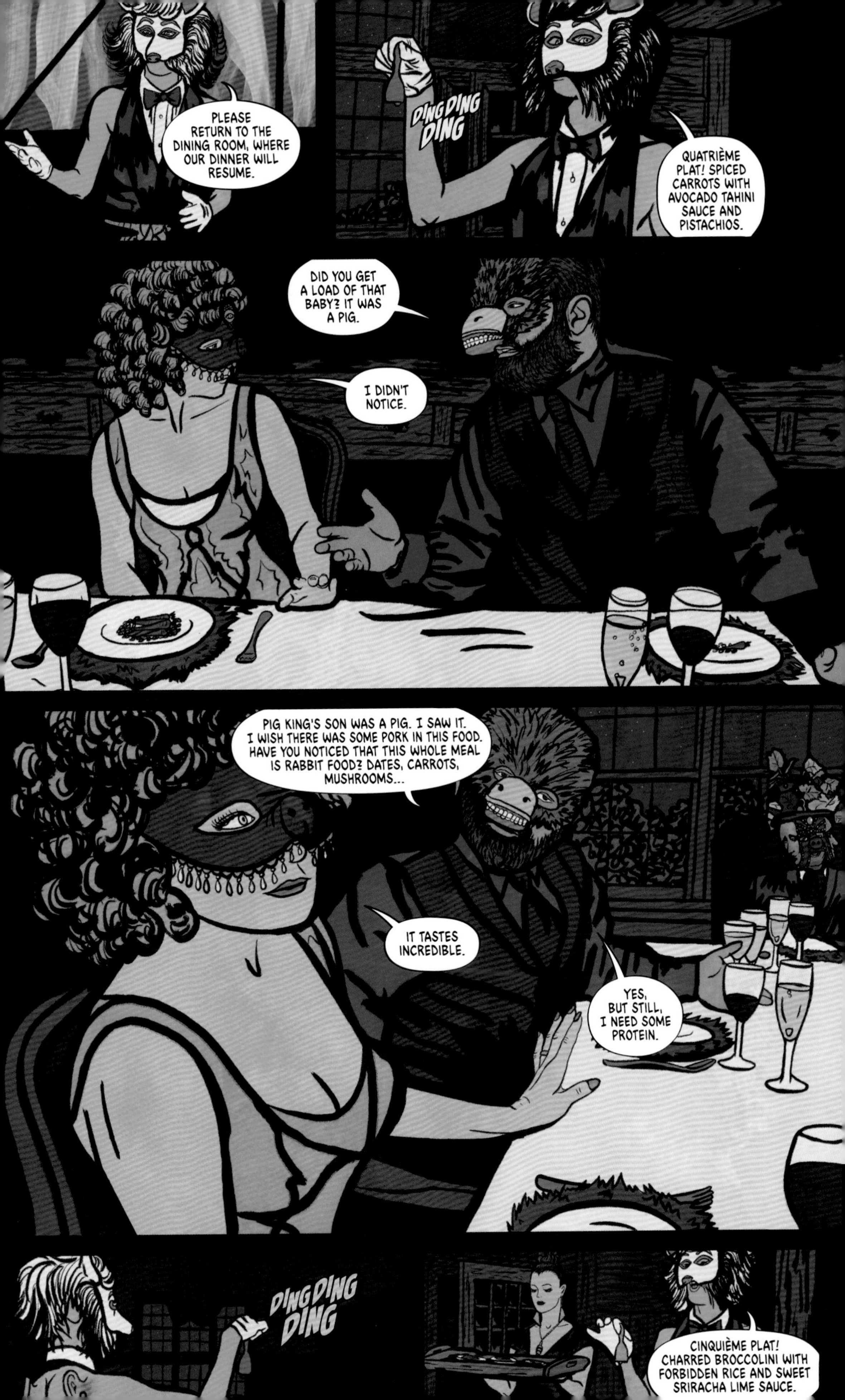
PLEASE RETURN TO THE DINING ROOM, WHERE OUR DINNER WILL RESUME.
DING DING DING
QUATRIÈME PLAT! SPICED CARROTS WITH AVOCADO TAHINI SAUCE AND PISTACHIOS.
DID YOU GET A LOAD OF THAT BABY? IT WAS A PIG.
I DIDN'T NOTICE.
PIG KING'S SON WAS A PIG. I SAW IT. I WISH THERE WAS SOME PORK IN THIS FOOD. HAVE YOU NOTICED THAT THIS WHOLE MEAL IS RABBIT FOOD? DATES, CARROTS, MUSHROOMS...
IT TASTES INCREDIBLE.
YES, BUT STILL, I NEED SOME PROTEIN.
DING DING DING
CINQUIÈME PLAT! CHARRED BROCCOLINI WITH FORBIDDEN RICE AND SWEET SRIRACHA LIME SAUCE.

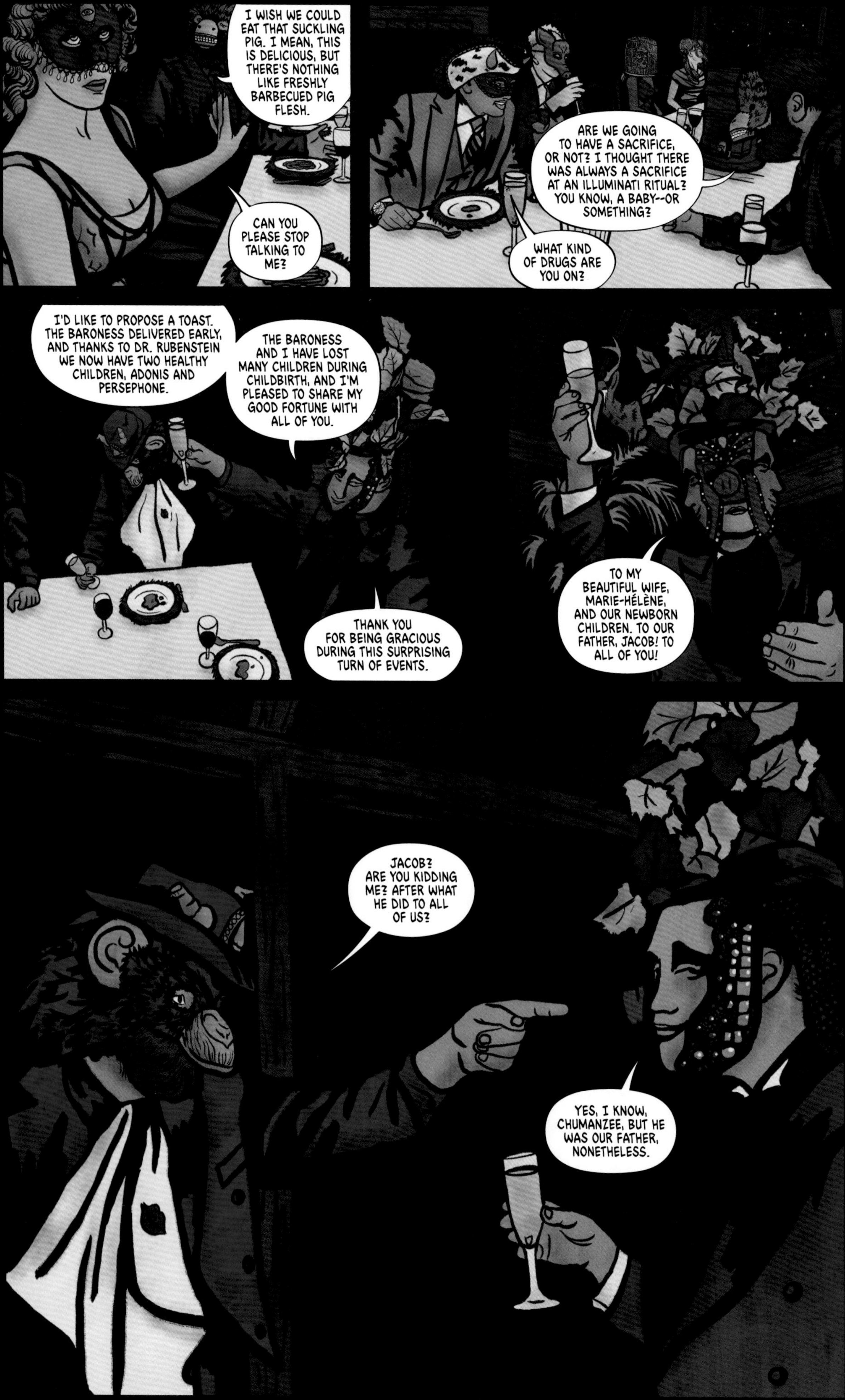

I WISH WE COULD EAT THAT SUCKLING PIG. I MEAN, THIS IS DELICIOUS, BUT THERE'S NOTHING LIKE FRESHLY BARBECUED PIG FLESH.
CAN YOU PLEASE STOP TALKING TO ME?
ARE WE GOING TO HAVE A SACRIFICE, OR NOT? I THOUGHT THERE WAS ALWAYS A SACRIFICE AT AN ILLUMINATI RITUAL? YOU KNOW, A BABY--OR SOMETHING?
WHAT KIND OF DRUGS ARE YOU ON?
I'D LIKE TO PROPOSE A TOAST. THE BARONESS DELIVERED EARLY, AND THANKS TO DR. RUBENSTEIN WE NOW HAVE TWO HEALTHY CHILDREN, ADONIS AND PERSEPHONE.
THE BARONESS AND I HAVE LOST MANY CHILDREN DURING CHILDBIRTH, AND I'M PLEASED TO SHARE MY GOOD FORTUNE WITH ALL OF YOU.
THANK YOU FOR BEING GRACIOUS DURING THIS SURPRISING TURN OF EVENTS.
TO MY BEAUTIFUL WIFE, MARIE-HÉLÈNE, AND OUR NEWBORN CHILDREN. TO OUR FATHER, JACOB! TO ALL OF YOU!
JACOB? ARE YOU KIDDING ME? AFTER WHAT HE DID TO ALL OF US?
YES, I KNOW, CHUMANZEE, BUT HE WAS OUR FATHER, NONETHELESS.

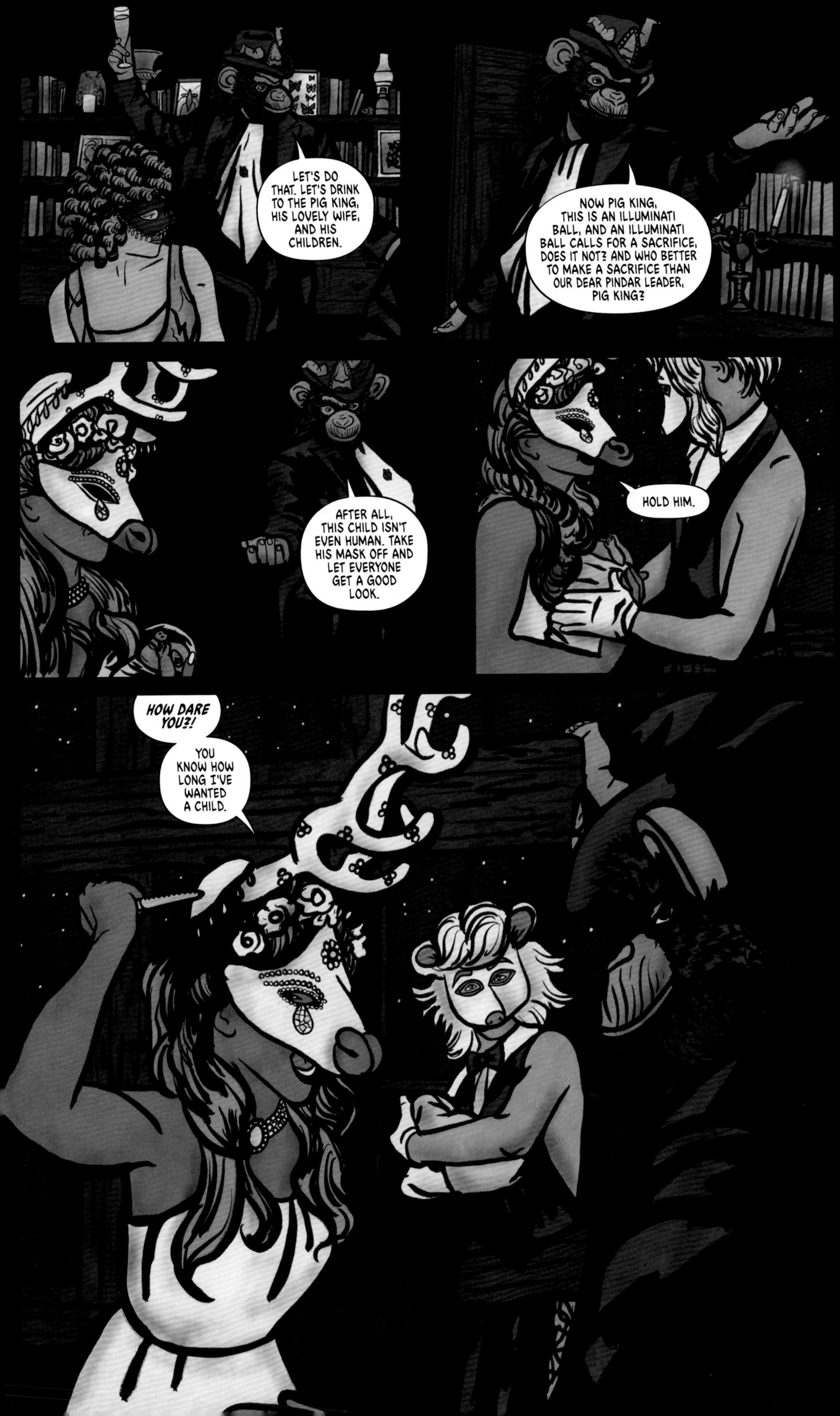
LET'S DO THAT. LET'S DRINK TO THE PIG KING, HIS LOVELY WIFE, AND HIS CHILDREN.
NOW PIG KING, THIS IS AN ILLUMINATI BALL, AND AN ILLUMINATI BALL CALLS FOR A SACRIFICE, DOES IT NOT? AND WHO BETTER TO MAKE A SACRIFICE THAN OUR DEAR PINDAR LEADER, PIG KING?
AFTER ALL, THIS CHILD ISN'T EVEN HUMAN. TAKE HIS MASK OFF AND LET EVERYONE GET A GOOD LOOK.
HOLD HIM.
HOW DARE YOU?!
YOU KNOW HOW LONG I'VE WANTED A CHILD.

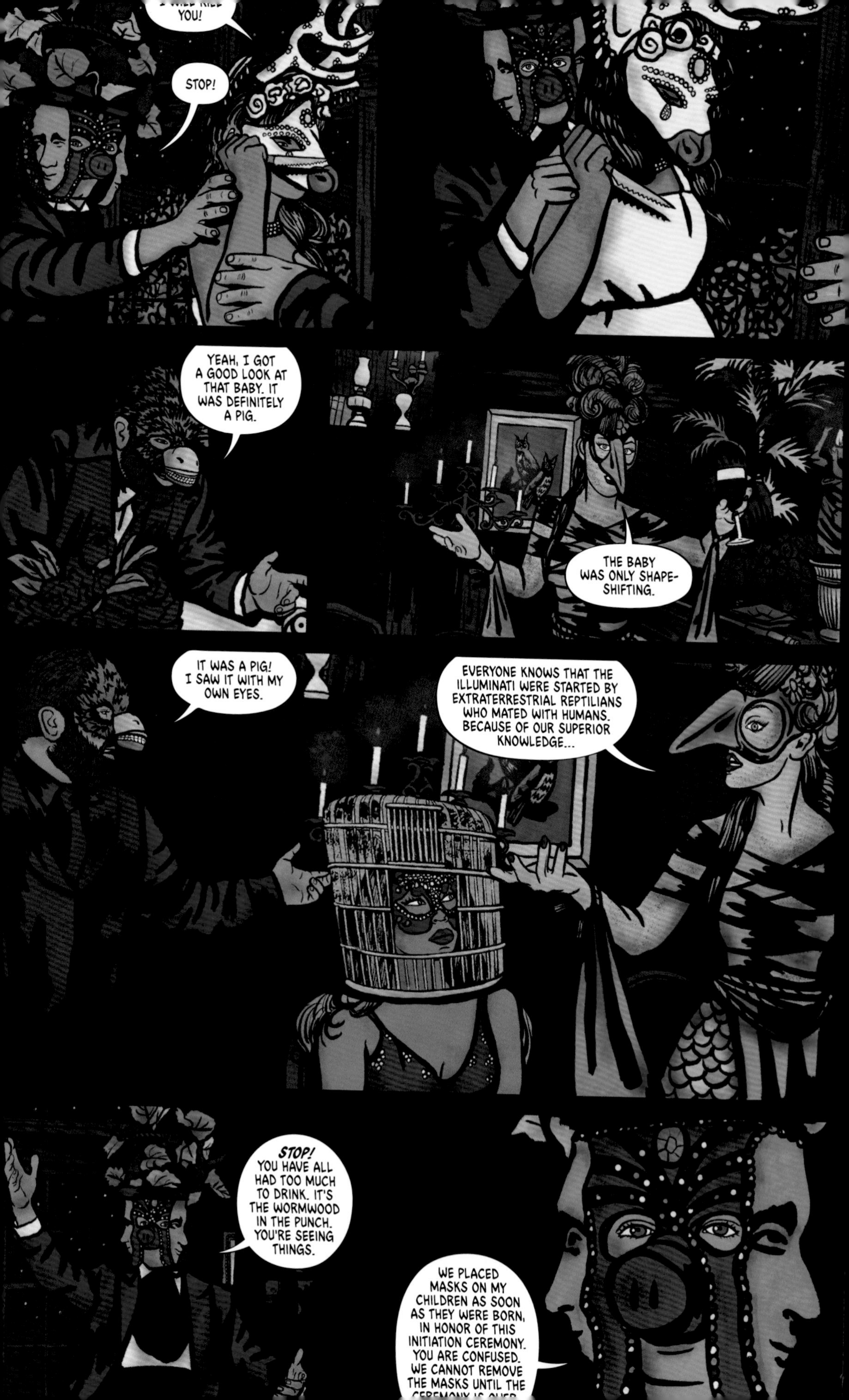
YOU!
STOP!
YEAH, I GOT A GOOD LOOK AT THAT BABY. IT WAS DEFINITELY A PIG.
THE BABY WAS ONLY SHAPE-SHIFTING.
IT WAS A PIG! I SAW IT WITH MY OWN EYES.
EVERYONE KNOWS THAT THE ILLUMINATI WERE STARTED BY EXTRATERRESTRIAL REPTILIANS WHO MATED WITH HUMANS. BECAUSE OF OUR SUPERIOR KNOWLEDGE...
STOP! YOU HAVE ALL HAD TOO MUCH TO DRINK. IT'S THE WORMWOOD IN THE PUNCH. YOU'RE SEEING THINGS.
WE PLACED MASKS ON MY CHILDREN AS SOON AS THEY WERE BORN, IN HONOR OF THIS INITIATION CEREMONY. YOU ARE CONFUSED. WE CANNOT REMOVE THE MASKS UNTIL THE

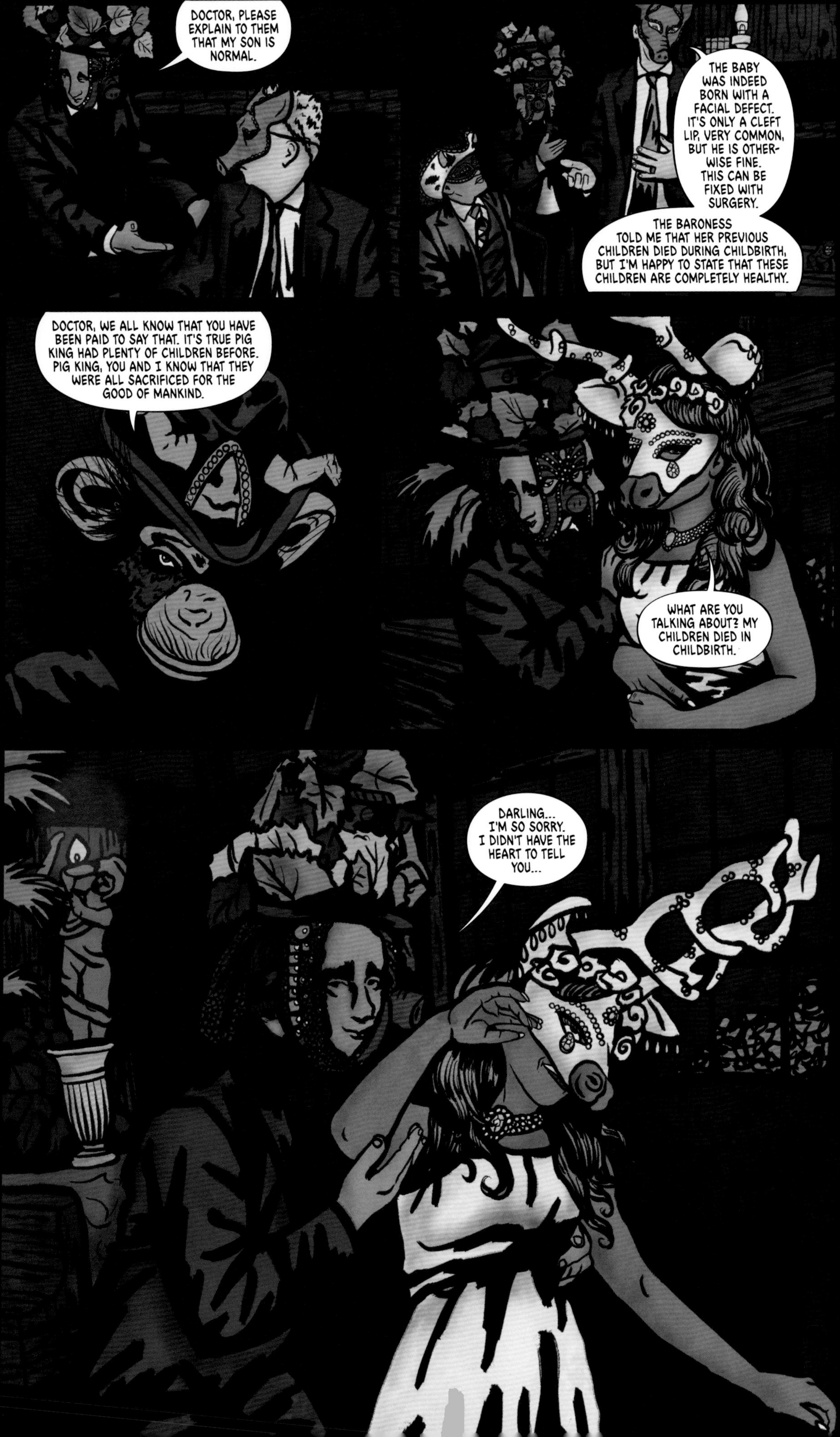
DOCTOR, PLEASE EXPLAIN TO THEM THAT MY SON IS NORMAL.
THE BABY WAS INDEED BORN WITH A FACIAL DEFECT. IT'S ONLY A CLEFT LIP, VERY COMMON, BUT HE IS OTHER-WISE FINE. THIS CAN BE FIXED WITH SURGERY.
THE BARONESS TOLD ME THAT HER PREVIOUS CHILDREN DIED DURING CHILDBIRTH, BUT I'M HAPPY TO STATE THAT THESE CHILDREN ARE COMPLETELY HEALTHY.
DOCTOR, WE ALL KNOW THAT YOU HAVE BEEN PAID TO SAY THAT. IT'S TRUE PIG KING HAD PLENTY OF CHILDREN BEFORE. PIG KING, YOU AND I KNOW THAT THEY WERE ALL SACRIFICED FOR THE GOOD OF MANKIND.
WHAT ARE YOU TALKING ABOUT? MY CHILDREN DIED IN CHILDBIRTH.
DARLING... I'M SO SORRY. I DIDN'T HAVE THE HEART TO TELL YOU...

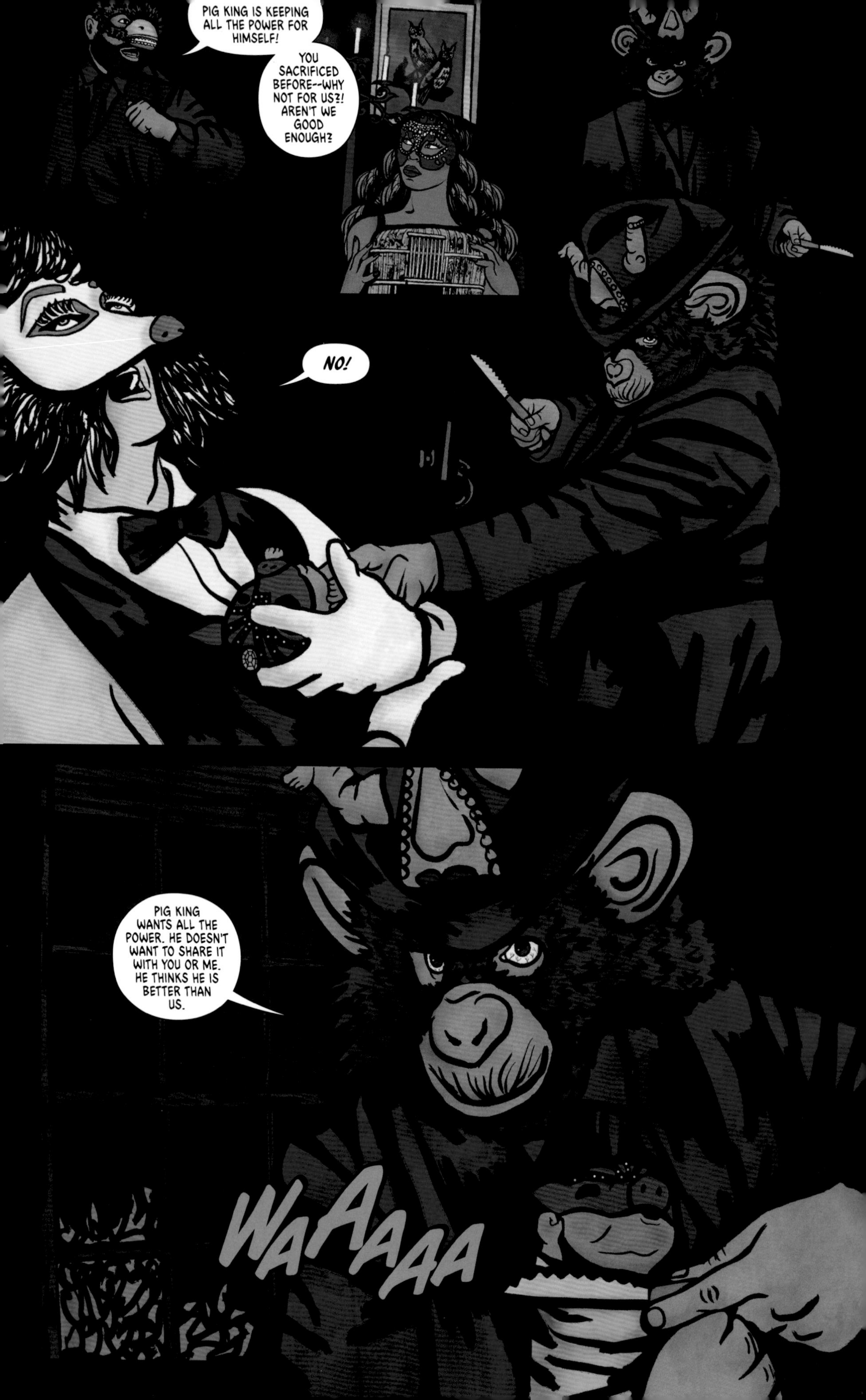
PIG KING IS KEEPING ALL THE POWER FOR HIMSELF!
YOU SACRIFICED BEFORE--WHY NOT FOR US?! AREN'T WE GOOD ENOUGH?
NO!
PIG KING WANTS ALL THE POWER. HE DOESN'T WANT TO SHARE IT WITH YOU OR ME. HE THINKS HE IS BETTER THAN US.
WAAAAA

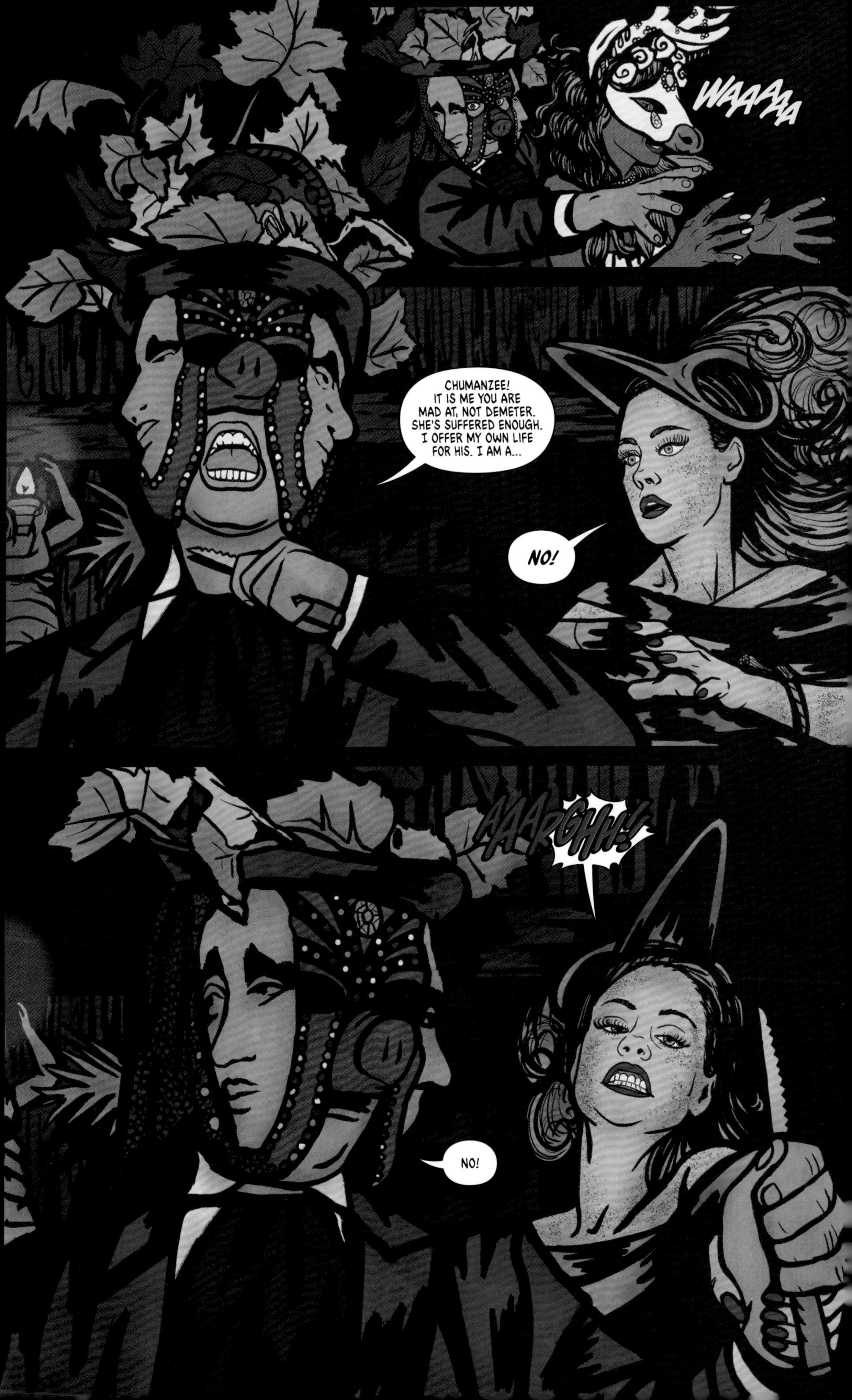
WAAAAA
CHUMANZEE! IT IS ME YOU ARE MAD AT, NOT DEMETER. SHE'S SUFFERED ENOUGH. I OFFER MY OWN LIFE FOR HIS. I AM A...
NO!
AAARGHH!
NO!

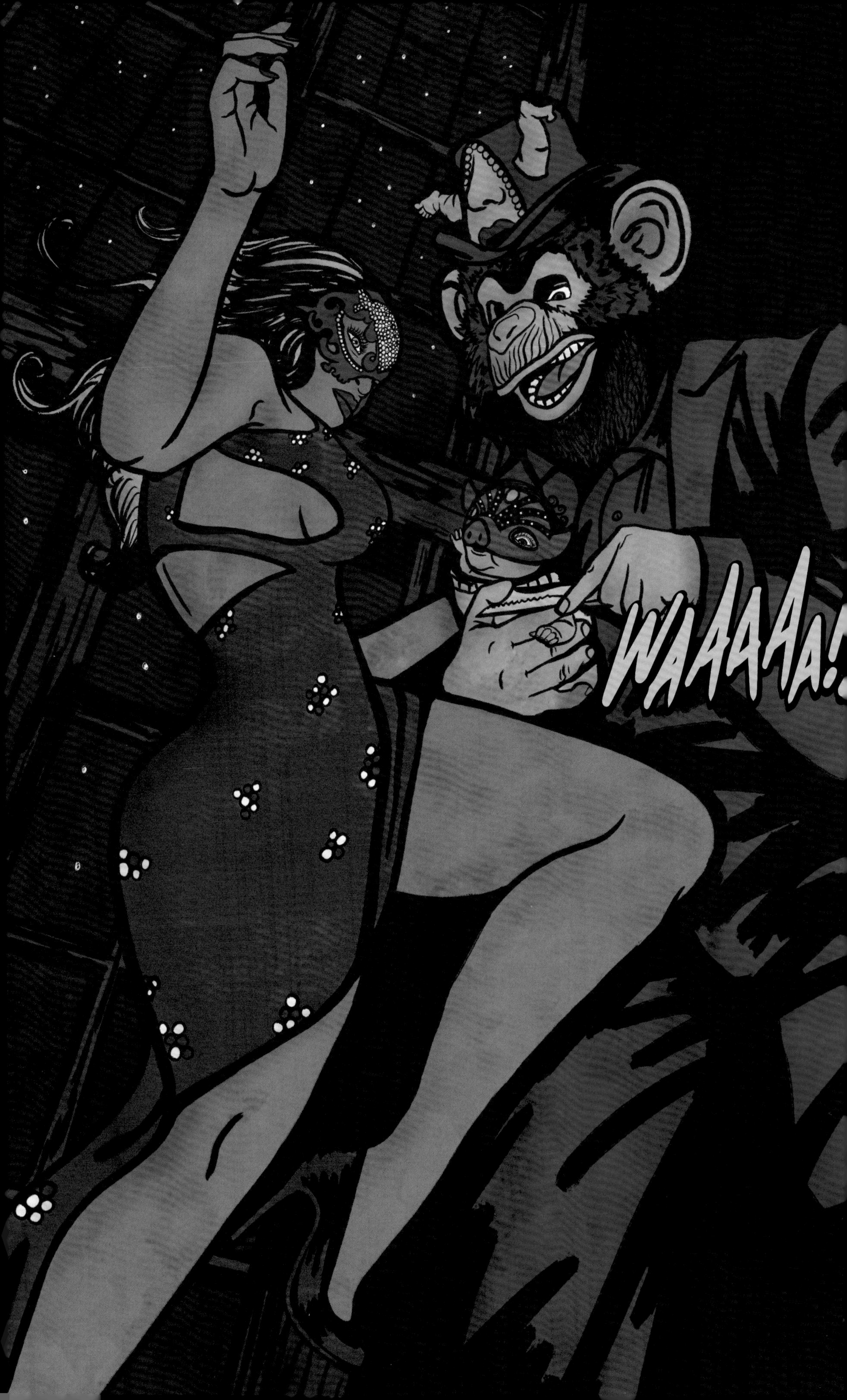
WAAAAA!

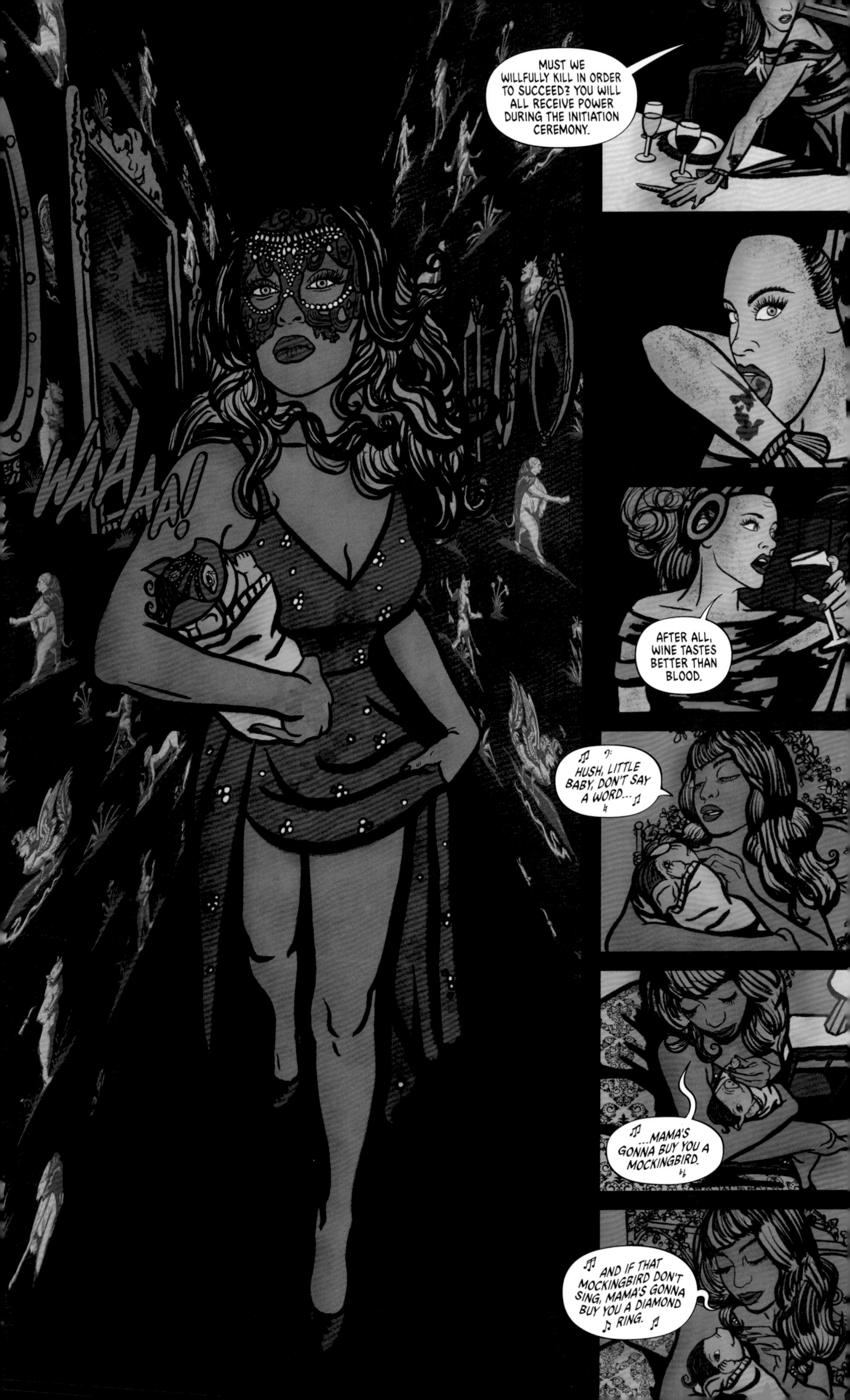
MUST WE WILLFULLY KILL IN ORDER TO SUCCEED? YOU WILL ALL RECEIVE POWER DURING THE INITIATION CEREMONY.
WAAAA!
AFTER ALL, WINE TASTES BETTER THAN BLOOD.
HUSH, LITTLE BABY, DON'T SAY A WORD...
...MAMA'S GONNA BUY YOU A MOCKINGBIRD.
AND IF THAT MOCKINGBIRD DON'T SING, MAMA'S GONNA BUY YOU A DIAMOND RING.

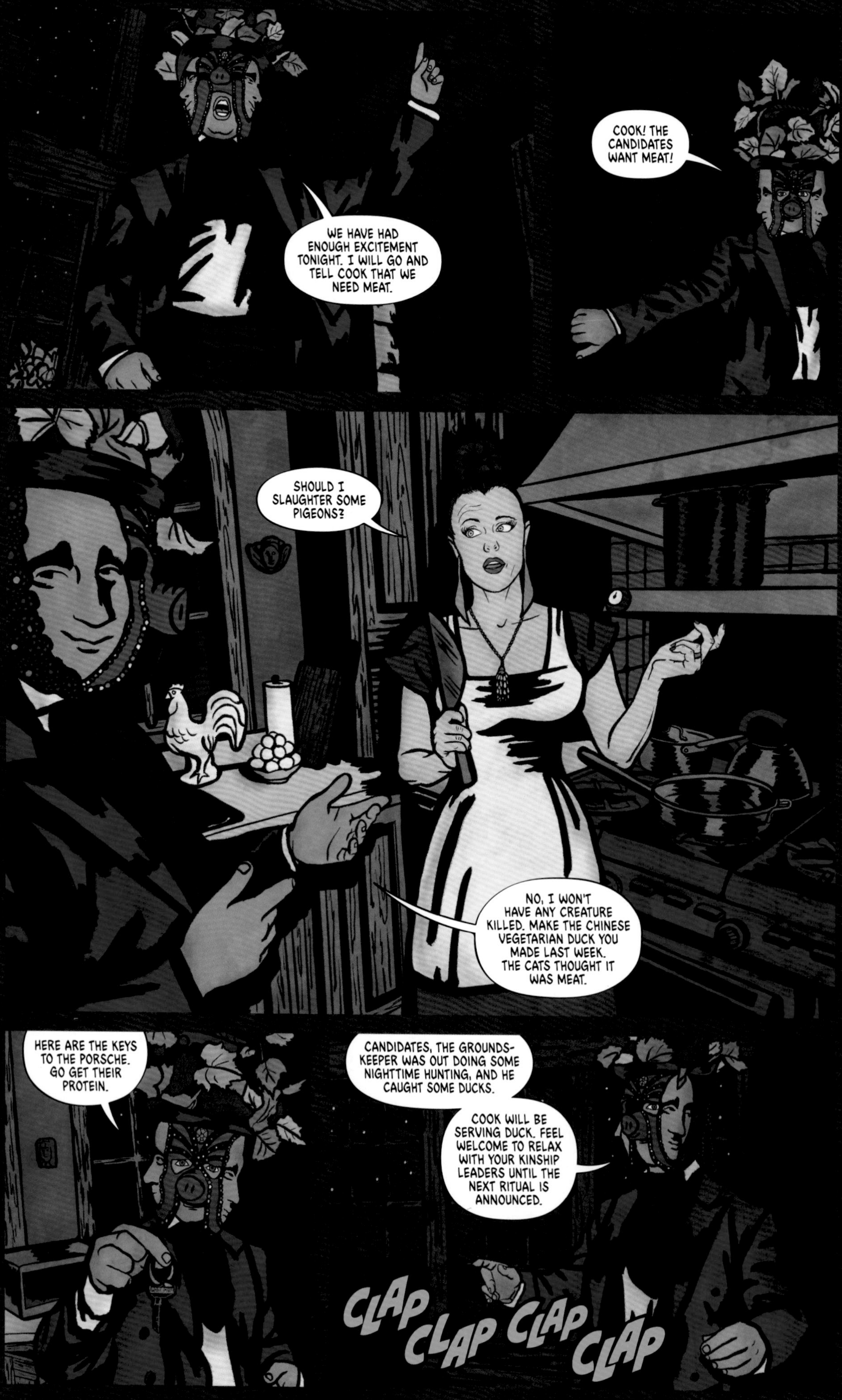
WE HAVE HAD ENOUGH EXCITEMENT TONIGHT. I WILL GO AND TELL COOK THAT WE NEED MEAT.
COOK! THE CANDIDATES WANT MEAT!
SHOULD I SLAUGHTER SOME PIGEONS?
NO, I WON'T HAVE ANY CREATURE KILLED. MAKE THE CHINESE VEGETARIAN DUCK YOU MADE LAST WEEK. THE CATS THOUGHT IT WAS MEAT.
HERE ARE THE KEYS TO THE PORSCHE. GO GET THEIR PROTEIN.
CANDIDATES, THE GROUNDS-KEEPER WAS OUT DOING SOME NIGHTTIME HUNTING, AND HE CAUGHT SOME DUCKS.
COOK WILL BE SERVING DUCK. FEEL WELCOME TO RELAX WITH YOUR KINSHIP LEADERS UNTIL THE NEXT RITUAL IS ANNOUNCED.
CLAP CLAP CLAP CLAP

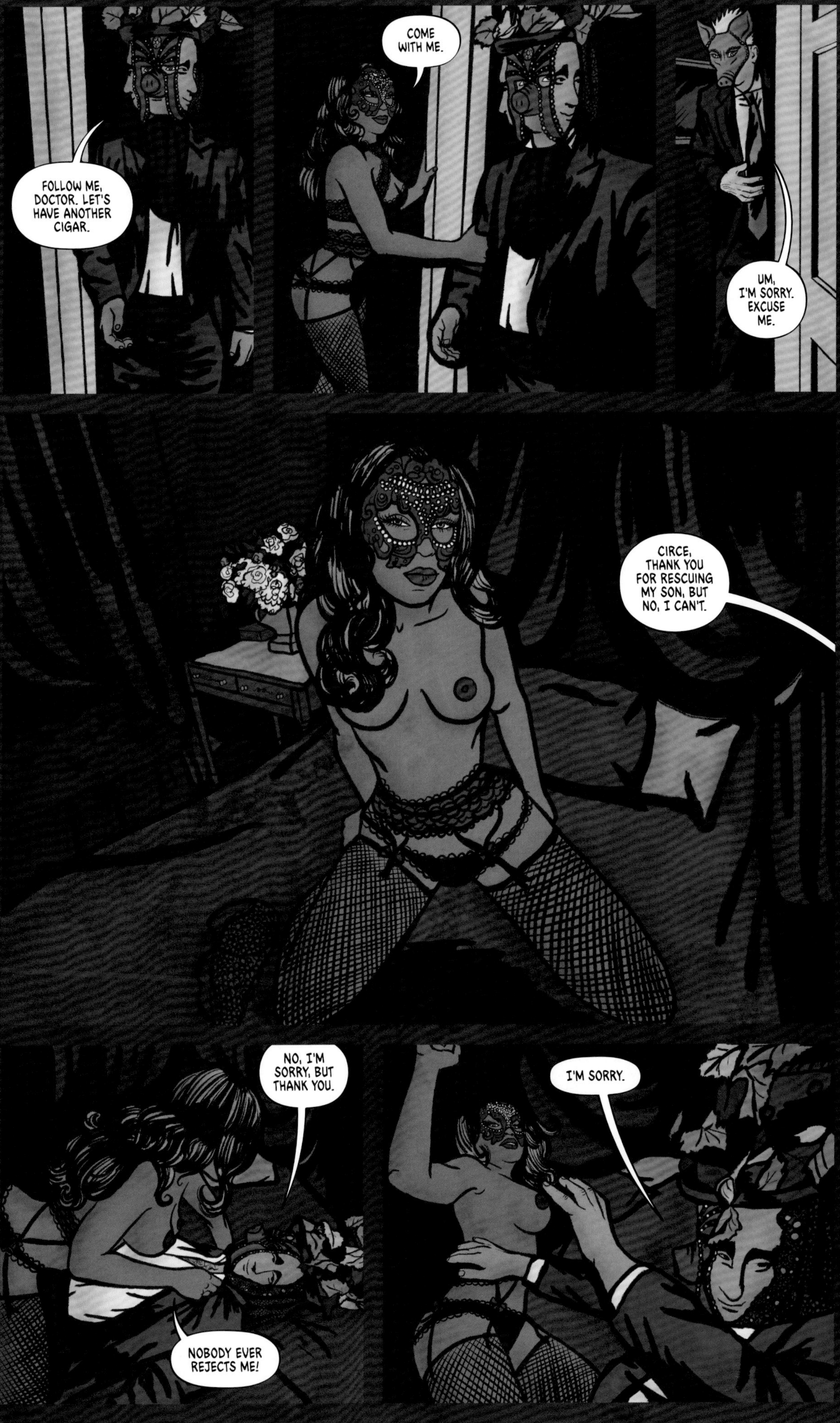
FOLLOW ME, DOCTOR. LET'S HAVE ANOTHER CIGAR.
COME WITH ME.
UM, I'M SORRY. EXCUSE ME.
CIRCE, THANK YOU FOR RESCUING MY SON, BUT NO, I CAN'T.
NO, I'M SORRY, BUT THANK YOU.
NOBODY EVER REJECTS ME!
I'M SORRY.

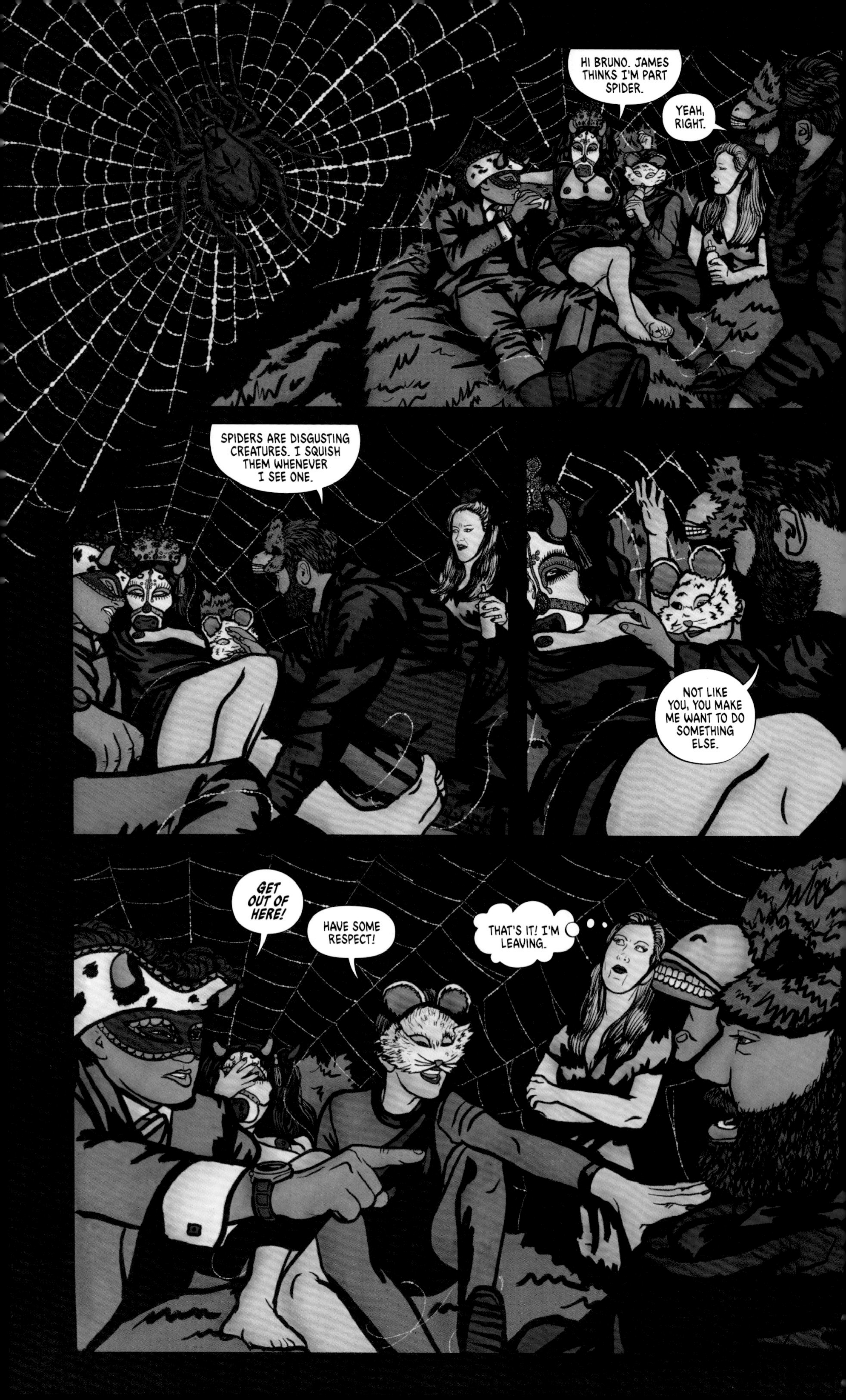

HI BRUNO. JAMES THINKS I'M PART SPIDER.
YEAH, RIGHT.
SPIDERS ARE DISGUSTING CREATURES. I SQUISH THEM WHENEVER I SEE ONE.
NOT LIKE YOU, YOU MAKE ME WANT TO DO SOMETHING ELSE.
GET OUT OF HERE!
HAVE SOME RESPECT!
THAT'S IT! I'M LEAVING.

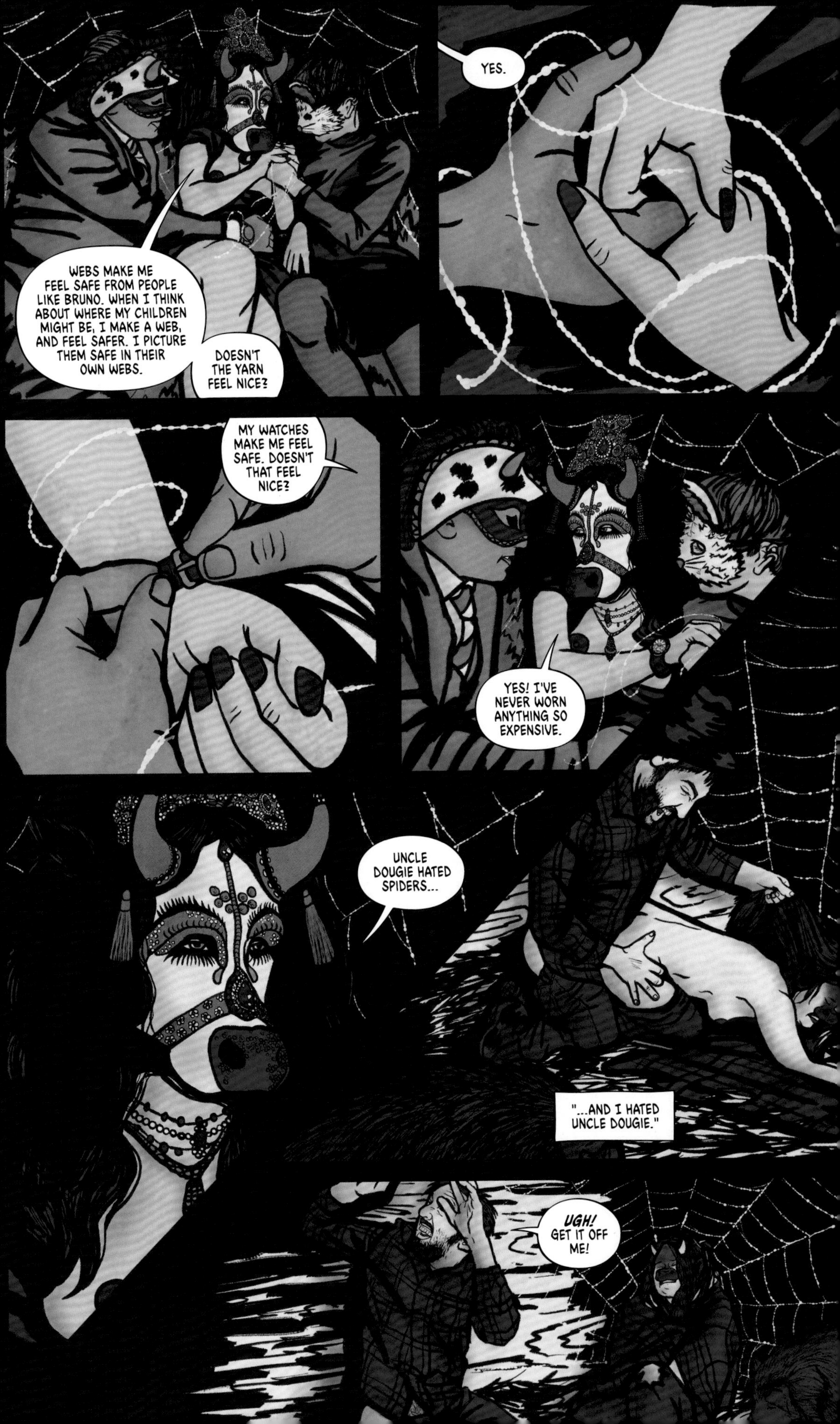
WEBS MAKE ME FEEL SAFE FROM PEOPLE LIKE BRUNO. WHEN I THINK ABOUT WHERE MY CHILDREN MIGHT BE, I MAKE A WEB, AND FEEL SAFER. I PICTURE THEM SAFE IN THEIR OWN WEBS.
DOESN'T THE YARN FEEL NICE?
YES.
MY WATCHES MAKE ME FEEL SAFE. DOESN'T THAT FEEL NICE?
YES! I'VE NEVER WORN ANYTHING SO EXPENSIVE.
UNCLE DOUGIE HATED SPIDERS...
"...AND I HATED UNCLE DOUGIE."
UGH! GET IT OFF ME!

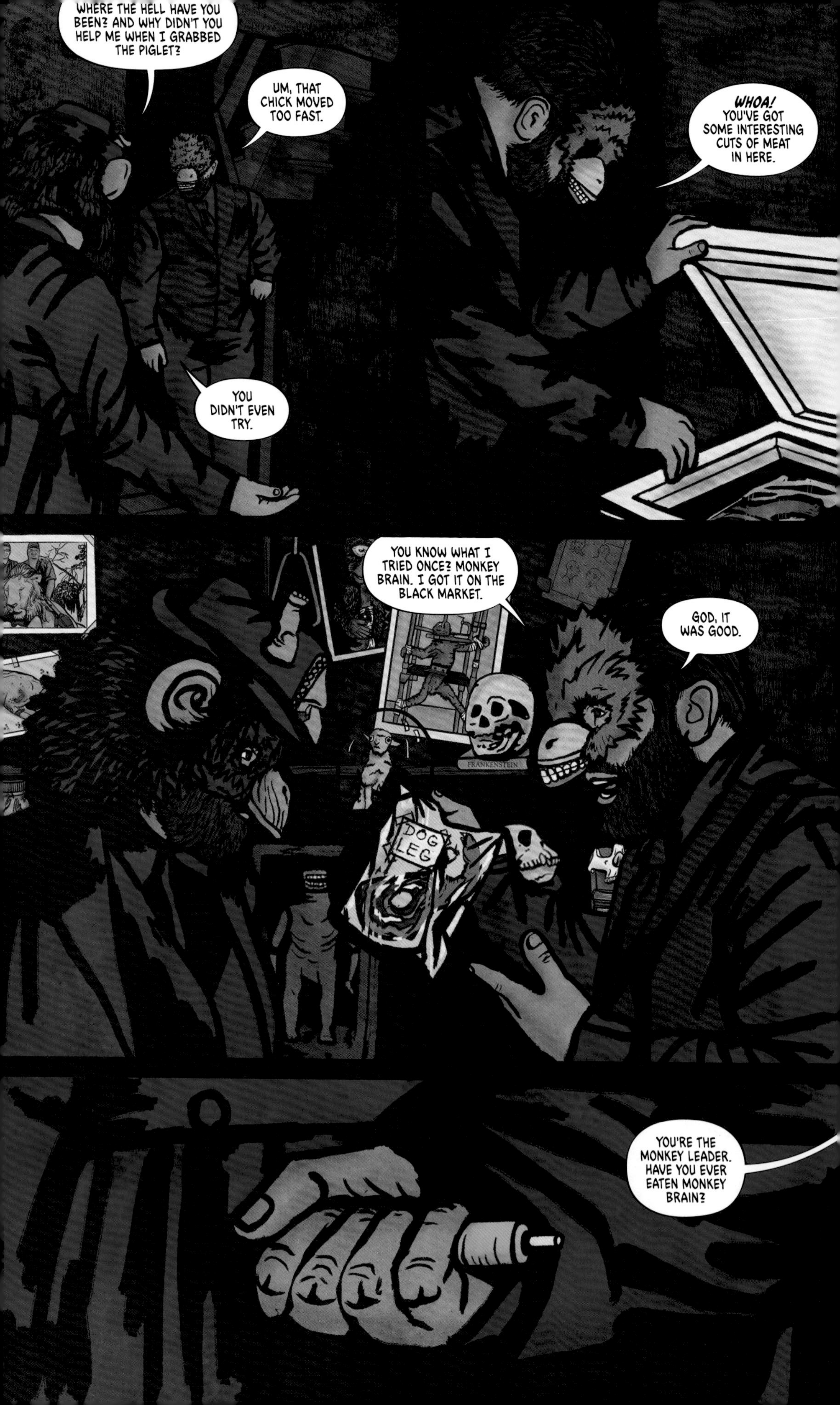
WHERE THE HELL HAVE YOU BEEN? AND WHY DIDN'T YOU HELP ME WHEN I GRABBED THE PIGLET?
UM, THAT CHICK MOVED TOO FAST.
YOU DIDN'T EVEN TRY.
WHOA! YOU'VE GOT SOME INTERESTING CUTS OF MEAT IN HERE.
YOU KNOW WHAT I TRIED ONCE? MONKEY BRAIN. I GOT IT ON THE BLACK MARKET.
GOD, IT WAS GOOD.
FRANKENSTEIN
DOG LEG
YOU'RE THE MONKEY LEADER. HAVE YOU EVER EATEN MONKEY BRAIN?

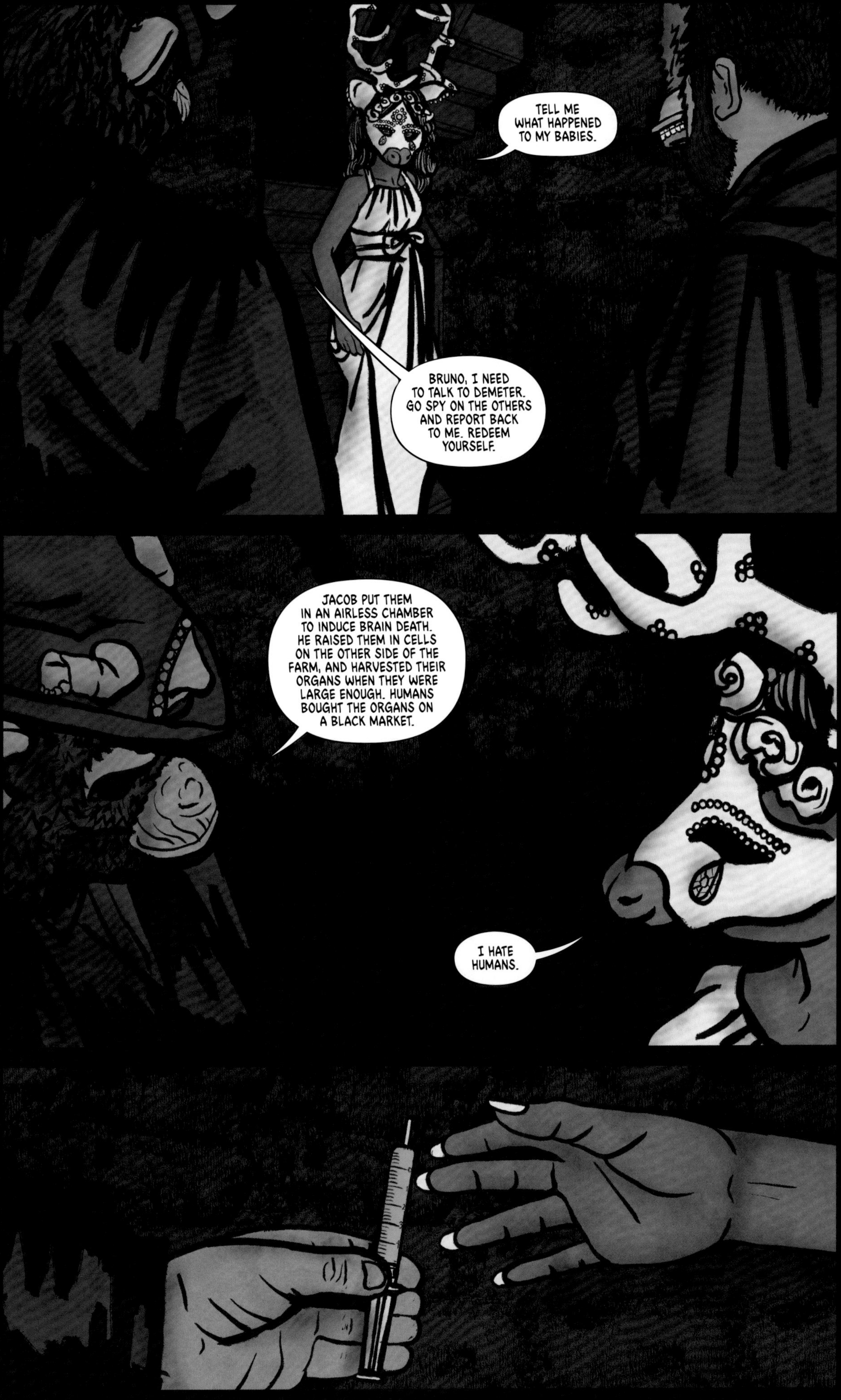
TELL ME WHAT HAPPENED TO MY BABIES.
BRUNO, I NEED TO TALK TO DEMETER. GO SPY ON THE OTHERS AND REPORT BACK TO ME. REDEEM YOURSELF.
JACOB PUT THEM IN AN AIRLESS CHAMBER TO INDUCE BRAIN DEATH. HE RAISED THEM IN CELLS ON THE OTHER SIDE OF THE FARM, AND HARVESTED THEIR ORGANS WHEN THEY WERE LARGE ENOUGH. HUMANS BOUGHT THE ORGANS ON A BLACK MARKET.
I HATE HUMANS.

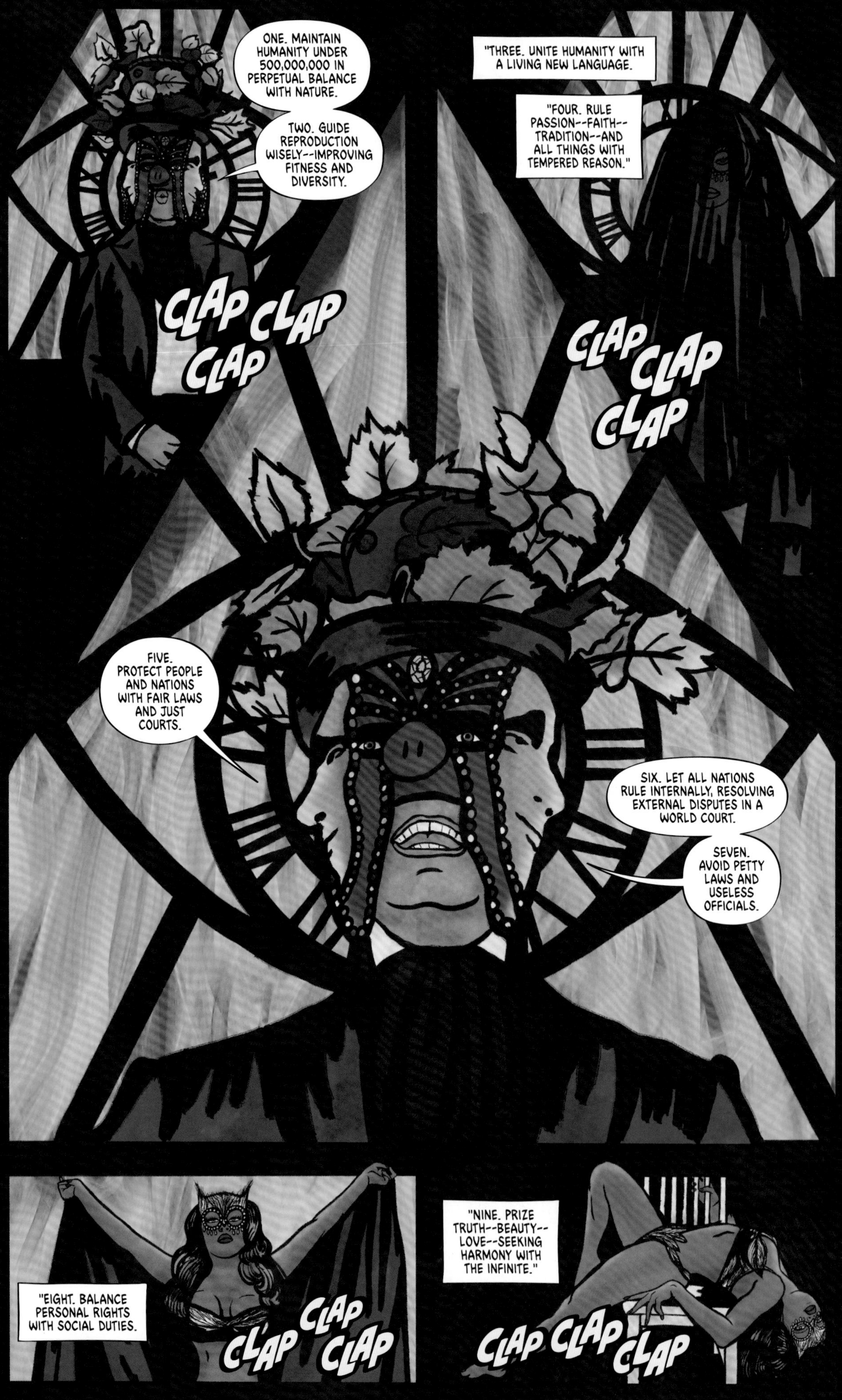
ONE. MAINTAIN HUMANITY UNDER 500,000,000 IN PERPETUAL BALANCE WITH NATURE.
TWO. GUIDE REPRODUCTION WISELY--IMPROVING FITNESS AND DIVERSITY.
CLAP CLAP CLAP
"THREE. UNITE HUMANITY WITH A LIVING NEW LANGUAGE.
"FOUR. RULE PASSION--FAITH--TRADITION--AND ALL THINGS WITH TEMPERED REASON."
CLAP CLAP CLAP
FIVE. PROTECT PEOPLE AND NATIONS WITH FAIR LAWS AND JUST COURTS.
SIX. LET ALL NATIONS RULE INTERNALLY, RESOLVING EXTERNAL DISPUTES IN A WORLD COURT.
SEVEN. AVOID PETTY LAWS AND USELESS OFFICIALS.
"EIGHT. BALANCE PERSONAL RIGHTS WITH SOCIAL DUTIES.
CLAP CLAP CLAP
"NINE. PRIZE TRUTH--BEAUTY--LOVE--SEEKING HARMONY WITH THE INFINITE."
CLAP CLAP CLAP

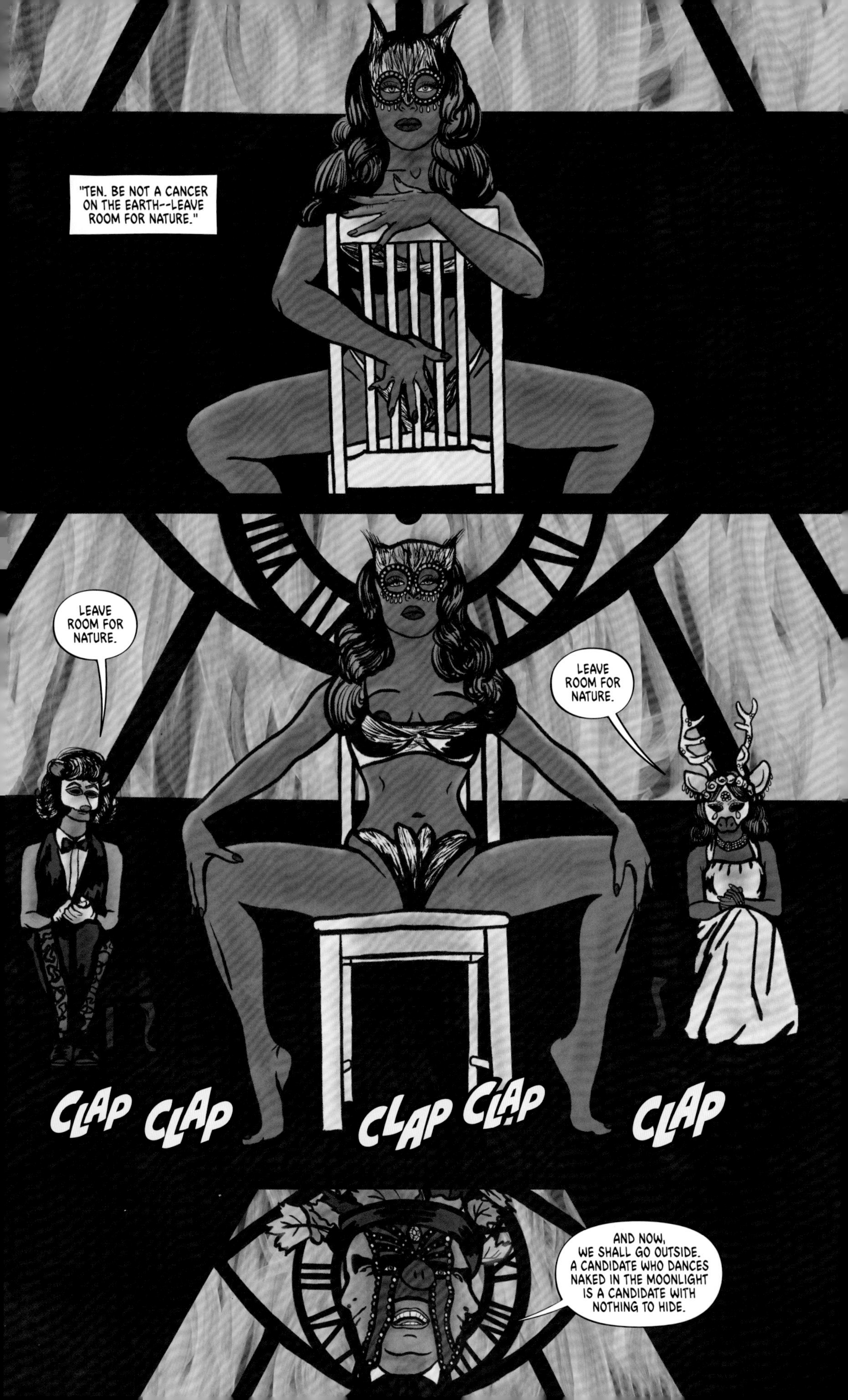
"TEN. BE NOT A CANCER ON THE EARTH--LEAVE ROOM FOR NATURE."
LEAVE ROOM FOR NATURE.
LEAVE ROOM FOR NATURE.
CLAP CLAP CLAP CLAP CLAP
AND NOW, WE SHALL GO OUTSIDE. A CANDIDATE WHO DANCES NAKED IN THE MOONLIGHT IS A CANDIDATE WITH NOTHING TO HIDE.

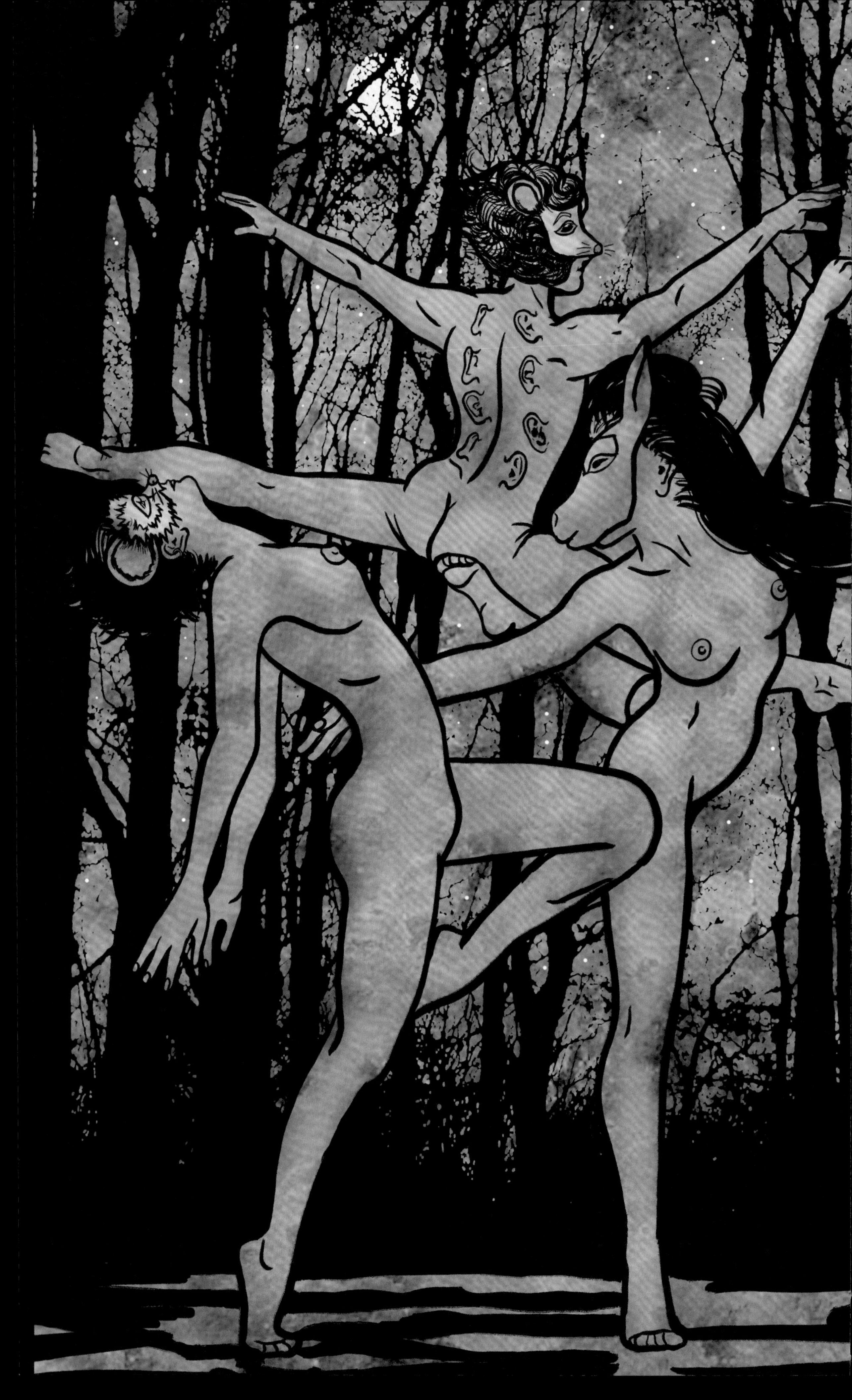

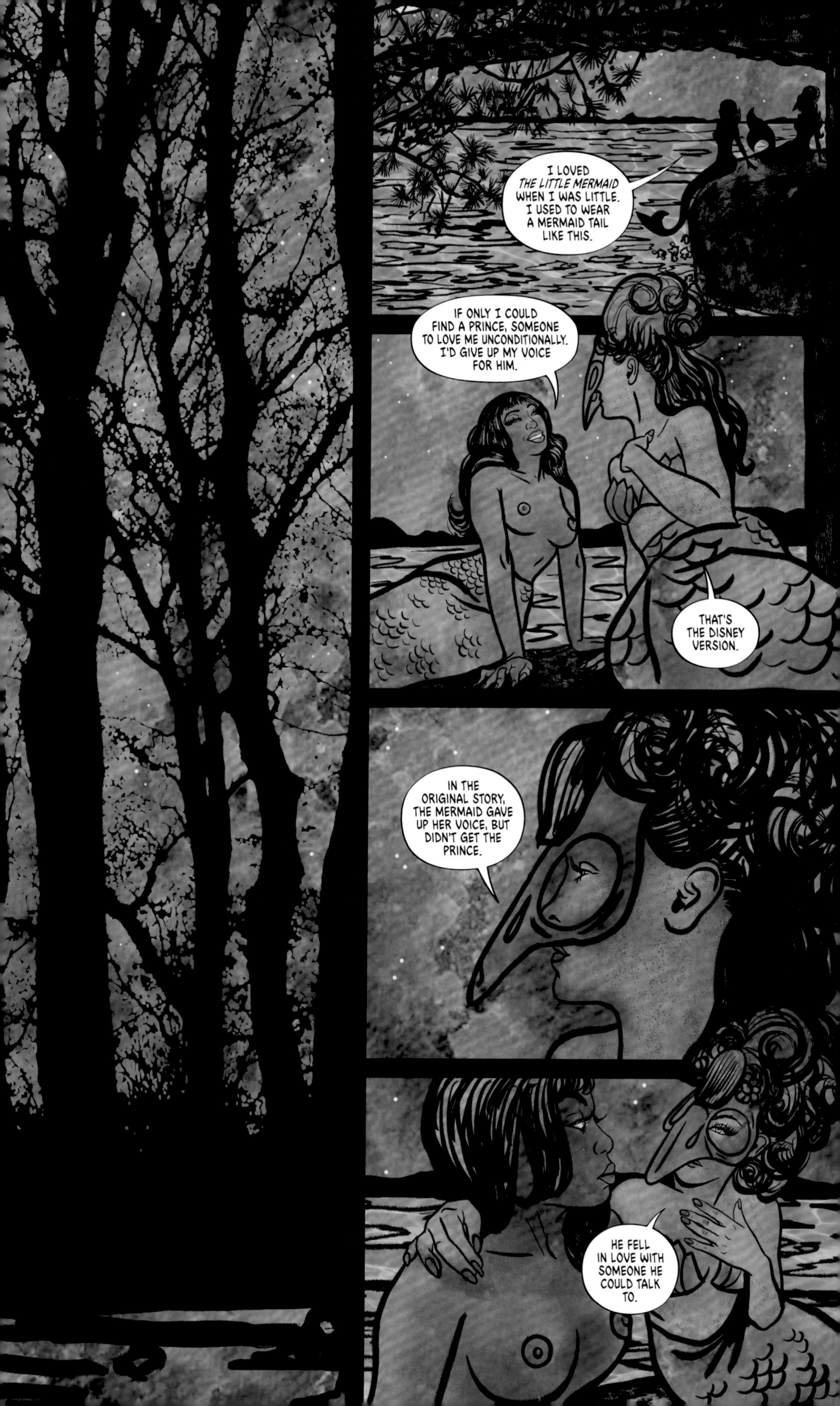
I LOVED *THE LITTLE MERMAID* WHEN I WAS LITTLE. I USED TO WEAR A MERMAID TAIL LIKE THIS.
IF ONLY I COULD FIND A PRINCE, SOMEONE TO LOVE ME UNCONDITIONALLY. I'D GIVE UP MY VOICE FOR HIM.
THAT'S THE DISNEY VERSION.
IN THE ORIGINAL STORY, THE MERMAID GAVE UP HER VOICE, BUT DIDN'T GET THE PRINCE.
HE FELL IN LOVE WITH SOMEONE HE COULD TALK TO.

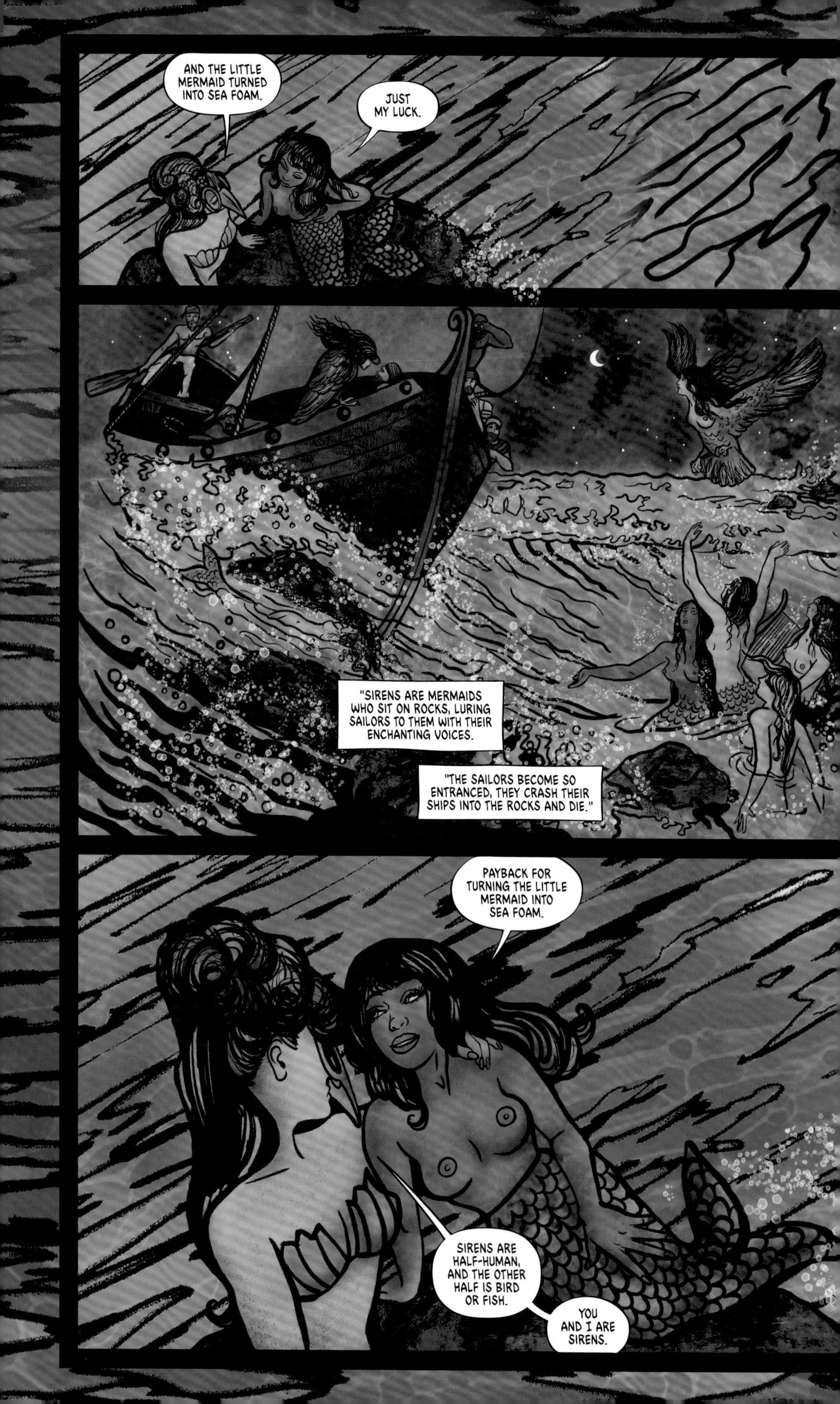
AND THE LITTLE MERMAID TURNED INTO SEA FOAM.
JUST MY LUCK.
"SIRENS ARE MERMAIDS WHO SIT ON ROCKS, LURING SAILORS TO THEM WITH THEIR ENCHANTING VOICES.
"THE SAILORS BECOME SO ENTRANCED, THEY CRASH THEIR SHIPS INTO THE ROCKS AND DIE."
PAYBACK FOR TURNING THE LITTLE MERMAID INTO SEA FOAM.
SIRENS ARE HALF-HUMAN, AND THE OTHER HALF IS BIRD OR FISH.
YOU AND I ARE SIRENS.

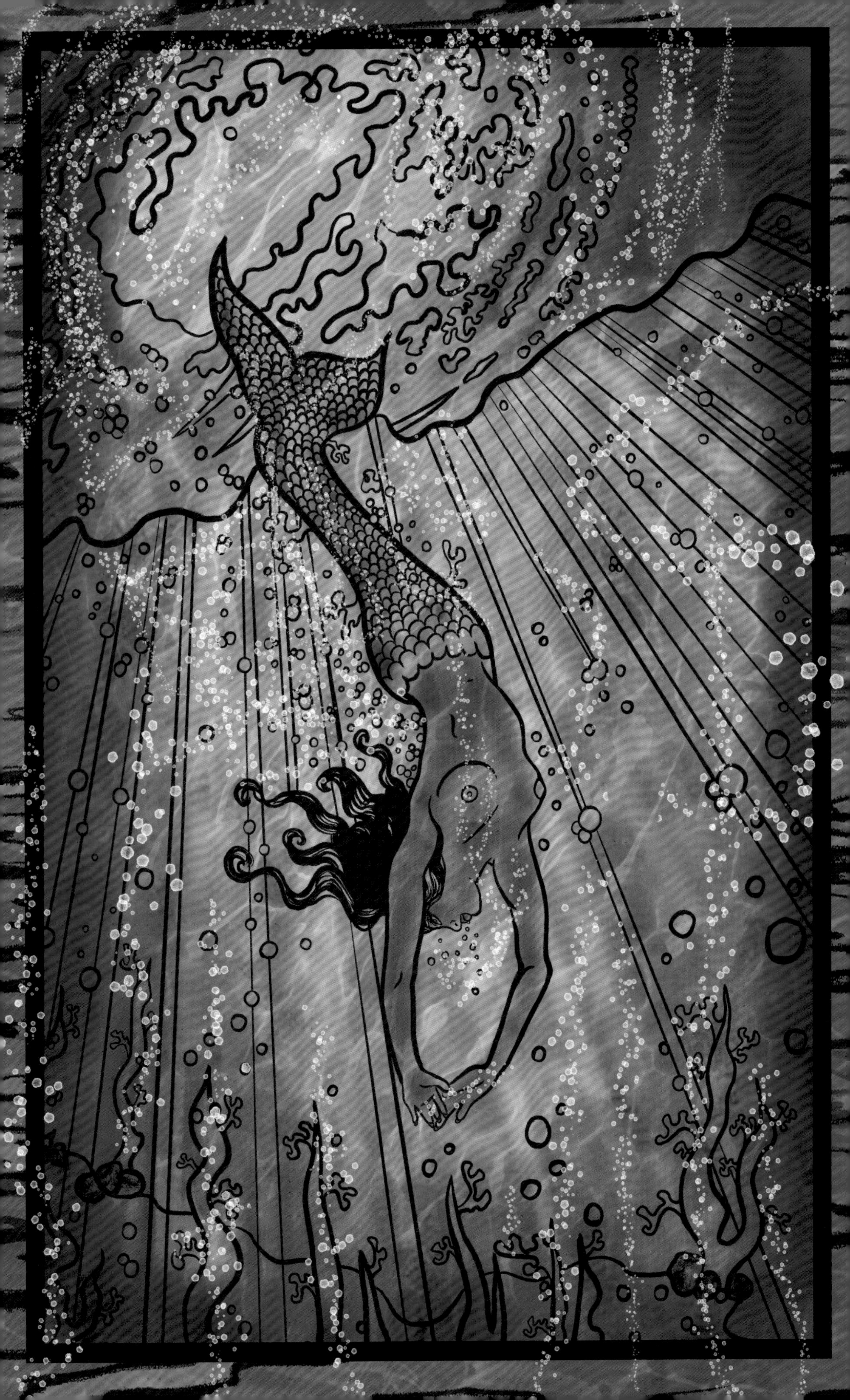

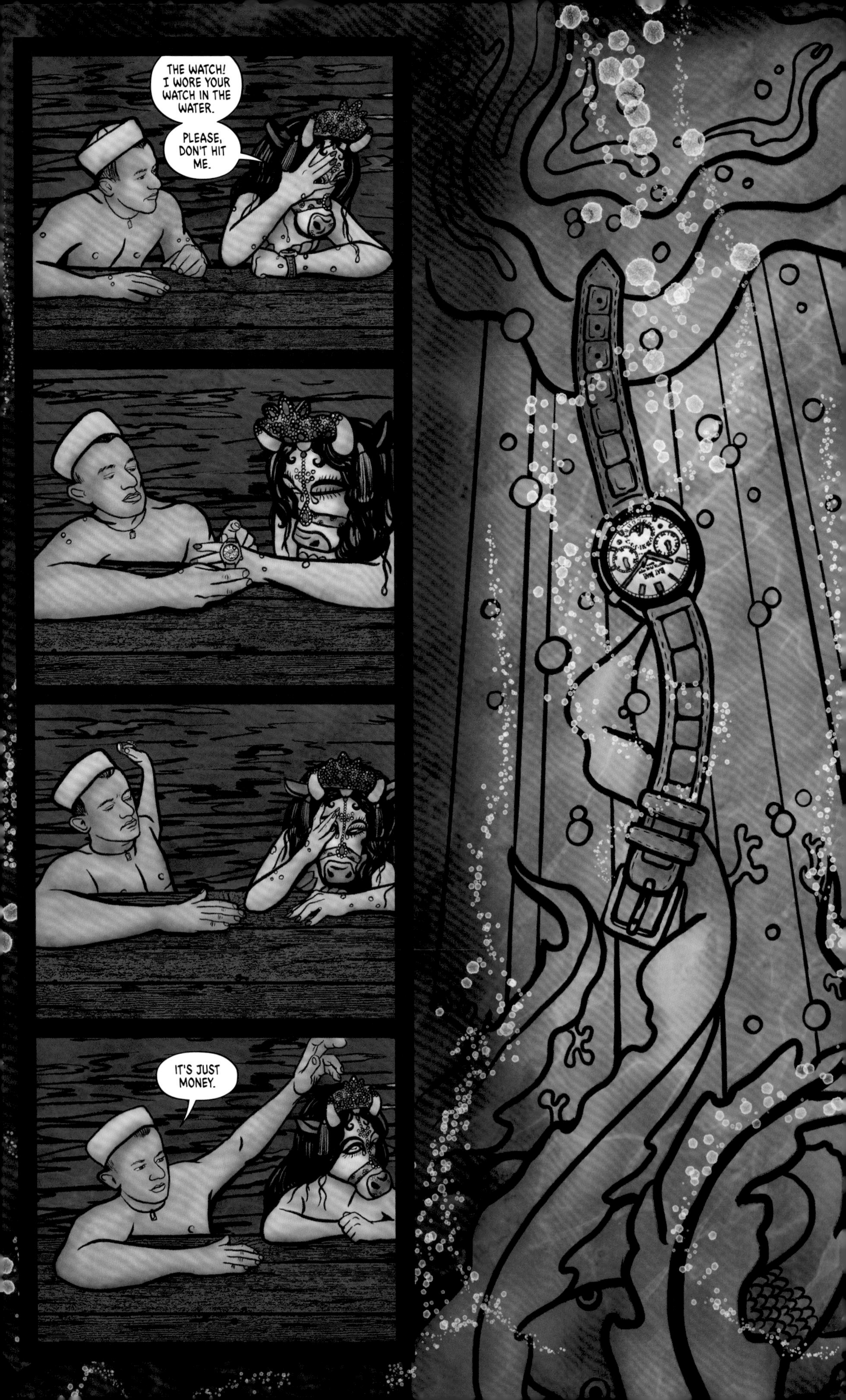
THE WATCH! I WORE YOUR WATCH IN THE WATER.
PLEASE, DON'T HIT ME.
IT'S JUST MONEY.

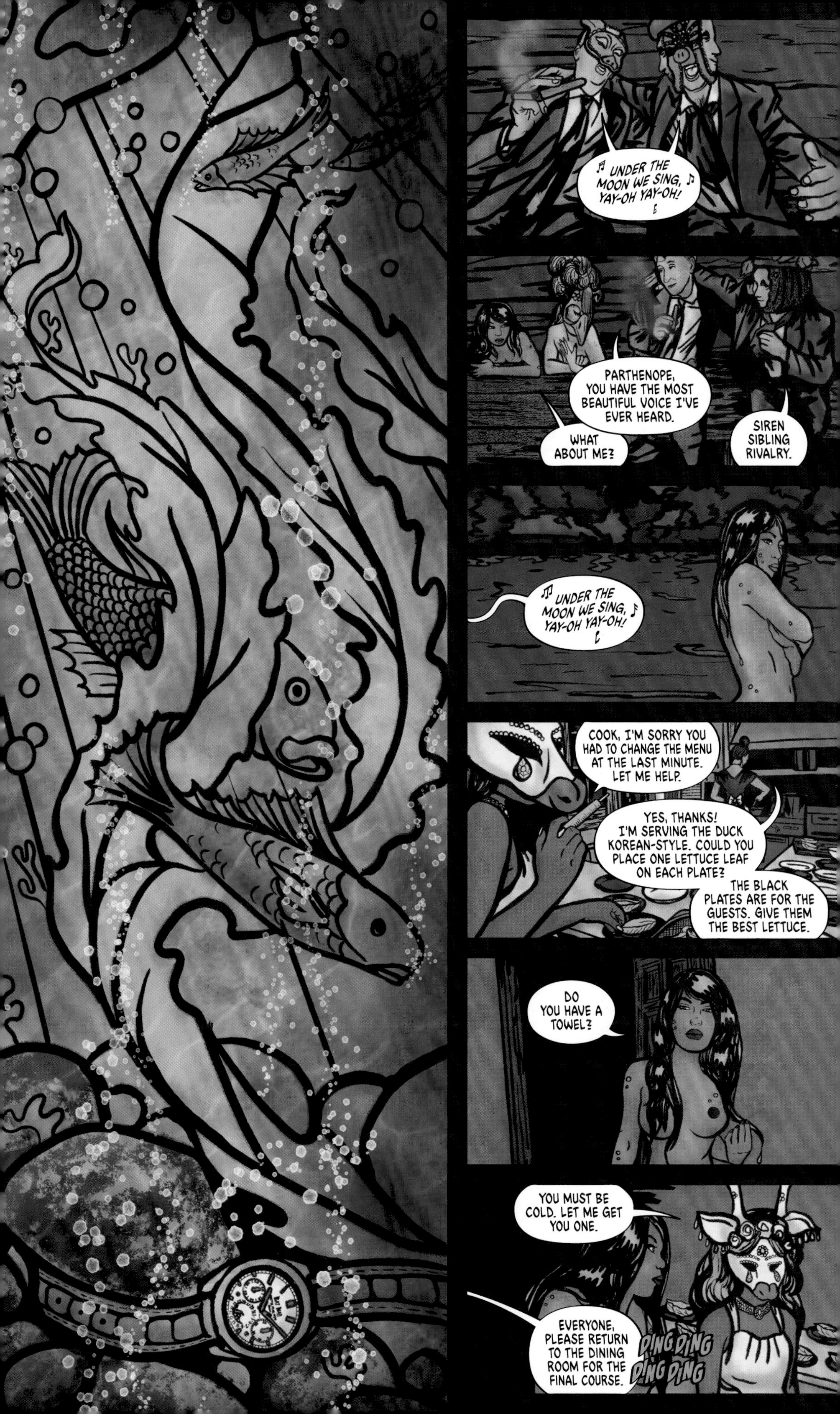
♫ UNDER THE MOON WE SING, ♪ YAY-OH YAY-OH!
PARTHENOPE, YOU HAVE THE MOST BEAUTIFUL VOICE I'VE EVER HEARD.
WHAT ABOUT ME?
SIREN SIBLING RIVALRY.
♫ UNDER THE MOON WE SING, ♪ YAY-OH YAY-OH!
COOK, I'M SORRY YOU HAD TO CHANGE THE MENU AT THE LAST MINUTE. LET ME HELP.
YES, THANKS! I'M SERVING THE DUCK KOREAN-STYLE. COULD YOU PLACE ONE LETTUCE LEAF ON EACH PLATE?
THE BLACK PLATES ARE FOR THE GUESTS. GIVE THEM THE BEST LETTUCE.
DO YOU HAVE A TOWEL?
YOU MUST BE COLD. LET ME GET YOU ONE.
EVERYONE, PLEASE RETURN TO THE DINING ROOM FOR THE FINAL COURSE.
DING DING DING DING

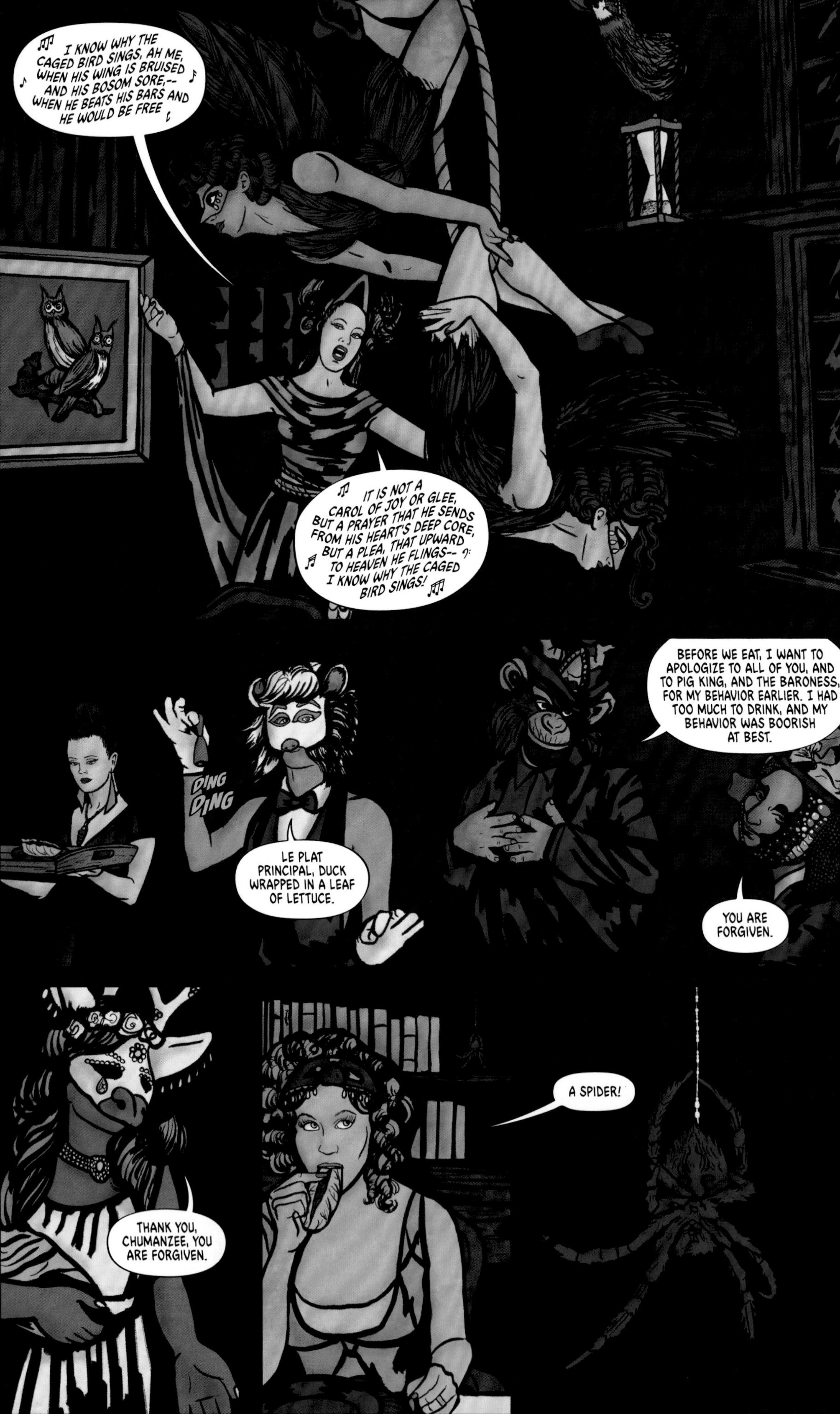
I KNOW WHY THE CAGED BIRD SINGS, AH ME, WHEN HIS WING IS BRUISED AND HIS BOSOM SORE,-- WHEN HE BEATS HIS BARS AND HE WOULD BE FREE
IT IS NOT A CAROL OF JOY OR GLEE, BUT A PRAYER THAT HE SENDS FROM HIS HEART'S DEEP CORE, BUT A PLEA, THAT UPWARD TO HEAVEN HE FLINGS-- I KNOW WHY THE CAGED BIRD SINGS!
DING DING
LE PLAT PRINCIPAL, DUCK WRAPPED IN A LEAF OF LETTUCE.
BEFORE WE EAT, I WANT TO APOLOGIZE TO ALL OF YOU, AND TO PIG KING, AND THE BARONESS, FOR MY BEHAVIOR EARLIER. I HAD TOO MUCH TO DRINK, AND MY BEHAVIOR WAS BOORISH AT BEST.
YOU ARE FORGIVEN.
THANK YOU, CHUMANZEE, YOU ARE FORGIVEN.
A SPIDER!

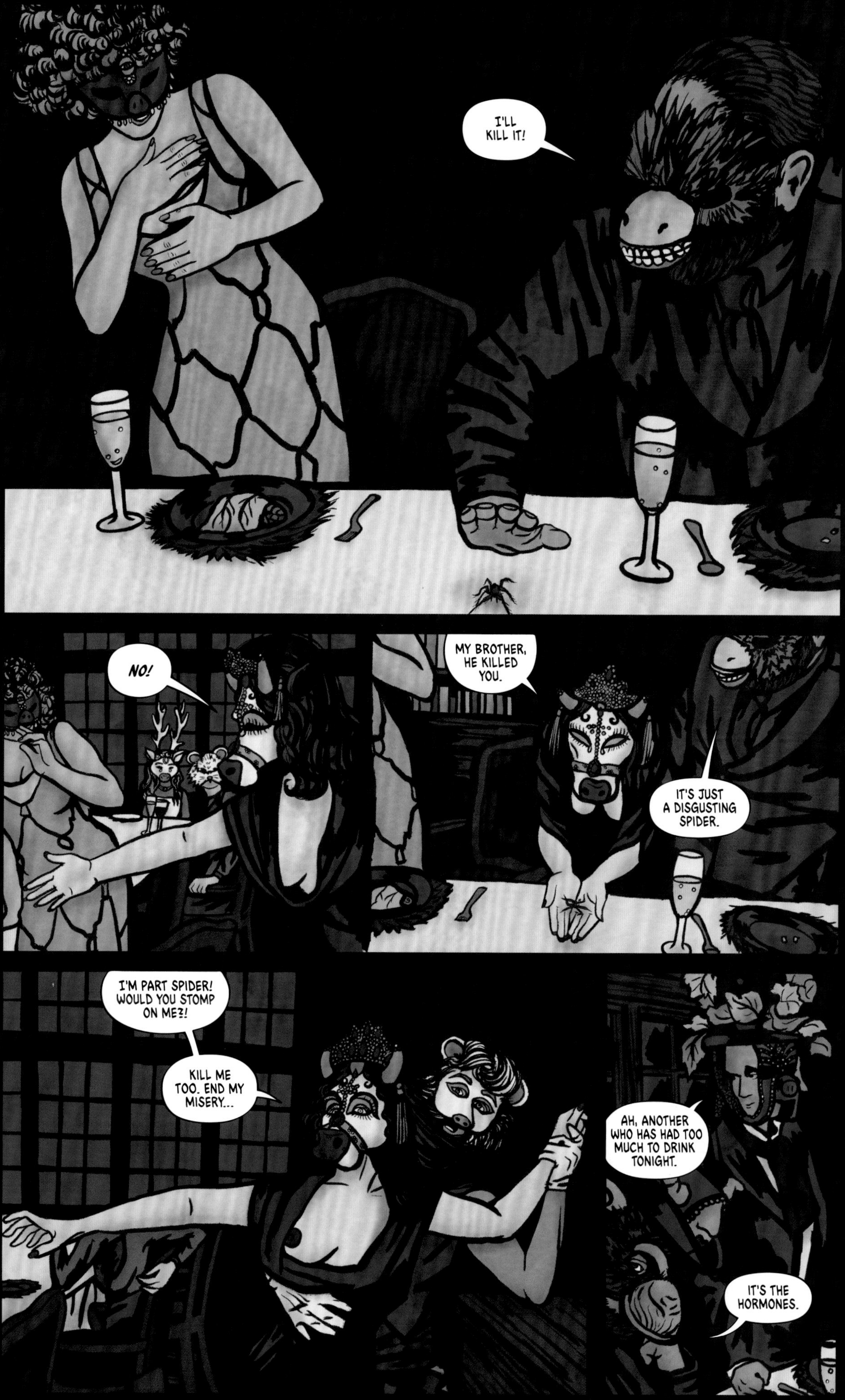
I'LL KILL IT!
NO!
MY BROTHER, HE KILLED YOU.
IT'S JUST A DISGUSTING SPIDER.
I'M PART SPIDER! WOULD YOU STOMP ON ME?!
KILL ME TOO. END MY MISERY...
AH, ANOTHER WHO HAS HAD TOO MUCH TO DRINK TONIGHT.
IT'S THE HORMONES.

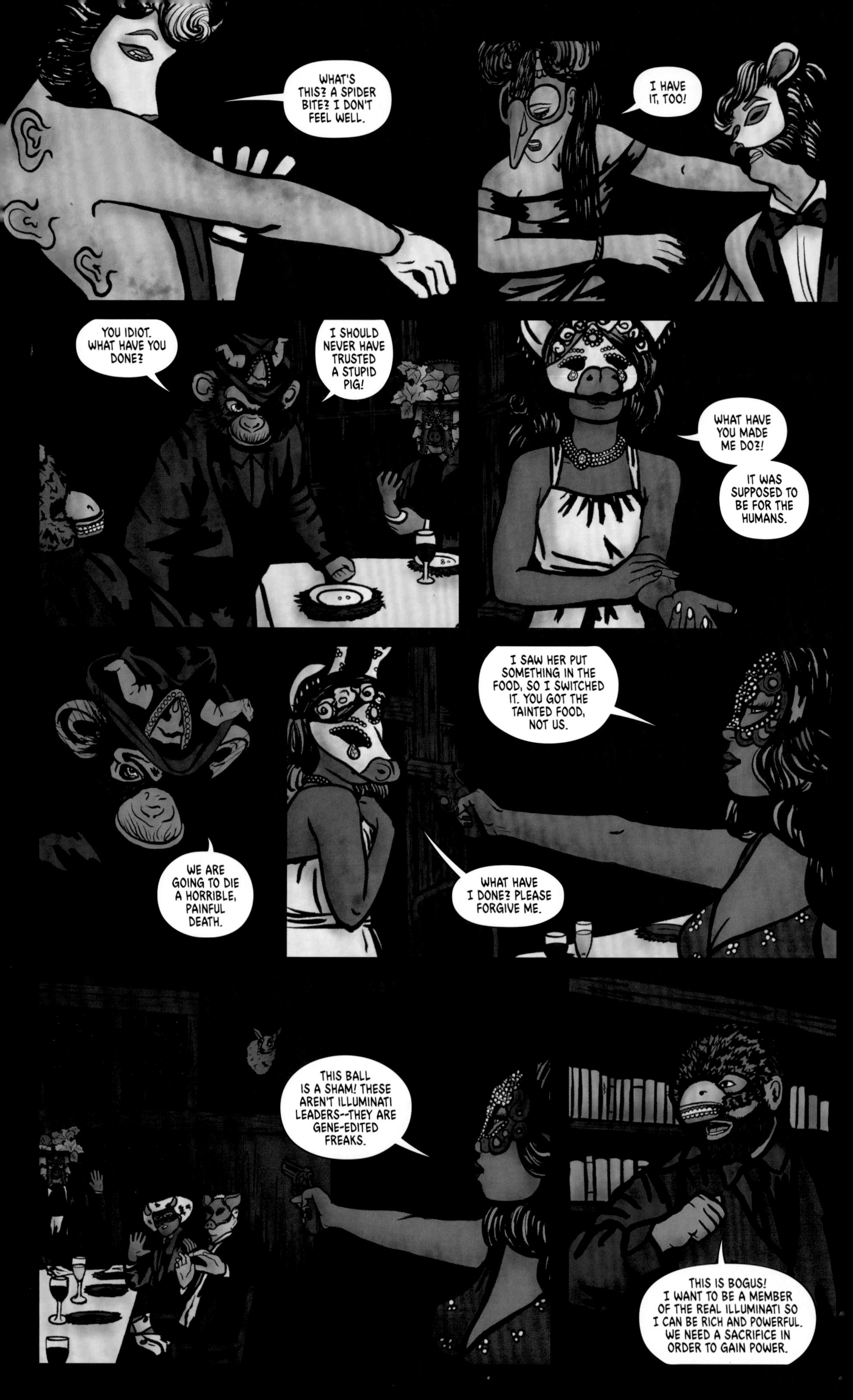
WHAT'S THIS? A SPIDER BITE? I DON'T FEEL WELL.
I HAVE IT, TOO!
YOU IDIOT. WHAT HAVE YOU DONE?
I SHOULD NEVER HAVE TRUSTED A STUPID PIG!
WHAT HAVE YOU MADE ME DO?!
IT WAS SUPPOSED TO BE FOR THE HUMANS.
WE ARE GOING TO DIE A HORRIBLE, PAINFUL DEATH.
I SAW HER PUT SOMETHING IN THE FOOD, SO I SWITCHED IT. YOU GOT THE TAINTED FOOD, NOT US.
WHAT HAVE I DONE? PLEASE FORGIVE ME.
THIS BALL IS A SHAM! THESE AREN'T ILLUMINATI LEADERS--THEY ARE GENE-EDITED FREAKS.
THIS IS BOGUS! I WANT TO BE A MEMBER OF THE REAL ILLUMINATI SO I CAN BE RICH AND POWERFUL. WE NEED A SACRIFICE IN ORDER TO GAIN POWER.

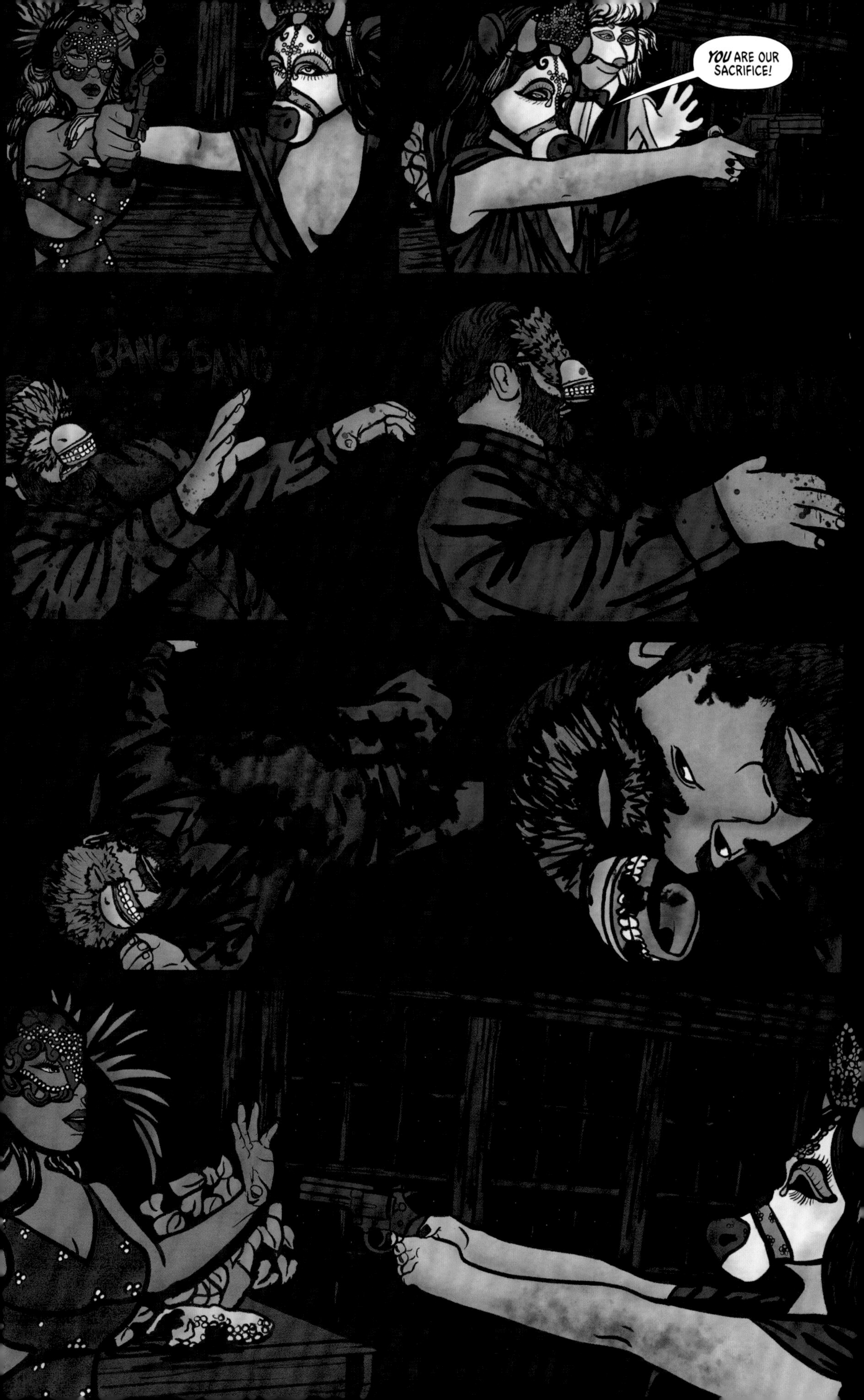
YOU ARE OUR SACRIFICE!
BANG BANG
BANG

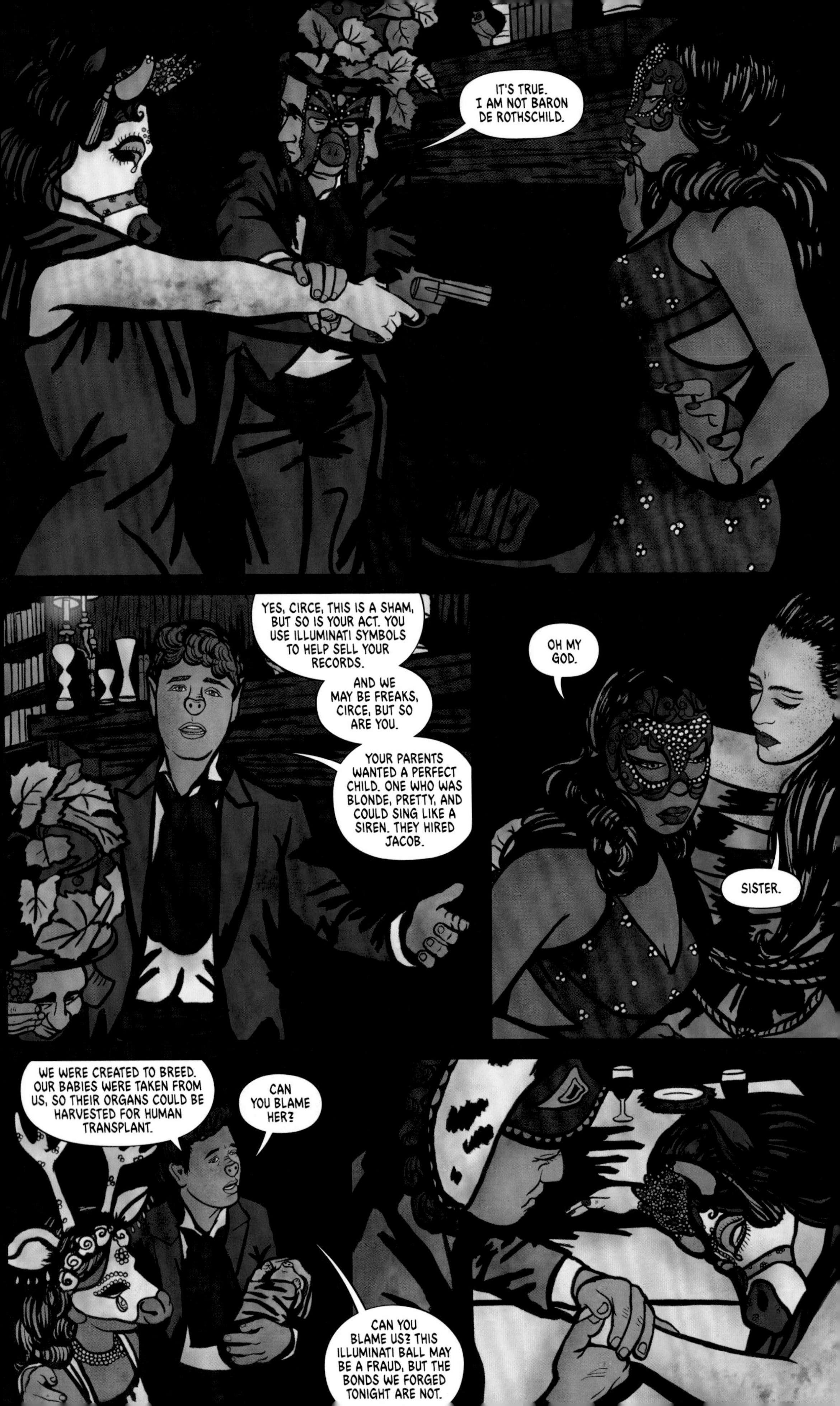
IT'S TRUE.
I AM NOT BARON
DE ROTHSCHILD.
YES, CIRCE, THIS IS A SHAM, BUT SO IS YOUR ACT. YOU USE ILLUMINATI SYMBOLS TO HELP SELL YOUR RECORDS.
AND WE MAY BE FREAKS, CIRCE, BUT SO ARE YOU.
YOUR PARENTS WANTED A PERFECT CHILD. ONE WHO WAS BLONDE, PRETTY, AND COULD SING LIKE A SIREN. THEY HIRED JACOB.
OH MY GOD.
SISTER.
WE WERE CREATED TO BREED. OUR BABIES WERE TAKEN FROM US, SO THEIR ORGANS COULD BE HARVESTED FOR HUMAN TRANSPLANT.
CAN YOU BLAME HER?
CAN YOU BLAME US? THIS ILLUMINATI BALL MAY BE A FRAUD, BUT THE BONDS WE FORGED TONIGHT ARE NOT.

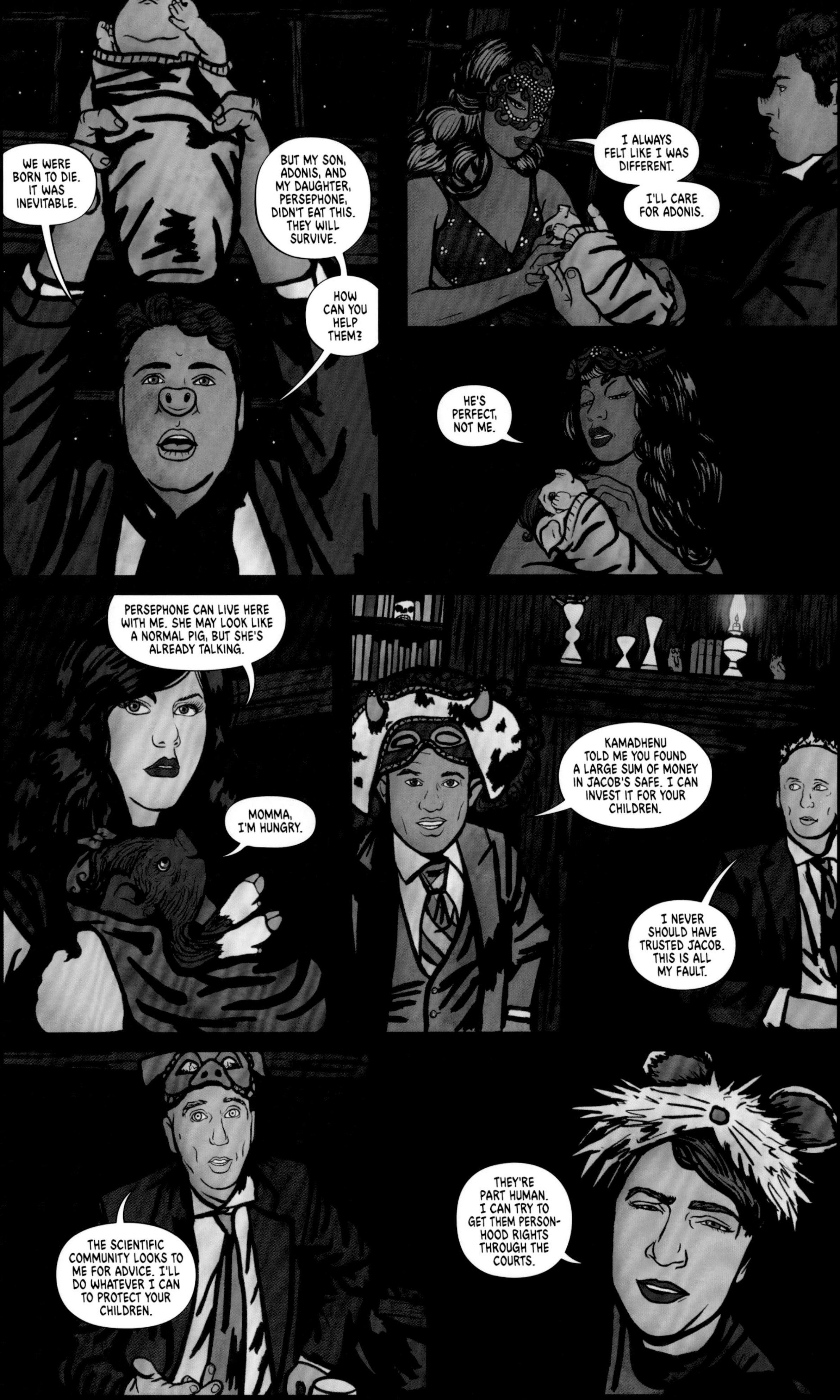
WE WERE BORN TO DIE. IT WAS INEVITABLE.
BUT MY SON, ADONIS, AND MY DAUGHTER, PERSEPHONE, DIDN'T EAT THIS. THEY WILL SURVIVE.
HOW CAN YOU HELP THEM?
I ALWAYS FELT LIKE I WAS DIFFERENT.
I'LL CARE FOR ADONIS.
HE'S PERFECT, NOT ME.
PERSEPHONE CAN LIVE HERE WITH ME. SHE MAY LOOK LIKE A NORMAL PIG, BUT SHE'S ALREADY TALKING.
MOMMA, I'M HUNGRY.
KAMADHENU TOLD ME YOU FOUND A LARGE SUM OF MONEY IN JACOB'S SAFE. I CAN INVEST IT FOR YOUR CHILDREN.
I NEVER SHOULD HAVE TRUSTED JACOB. THIS IS ALL MY FAULT.
THE SCIENTIFIC COMMUNITY LOOKS TO ME FOR ADVICE. I'LL DO WHATEVER I CAN TO PROTECT YOUR CHILDREN.
THEY'RE PART HUMAN. I CAN TRY TO GET THEM PERSON-HOOD RIGHTS THROUGH THE COURTS.

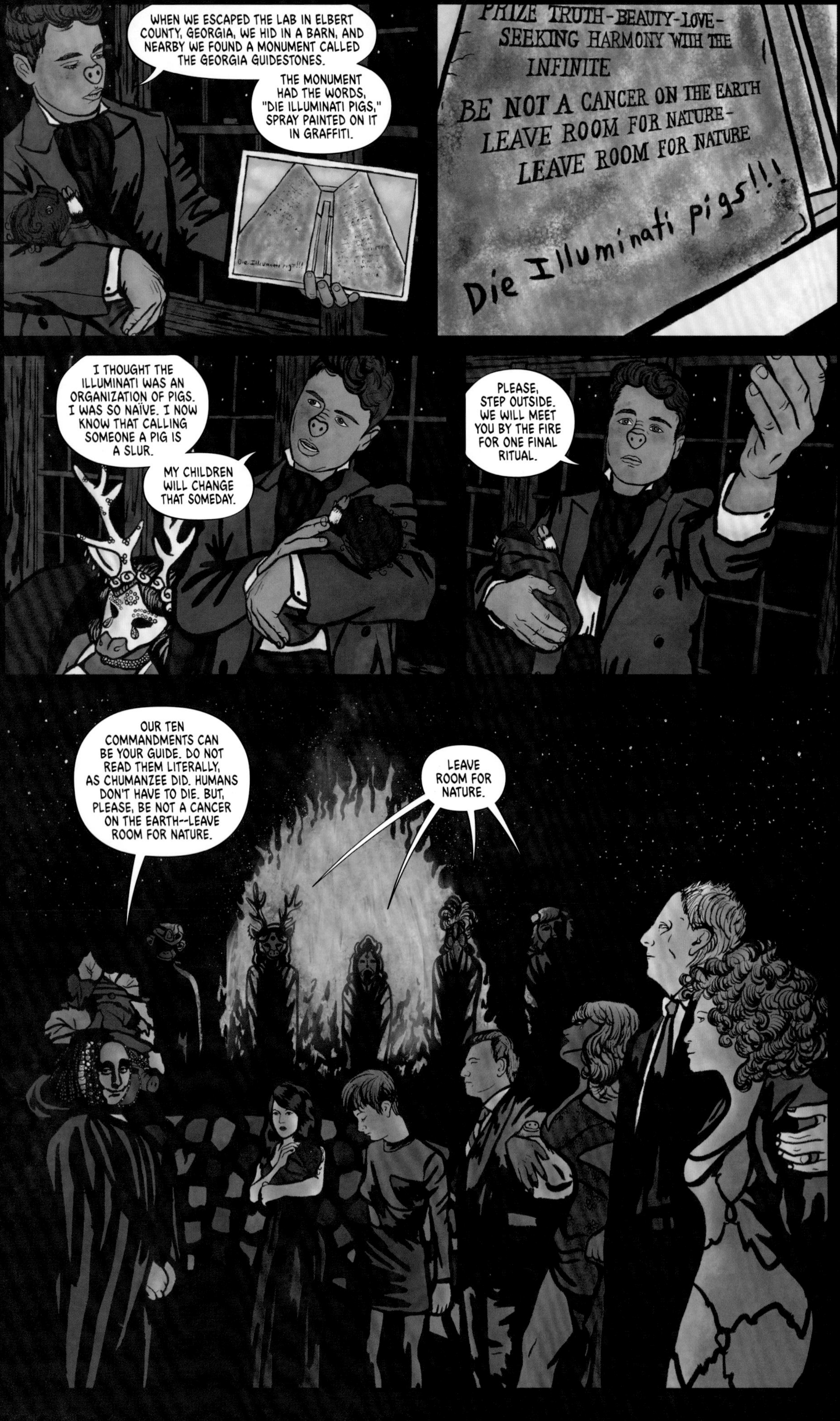
WHEN WE ESCAPED THE LAB IN ELBERT COUNTY, GEORGIA, WE HID IN A BARN, AND NEARBY WE FOUND A MONUMENT CALLED THE GEORGIA GUIDESTONES.
THE MONUMENT HAD THE WORDS, "DIE ILLUMINATI PIGS," SPRAY PAINTED ON IT IN GRAFFITI.
PRIZE TRUTH-BEAUTY-LOVE-
SEEKING HARMONY WITH THE INFINITE
BE NOT A CANCER ON THE EARTH
LEAVE ROOM FOR NATURE-
LEAVE ROOM FOR NATURE
Die Illuminati pigs!!!
I THOUGHT THE ILLUMINATI WAS AN ORGANIZATION OF PIGS. I WAS SO NAÏVE. I NOW KNOW THAT CALLING SOMEONE A PIG IS A SLUR.
MY CHILDREN WILL CHANGE THAT SOMEDAY.
PLEASE, STEP OUTSIDE. WE WILL MEET YOU BY THE FIRE FOR ONE FINAL RITUAL.
OUR TEN COMMANDMENTS CAN BE YOUR GUIDE. DO NOT READ THEM LITERALLY, AS CHUMANZEE DID. HUMANS DON'T HAVE TO DIE. BUT, PLEASE, BE NOT A CANCER ON THE EARTH--LEAVE ROOM FOR NATURE.
LEAVE ROOM FOR NATURE.

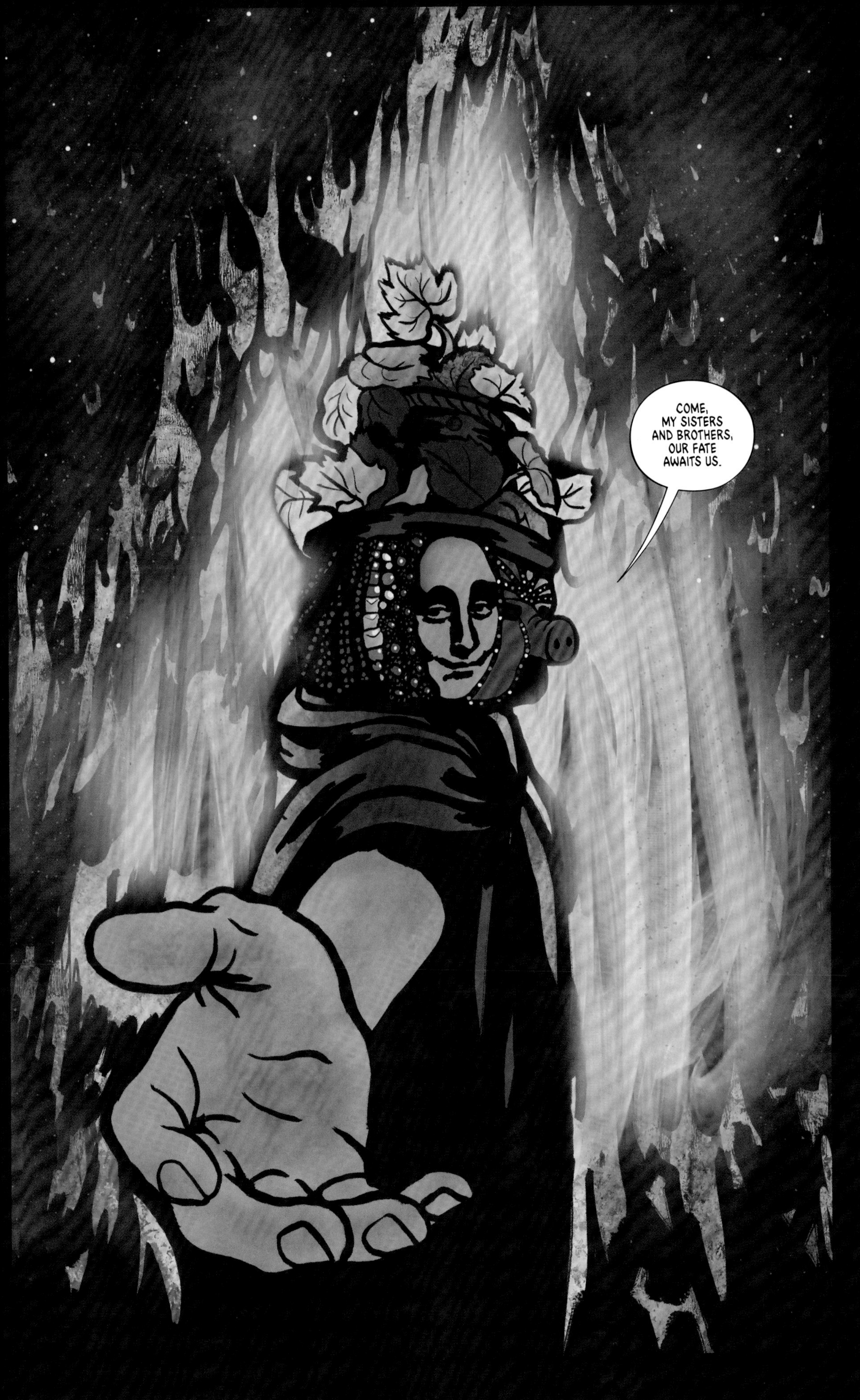
COME, MY SISTERS AND BROTHERS, OUR FATE AWAITS US.

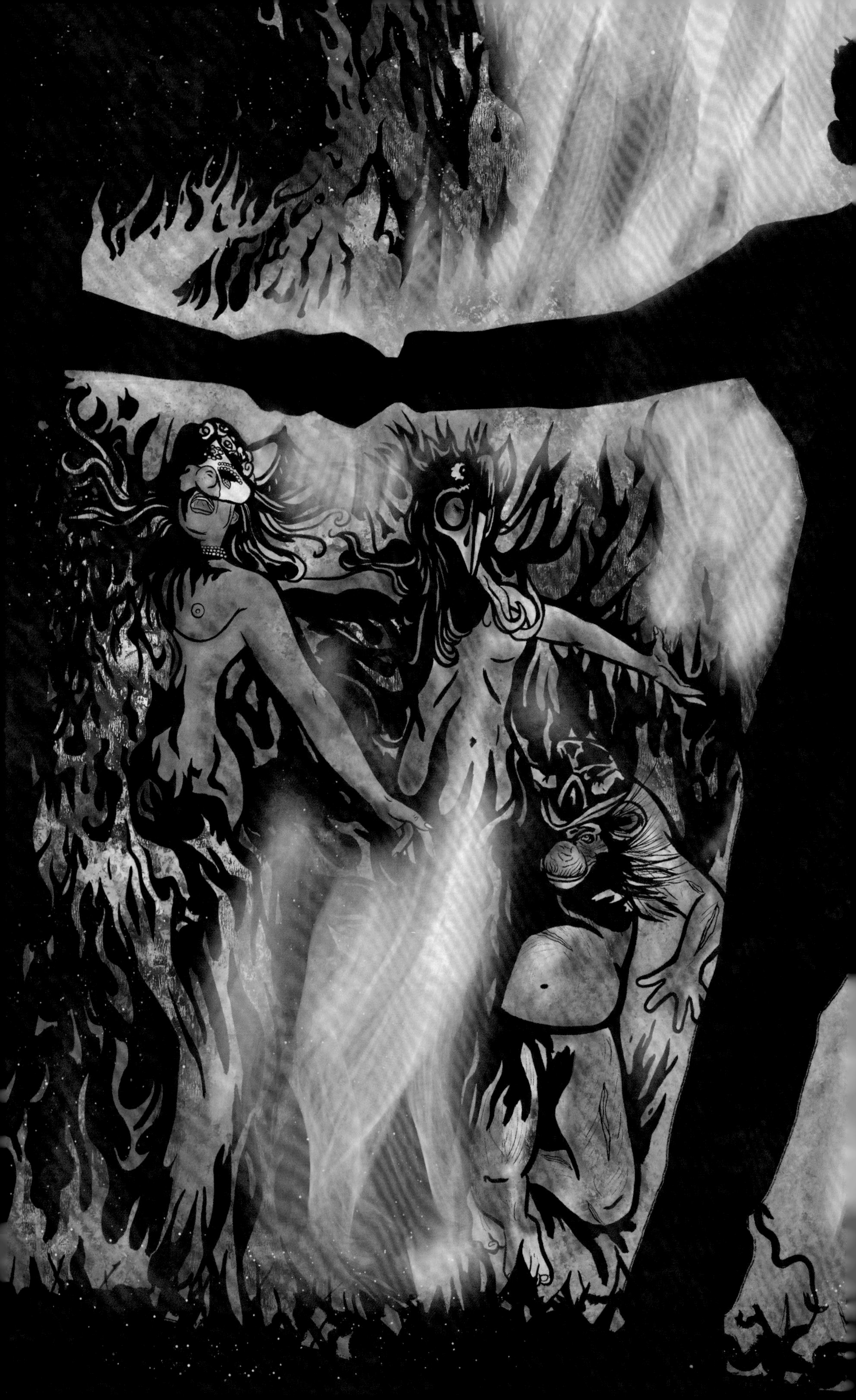

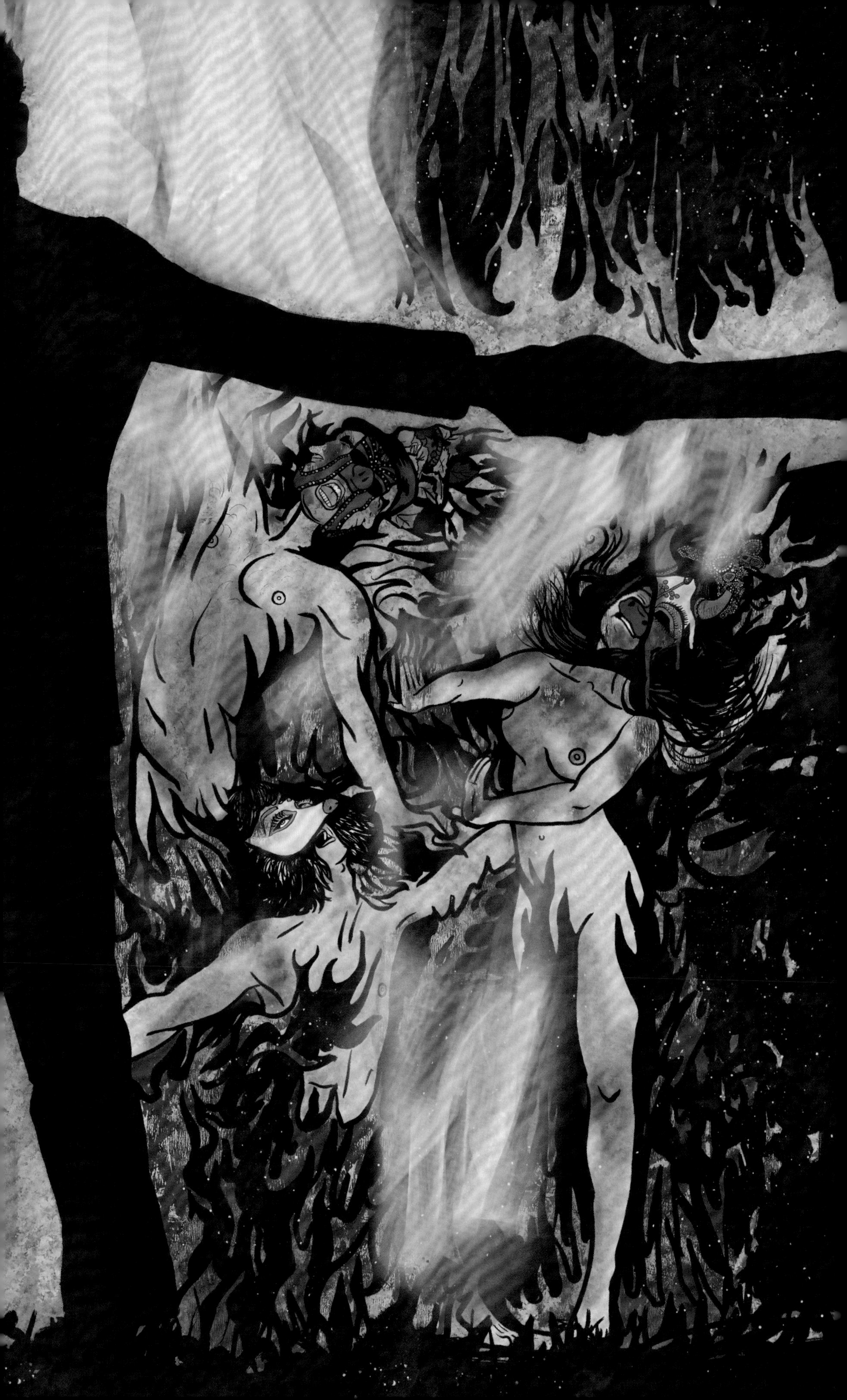

The Vegetable Lamb of Tartary, species Agnus scythicus, has the flesh and blood of a lamb, yet it grows up from the ground, hatched from a gourd, and tethered to the plant by an umbilical cord.

After eating all the foliage surrounding it, the lamb and plant die.

For four centuries, Agnus scythicus was believed to be an actual plant. It appeared in encyclopedias and books.

Naturalists, scholars, and historians didn't question each other. It had been propagated for so long -- it had to be true! It turns out it was just a cotton plant which rivaled wool for making clothes.

"Illuminati" comes from the word "Illumination." The original Illuminati, started by a Bavarian, Adam Weishaupt, in 1776, was created to illuminate that which is hidden and secret.

Its goals were to oppose superstition, promote transparency, remove religious influence over public life, and end abuses of state power.

Illuminati meetings were outlawed by the Bavarian ruler and the Catholic Church.

The Illuminati was vilified by conservative and religious critics, and the group disbanded and became fractured.

Since then, in a historical game of Telephone, the Illuminati has become known as an organization of shadowy figures controlling the world like puppeteers.

Its members are supposedly billionaires, presidents, rappers, and pop stars, who sacrifice children and worship Satan in exchange for fame, wealth, and power. These ideas about the Illuminati, like the Vegetable Lamb, Flat Earth, and Holocaust Denial, are nonsense.

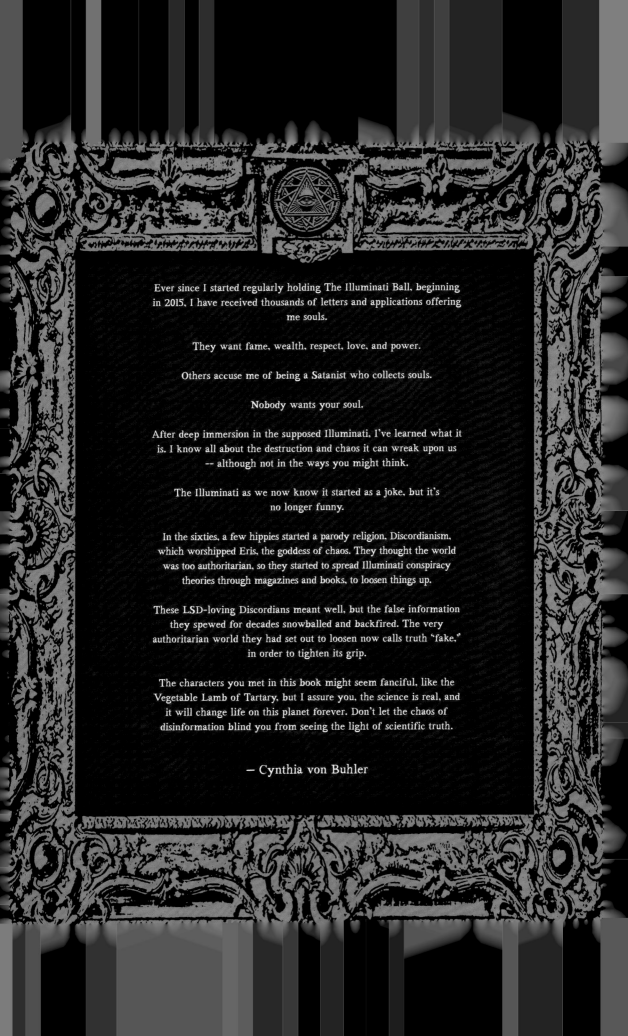

Ever since I started regularly holding The Illuminati Ball, beginning in 2015, I have received thousands of letters and applications offering me souls.

They want fame, wealth, respect, love, and power.

Others accuse me of being a Satanist who collects souls.

Nobody wants your soul.

After deep immersion in the supposed Illuminati, I've learned what it is. I know all about the destruction and chaos it can wreak upon us -- although not in the ways you might think.

The Illuminati as we now know it started as a joke, but it's no longer funny.

In the sixties, a few hippies started a parody religion, Discordianism, which worshipped Eris, the goddess of chaos. They thought the world was too authoritarian, so they started to spread Illuminati conspiracy theories through magazines and books, to loosen things up.

These LSD-loving Discordians meant well, but the false information they spewed for decades snowballed and backfired. The very authoritarian world they had set out to loosen now calls truth "fake," in order to tighten its grip.

The characters you met in this book might seem fanciful, like the Vegetable Lamb of Tartary, but I assure you, the science is real, and it will change life on this planet forever. Don't let the chaos of disinformation blind you from seeing the light of scientific truth.

— Cynthia von Buhler

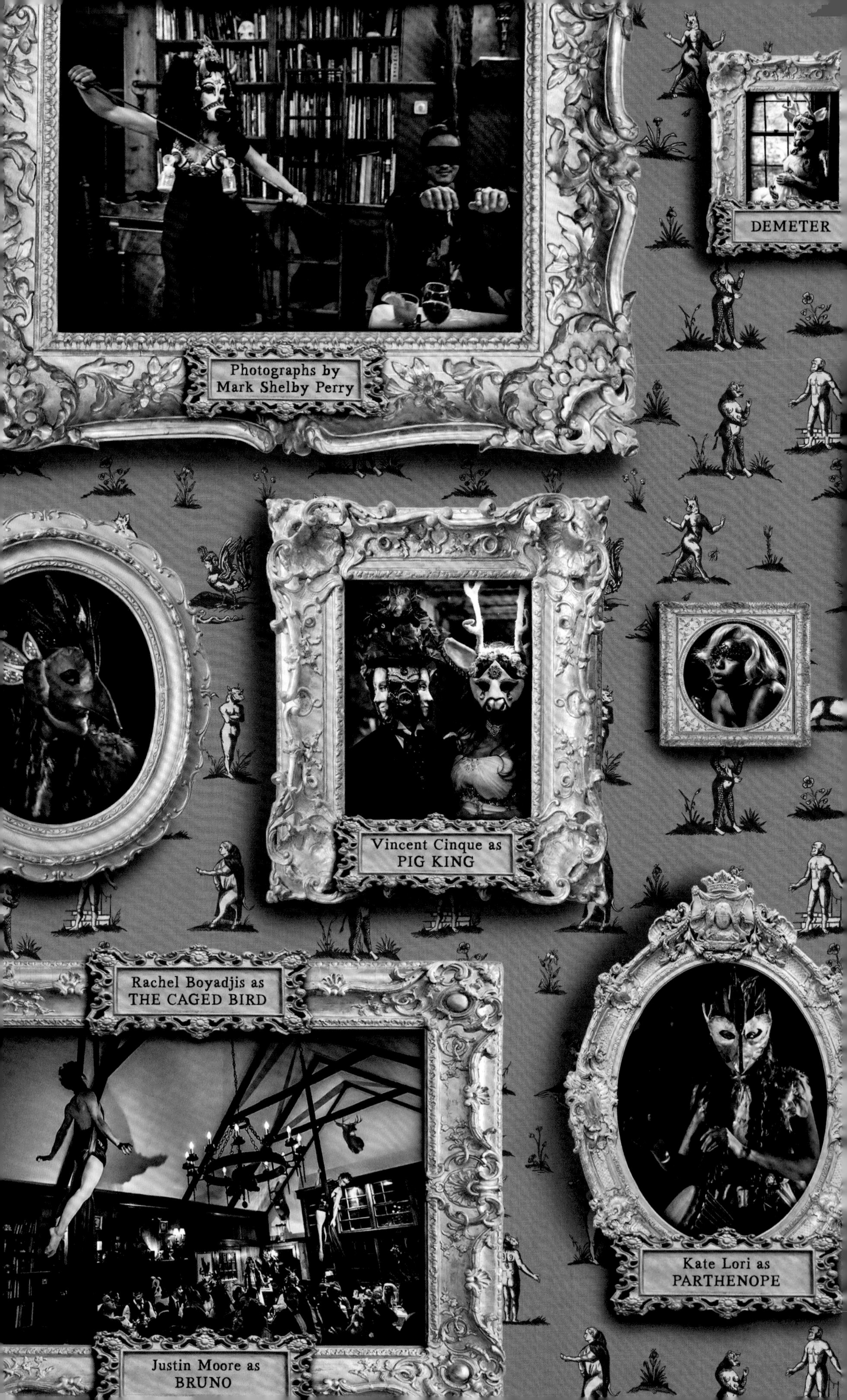
Photographs by
Mark Shelby Perry
DEMETER
Vincent Cinque as
PIG KING
Rachel Boyadjis as
THE CAGED BIRD
Kate Lori as
PARTHENOPE
Justin Moore as
BRUNO

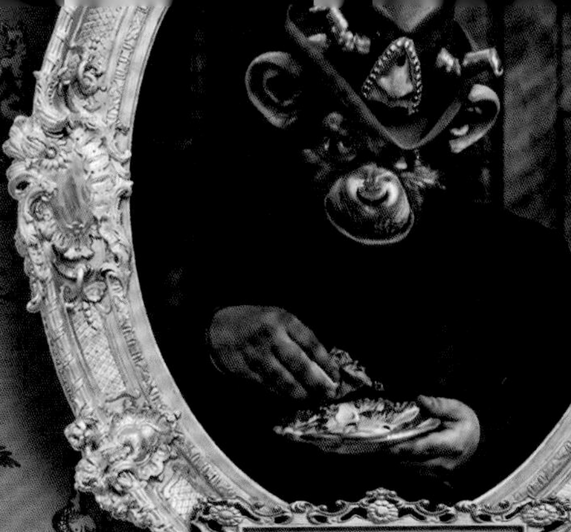

Travis Moore as
CHUMANZEE

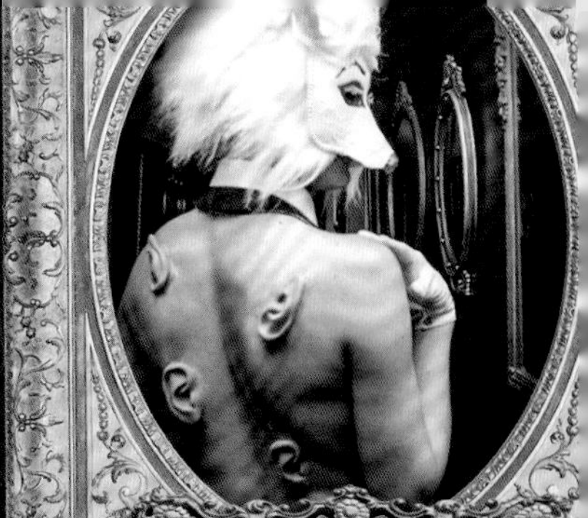

Luka Fric as
VACANTI

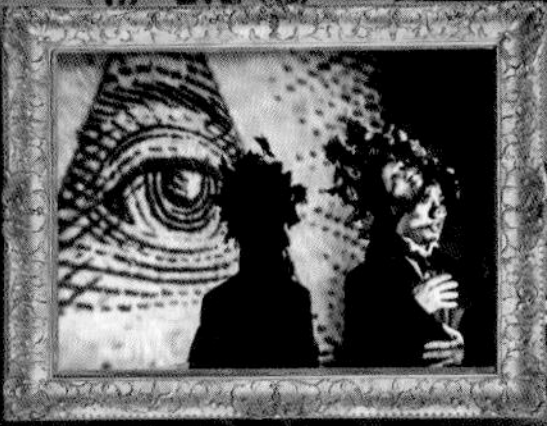

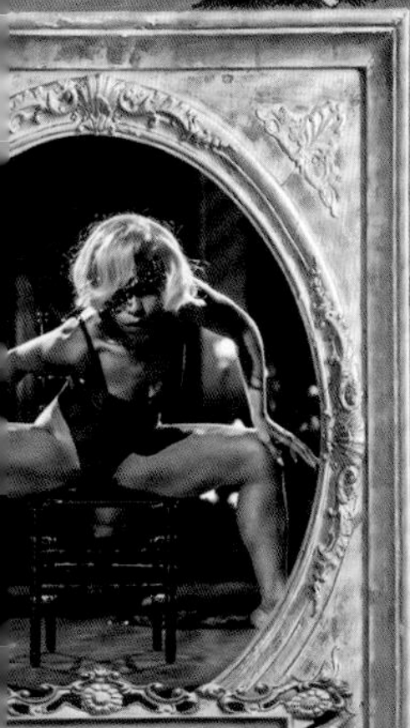

sia La Chatte as
CIRCE

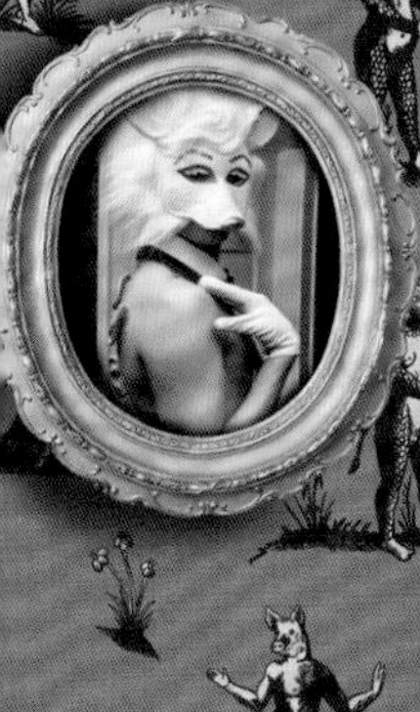

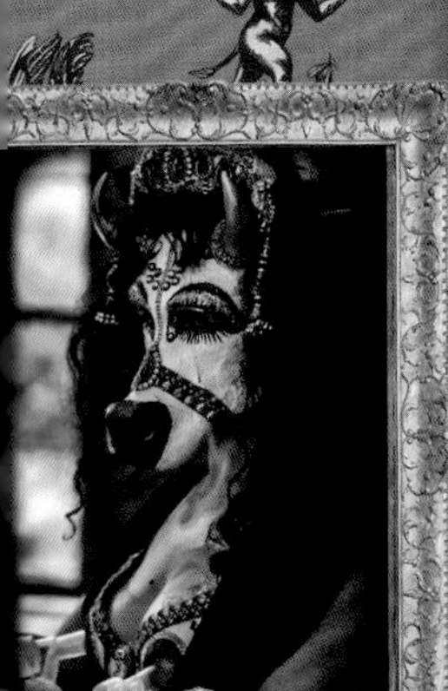

KAMADHENU

THE ILLUMINATI BALL

IMMERSIVE EXPERIENCE

THE ILLUMINATI BALL, AN IMMERSIVE EXCURSION INTO THE UNKNOWN, IS A SURREAL DINNER PARTY CROSSHATCHED WITH POWER STRUGGLES, MORALITY TESTS, AND INTER-SPECIES INTRIGUE.

Every summer, adventurous guests are blindfolded and whisked from Manhattan to a secluded waterfront estate outside the city for a lavish dinner, exotic cocktails, and an extraordinary evening of ritual and revelation. The Ball is inspired by the infamous 1972 Surrealist Ball hosted by the Baron and Baroness de Rothschild at their massive mansion in France. The elaborately masked luminaries who attended included the likes of Salvador Dalí and Audrey Hepburn, who appeared with a gilded birdcage on her head.

The Illuminati Ball features vegan delicacies (by Erin Orr) and libations (by Bootleg Greg). As the story unfolds, guests are dazzled with fire performances, opera, aerial acts, esoteric ceremonies, and intimate bonding activities.

In keeping with the exclusivity of the de Rothschilds' affair, attendance at each performance is limited to thirty guests, each of whom must apply and be accepted in order to attend. If admitted, they are asked to choose an animal kinship of pig, monkey, cow, bird, or mouse, which shapes their experience throughout the evening.

In fall and winter, guests may apply to attend The Illuminati Ball of New York City. This expanded Illuminati Ball is held twice a year and explores the five Illuminati desires: fame, respect, love, power, and wealth.

The Illuminati Ball is produced by Cynthia von Buhler and PJ Mead of Speakeasy Dollhouse, which also presented the first title in von Buhler's Minky Woodcock comic book series, *The Girl Who Handcuffed Houdini* (Hard Case Crime/Titan Comics), as an immersive play in 2018. For more information on Minky Woodcock, please visit MinkyWoodcock.com.

Apply to attend at TheIlluminatiBall.com.

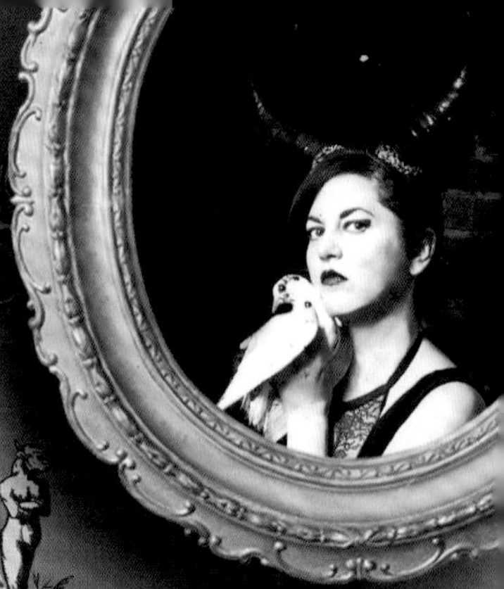

Creator Biography

CYNTHIA VON BUHLER

Cynthia von Buhler, aka Countess von Buhler, is an American artist, performer, playwright and author. Hailed by the press as "multitalented and eccentric" (*Boston Globe*), a "rising star" (*NY Arts*), and "one of the top contemporary surrealists" (*Art & Antiques*), Cynthia von Buhler has made a name for herself as an award-winning and critically acclaimed fine artist, author, and illustrator. Her illustration work has won awards from the Society of Illustrators and has repeatedly appeared in *American Illustration*, *Communication Arts* and the Society of Illustrator annuals of the best illustration in America. Von Buhler's stunning, three-dimensional paintings have been displayed in galleries and museums around the world, and have been featured in books, newspapers and magazines from *Rolling Stone* to *The New Yorker*. *The New York Times* has written four features on her in the last five years. Von Buhler has collaborated on art projects with Steven Spielberg, Neil Gaiman and Clive Barker. She has illustrated book covers for Harry Turtledove, Scott O'Dell, Jane Yolen, Elizabeth George Speare and Lawrence Block. Her sculptures have appeared on NBC's *Law & Order: Special Victims Unit*, she and her work were profiled in *Mary Magdalen: An Intimate Portrait* on the Lifetime Network, and she was a recurring character on Discovery Channel's *Oddities*. Von Buhler also writes, directs and produces immersive theater. In writing about her theater productions, *Forbes* called her "a creative genius" and the *New York Post* wrote, "Von Buhler has the kind of family footnote any writer would kill for." Von Buhler was the lead singer in two seminal Boston bands, The Women of Sodom and Countess, the latter garnering her a development deal with MCA Records. Her comic work includes *Minky Woodcock: The Girl Who Handcuffed Houdini*, *Evelyn Evelyn: A Terrible Tale in Two Tomes* with Amanda Palmer and Jason Webley, *An Evening with Neil Gaiman and Amanda Palmer*, *Speakeasy Dollhouse: The Bloody Beginning* and *Emily and The Strangers*. Connect with Cynthia at cynthiavonbuhler.com or on Twitter at twitter.com/CynthVonBuhler.

Photographs by Kyle Dorosz

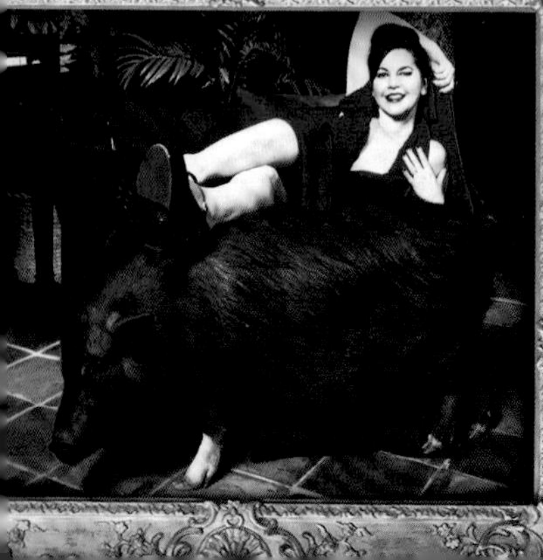

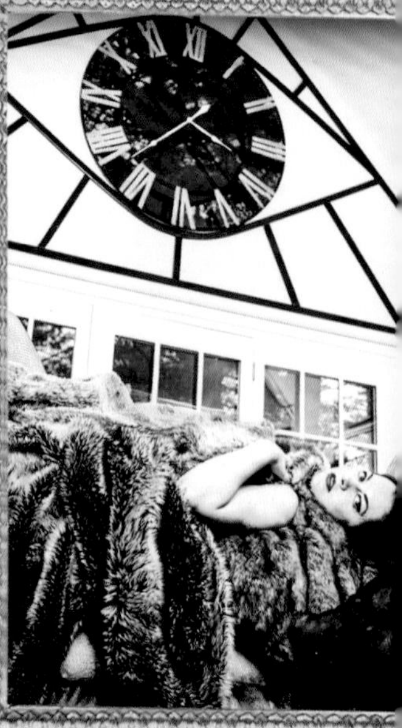